D0521492

California Real Estate Finance

Robert Handwerker and Jerry Frankel

Copyright © 2019 License Solution

License Solution, Inc.

2700 Neilson Way, Suite 731

Santa Monica, CA

888-714-0566

Table of Contents

CHAPTER 1

THE ORIGINS OF MONEY

Overview

Money has value because people perceive it to be valuable. Money has evolved over the past several thousand years from the exchange of goods and services that two parties believed were of equal value to the exchange of physical money or digital numbers with others that are backed by assets or things of value. Without money, the field of real estate would not exist. Money allows buyers and sellers the option to leverage a purchase transaction with very little money down on the buyer's side, and assists sellers with various creative ways to take cash out of the property and walk away from hopefully significant profits. To best understand how money exists in its many forms today, we must first go back in time to learn about how access to money changed and improved over time.

What gives money value?

Barter

Barter is a system of exchange where goods and services are directly exchanged between two or more parties for other types of goods or services without using any medium such as money, gold, or silver. Barter probably first began with the trading of farm crops and livestock from local ranches thousands of years ago. Most people are motivated to eat on a daily basis, so the exchanging of products that could be eaten had plenty of interested parties ready, willing, and able to offer other items of value to farmers and ranchers who could help feed them.

Bartering dates at least as far back as 6000 BC. It was allegedly introduced by Mesopotamia tribes who lived in regions near where Iraq and Iran are located today. The word "mesopotamia" is derived from Greek origins to mean "between two rivers" due to the fact that the main land region was located between the Tigris and Euphrates rivers. Mesopotamia is described by many historians as the **"cradle of civilization."** The origins there of the barter system -- coins and money that became more prevalent in 5000 BC with the introduction of clay tokens -- improved writing techniques (such as script), the wheel, and allowed for the development of more efficient transportation systems.

In 700 BC, the Lydians (tribes based in what is now Turkey) would become the first Western culture to make its own coins. Other civilizations and countries would soon follow the Lydians with the creation of their own coins or shells that had some consistent representation of value. Each coin or shell had a particular value range that fluctuated up and down depending upon supply and demand at the time. With more uniformity of value for the coins or shells, it was much easier to compare and exchange goods and services. The first coins that were created out of gold and/or silver might have begun with coins minted by the Lydians circa 600 BC.

Money is defined by economists as "anything commonly accepted by people for the exchange of goods and services." Because there were no centralized currency systems in place thousands of years ago, products that could be eaten were akin to the "gold standard" when it came to the barter system. Cattle was considered the most valuable asset to trade back near the start of the barter system. Lambs, sheep, chickens, rice, wheat, fruits, and vegetables were quite valuable commodities to exchange between local townspeople or tribe members.

With a barter system, the people involved in the exchanging of goods and services are usually just as important as the actual items being exchanged. Several hundred or thousand years ago, there were no third-party services in place to verify whether or not an item being exchanged actually had the same value that was claimed by one party. Items that a person could eat or drink were fairly easy to value in a relatively short period of time thanks to a person's taste buds. However, the exchange of something that was considered as valuable, like gold or silver jewelry or furniture, might later be proven to be of little value or defective and easily broken.

Parties in a barter system usually had to have some sort of trust and good faith between each other for the barter system to work efficiently. Most parties to a barter were neighbors who knew one another as opposed to strangers from some far-off land. Some parties to a barter might travel several miles on foot, or by horse or wagon to exchange goods and services with other tribal people. But this was considered much riskier because the parties had not established any sort of rapport or trust between one another. Sometimes, the "gold" ring was really just a yellow tin ring that had a fraction of the value that was originally claimed by the salesperson.

The barter system did offer lots of flexibility for neighbors and strangers to trade just about any sort of product or commodity that they felt had value. There really were no restrictions or limitations in regard to which items of value could be exchanged between two or more willing parties. One neighbor might consider a new hand-made bed to be more valuable than his prized largest cow in his backyard. If so, the neighbor would wholeheartedly agree to accept his carpenter friend's brand new bed in exchange for one of his 10 cattle. Because each neighbor knew that they could create more woodwork by building, and more cattle by breeding, both parties knew that their sources were not finite and could later be duplicated or replaced.

Farmers and ranchers usually had to own or at least control their land in some way in order to have enough time to grow their crops and feed their livestock. As a result, the money system really had its earliest origins from a type of real estate transaction. As the years moved forward, the item that had the most value was the land under the farmers, ranchers, and livestock.

The barter system lives on in the 21st century by way of some of the best known company personnel who exchange goods, services, accommodations, content, and time with or without actually owning the items of value that are being exchanged. Regardless of whether an item is legally owned, the most value can originate from a company's *control* of the asset being exchanged. It has been said that "time is the most valuable commodity of all" because it is truly finite and priceless to so many people.

Some of the most valuable companies in the world are really just online versions of modern day barter systems such as the following entities:

- Uber: The world's largest taxi company owns no vehicles.

- Facebook: The most-viewed media provider on the planet creates no actual content.

- Instagram: The most valuable photo company sells no cameras or film (owned by Facebook).

- Netflix: The fastest growing television network does not own or lay any cables.

- Airbnb: The largest accommodation provider in the world owns no real estate.

- Alibaba: The world's largest retailer out of China that surpasses Walmart in annual sales even though they have no inventory to actually sell.

- EBay: The world's largest online marketplace does not really have a physical presence or central retail building for customers to exchange goods and services.

EBay is the oldest of these companies listed above with a foundation date of 1995. The rest of the multi-billion dollar companies listed did not exist just 20 years ago. Yet these glorified online barter companies now dominate the retail, transportation, travel, and entertainment industries without actually offering real goods and services to offer another party. However, they do offer ease of access and overall positive reputations that allow their customers to have at least some faith that the product or service being purchase will arrive or be accessible at some point in the near term.

Commodity Money[1]

Often, the two parties could not agree on the exact value, size, or quantity for the exchange of certain goods. For example, a bag of rice might be worth a similar-sized bag of wheat to one neighbor and 10 eggs to another. The market value for any item is dependent upon the need, interest, and the "eye of the beholder" at the time of purchase. A man

---

[1]   All statistics in this chapter are borrowed from *PaymentsSource*.

who has not eaten any food for three days might be willing to exchange an ounce of gold for a loaf of bread. To another party who has plenty of food, the loaf of bread may be worth only three eggs in a barter exchange.

Barter began to evolve from values determined by two parties in the exchange of just about any two items, commodities, or assets based upon personal perceptions and needs to one that evolved into **commodity money** that was a bit more uniform and consistent with valuation. Commodity money is a form of money whose value originates from a commodity of which it is made. The commodity money consists of objects that have value in themselves (intrinsic value) in addition to value that is derived from their use as money.

The most popular types of commodity money used thousands of years ago as **media of exchange** include gold, silver, copper, tea, salt, shells, candy, cocoa beans, cowries, sugar, wheat, alcohol, and cigarettes. Each individual item being exchanged was pegged somewhat with corresponding value to another item of value. For example, one pound of tea may trade equally for one pound of wheat. Salt was considered so valuable that many Roman soldiers were paid in the form of salt rather than any other type of commodity.

Some of these items were very heavy to transport over a few miles or several hundred miles prior to exchanging them with other people. So, it wasn't very practical to place 300 pounds of shells on the back of a horse and walk alongside the horse for 50 miles to deliver the shells to another person who had a product of almost equal weight to exchange. Sometimes, the items were perishable, difficult to store, and would decay in a relatively short period of time causing them to lose their value.

Commodity money began to change over the years partly due to transportation and storage issues, especially for the heaviest food items that would not last too long in the hot sun. Commodity money changed into a type of **representative money** system in which a coin, shell, or paper certificate would represent the underlying commodity that was about to be exchanged between two or more parties. For this system to work, both parties must have full faith that the object or symbol being exchanged did in fact truly represent some type of valuable underlying asset such as 10 cattle or 50 chickens.

The effect of holding a token in exchange for a 100-gallon container of fresh well water must be the same economically as actually having the large water container by the buyer's side at the time of purchase. The commodity money system only worked if both parties trusted one another, and later delivered the items that the token or paper certificates represented. Few people could carry around heavy buckets of water to use as barter in exchanges, so new money methods would develop over time.

Commodity Market

In more modern times in the 20th and 21st centuries, the **Commodity Market** still exists, but now it is a global marketplace where items of value are exchanged and transferred all around the world. These trades are primarily associated with the economic sector more so than manufactured products that are sold at retail stores.

Commodities are categorized as **hard commodities** and **soft commodities** and include the following items of value:

- **Hard commodities:** Items that are mined from the ground or vegetation such as gold, diamonds, silver, rubber, and oil.

- **Soft commodities:** Agricultural items that are grown on farms and ranches such as wheat, sugar, coffee, cocoa, pork, and fruits.

A commodity market can be a physical or virtual marketplace for the buying, selling, and trading of raw or primary products. There are about 50 major commodity markets worldwide that assist with the trades of at least 100 primary commodities.

The main physical exchange headquarters for commodities in the United States are at the Chicago Board of Trade (CBOT) and at the Chicago Mercantile Exchange (CME), and at the New York Board of Trade (NYBOT) and the New York Mercantile Exchange (NYMEX). The Chicago Board of Trade was established in 1848.

Each of these commodities exchanges specializes in certain types of hard and soft commodities such as:

- **Chicago Board of Trade:** Gold, silver, soybeans, wheat, rice, oats, corn, and ethanol

- **Chicago Mercantile Exchange:** Cattle, pork bellies, lumber, milk, and butter

- **New York Board of Trade:** Coffee, orange juice, cocoa, sugar, and ethanol

- **New York Mercantile Exchange:** Gold, silver, copper, platinum, aluminum, heating oil, propane gas, and electricity

Two additional large regional centers for the exchange of commodities can be found at the Kansas City Board of Trade (KCBT) and the Minneapolis Grain Exchange (MGE). Both of these Midwestern regional exchange centers focus primarily on agricultural commodities. Two of the best known international commodity exchange headquarters are located at the London Metal Exchange and at the Tokyo Commodity Exchange.

Unlike the exchange of commodities thousands of years ago, most commodities are exchanged electronically through an online exchange system. Investors can purchase stock in corporations with ownership or control interests in a certain type of commodity such as gold, oil, or coffee, or the investor can purchase mutual funds, index funds, or exchange-traded funds (ETFs) that have underlying commodity assets that directly impact their overall market value every day.

Gold and Silver

California is nicknamed the "golden state" more for the gold rush years of mining a year or two before California officially became a state in 1850, than for our seemingly endless sunshine. The demand for gold and silver dates back at least 8,000 years. One of the earliest massive discoveries of gold treasures was found at a burial site in Bulgaria in 4000 BC. At the time, gold was so treasured that people were buried with it.

By 3600 BC, goldsmiths in Egypt began to melt gold ores as a technique to separate the metals inside. Blowpipes were made from fire-resistant clay to heat the smelting furnaces. The first value of exchange method for gold might date back to 3100 BC when Menes, the founder of the first Egyptian dynasty, decided that the gold-to-silver value ratio would transfer as "one part of gold would be equal to two and one half parts of silver in value," called the Menes gold-to-silver value ratio code.

The establishment of more consistent value for silver as compared with the more valuable and harder to find gold made silver more appealing to people. In 3000 BC, near modern day Turkey, more people began to mine for silver. Additionally, pure silver had many healing qualities such as the ability to destroy harmful bacteria found on a dinner plate. In fact, sterling silver utensils were originally created to kill off harmful bacteria before they went from the dinner plate to the person's mouth. The phrase "born with a silver spoon in his mouth" is partially a reference to the wealthier families who could afford to eat with healing and expensive sterling silver utensils.

Spanish sailors who arrived in the "New World" of Central and South America during the 15th and 16th centuries encountered a wide variety of native Incas or Indians that spoke many different languages than the European Spaniards were accustomed to at the time. The Spaniards and the natives did not have much in common besides the fact that they all seem to hold gold and silver items in high regard. Specifically, items made for religious purposes or rituals, jewelry, and coins for trade were usually made of some kind of gold or silver component.

Over the next few centuries, Spanish and British sailors discovered vast riches of gold and silver up and down the region that would later become the state of California. Sutter's Mill in Northern California was one of the largest gold mine strikes found anywhere in the western states. The years of 1848 and 1849 were two of the best years for the discovery of gold in the land that would later be added to the Union as an official state on September 9, 1850. Some historians have made the claim that the state might not ever have been formed without the discovery of so much vast gold and silver wealth. Once California became a state, the Spaniards and British soldiers were eventually pushed out.

Paper Money in the U.S.

The Massachusetts Bay Colony issued the first paper money in the U.S. territory on February 3, 1690. The main stated reason for the creation of paper money was to pay for war. The Massachusetts region was also the first place in the American colonies to mint its own silver coins in 1652 in spite of the British law against it at the time.

The original paper money was called a **bill of credit**; the money represented the colony's financial obligations to the soldiers fighting for independence. The soldiers could spend or trade the colony's bill of credit or fancy IOU just like they could silver and gold coins.

During the American Revolution (1775 - 1783), several other colonial leaders tried to replicate the Massachusetts Bay Colony's paper currency in their own regions on a much larger scale. The new currency system was called the **"continentals"** and was used to help finance the war. Sadly, the new currency quickly lost its value because it was not backed by any physical assets such as gold or silver. The value of the continental currency fell tremendously, inflation began to skyrocket for goods and services purchased by the weakening currency, and eventually most people would refuse to accept the continental currency.

The invention of the U.S. Mint, the federal monetary system, and the U.S. Coinage Act of 1792 would eventually replace other types of currency systems in existence at the time. The National Banks Act that was enacted after the end of the Civil War led to the federal government introducing a monetary system where banks could issue paper notes based on their holdings of government bonds. National bank notes followed over the next few decades as the U.S. finally had its first uniform paper currency.

The first type of more modern paper money issued in the U.S. came into existence on March 10, 1862. The $5, $10, and $20-bills that were issued were called "legal tender" after the passage of an act by Congress on March 17, 1862. The currency and financial systems would continue to change over the next few centuries as a result of actions taken by Congress, the Federal Reserve (the "Fed"), and consumers.

Checks

Some historians have claimed that the earliest version of the check dates as far back as with the Romans circa 352 BC. There were banks or bank-like institutions that existed in ancient Mesopotamia, Greece, and Rome that may have transferred deposits or provided some sort of a credit or debit system that was somewhat like a checking account, so the earliest versions of checks may date back hundreds or even thousands of years before that.

The first known "cheque," the name that was offered by financial institutions, was associated with financial firms in medieval Italy and Catalonia. Back then, someone making a deposit or withdrawal of funds had to appear in person before a banker to either withdraw the funds or transfer them to another customer. The "cheque" practice later evolved to the use of written instruments that were exchanged between people as opposed to the personal attendance in front of a banker before the funds could be withdrawn or transferred.

In the early 1500s in Holland, checks became increasingly popular with their residents. Amsterdam, now the capital of the Netherlands, was a major shipping and trading center at the time. Many people had accumulated large cash deposits as a result of these international trades, and decided to place their money with local Dutch "cashiers" for a small fee. It was thought that it was safer to leave the valuable money with a reputable cashier than to leave it in an empty home while sailing far away for weeks or months at a time.

The Dutch cashiers would use an accounting method that would keep track of all credits and debits made to a person's account. The cashiers would pay their depositors' debts out of their cash funds from each account as instructed by the written order or "note" issued by the depositor. This may have been the very first account-based bill payment. It would take another two or three-hundred years for the concept of check writing to catch on in England in the late 1700s. Many Brits were hesitant to try the check-writing system because the pieces of paper could easily be forged or replicated with phony accounts.

The concept of check writing became more common in the land areas that would later become the United States as far back as 1681. So, the residents of the land in America would be using check systems almost a hundred years before many British residents. The checks were cashed against the value of a person's land holdings that first began in the Boston region. Cash-strapped property owners would effectively mortgage their land to a fund, or put up the property as a form of collateral for a loan against which they could write checks.

The first printed checks were traced to a British banker named Lawrence Childs in 1762. Even though the Brits were late to join the check-writing system after the Dutch and Americans, it is thought that the word "check" was coined in England in the late 1700s. The Brits were claimed to be the first people to add serial numbers to these small pieces of paper as a more efficient way to keep track of them for this credit and debit system.

As checks became more widely used around the world, bankers realized that it became more challenging to collect actual cash funds from these accounts if the issuing bank was located far away. In the early years, each bank had to send a personal messenger to other banks to present the checks for the collection of cash. As the distances between banks increased over the years, it became almost impossible to send individuals to multiple financial institutions across a town, city, or much wider region. It was also dangerous for the bank messengers to carry large amounts of cash on them if they met face-to-face with a robber. Other times, the bank's messenger might run off with the money after collecting more money than the messenger may earn in an entire year.

The creation of a bank "clearinghouse" system was established sometime in the late 1700s at a pub somewhere in Great Britain after two bankers who were sharing drinks had the idea. At this pub gathering, the two bankers learned that they each held checks in their possession that were issued by the other person's bank. To save them both time and expenses related to messenger and travel costs, the bankers decided to form a check clearinghouse system that consisted of paper networks of banks that would exchange checks with one another.

In the 20th and 21st centuries, the clearinghouse system in the U.S. would become more efficient at a much faster pace. Now, banks can present checks to private clearinghouses or to the Federal Reserve System for regional, national, and international check collection. Checks will pass through large sorting machines that read the magnetic ink characters (**MICR - Magnetic Ink Character Recognition**) at the bottom of each check and place the check in sorting "pockets" during the automation process. The MICR standard was developed in the 1950s, and contains information such as the routing number that identifies the specific issuing or drawee bank, the payment amount, and the payor's unique account number.

The bank for the payee, or the person receiving the funds that are represented by the check, will then be credited for the entire payment amount. The funds will be instantaneously moved from the payor's account to the payee's account once the funds are cleared as "good" or valid. In the earliest years of the MICR check-clearing system, the actual physical check would be transported to the payee's bank by car, truck, or airplane. The payor, in turn, would receive a copy of the canceled check from their bank in the next statement. In more recent years, most of these credits, deposits, and check records are shared digitally between banks and customers.

In the 21st century, check writing has been declining at a rapid pace as new forms of virtual money technologies advance with options such as credit and debit cards and online bill paying options. Per a Federal Reserve report issued in 2013, the number of check payments in the U.S. had fallen from a high of almost 30 billion checks per year down to 17.3 billion over the period of 10 years.

The world's largest bank over the past several thousand years is thought to be the Vatican Bank near Rome, Italy. Most types of modern-day banking systems may be linked to origins tied to financial centers in the Vatican or Rome. In fact, the first "moneychangers" appointed by the Vatican to act as official bankers and currency managers was the Rothschild ("Red Shield") group. The Rothschild group members had a red shield sign on their front door. Later, larger regional banks and central banks like the Federal Reserve Bank and the Bank for International Settlements in Basel, Switzerland (the world's most powerful bank that governs all central banks worldwide) would evolve. Interestingly, the original name of Bank of America was the Bank of Italy.

Bretton Woods Conference

The Bretton Woods Agreement was the most important and influential monetary and exchange-rate management system established in the first half of the 20th century near the end of World War II. The meeting was scheduled at the United Nations Monetary and Financial Conference in Bretton Woods, New Hampshire that was held between July 1 and July 22, 1944. The World Bank Group was also established out of Bretton Woods as a financial entity that would provide financial assistance for countries in the midst of rebuilding after the two previous world wars.

Just like the year of '44, there were 44 member nations in attendance with 730 delegates to create a foreign exchange-rate system, prevent significant currency devaluations for member nations, promote economic growth and trade, and form a new international monetary system that would be pegged to the price of gold. The original price of gold was just $35 per ounce. In addition, the U.S. dollar was established as a **reserve currency** that was directly linked to the underlying price of gold. Out of Bretton Woods, the dollar became the most powerful and respected paper currency in the world partly since it was the main currency tied to gold.

The chief architects of the Bretton Woods Agreement were the noted economist named John Maynard Keynes of the United Kingdom and Harry Dexter White, the chief international economist of the U.S. Treasury Department. It was Keynes' intent to try to establish a global central bank called the Clearing Union. White's plan was more to limit the powers and resources of each member nation. The final adopted plan took ideals from both sides while reaching some type of compromise.

The establishment of the **International Monetary Fund (IMF)** came as a result of the Bretton Woods Agreement one year later in 1945. Twenty-nine original members of the IMF signed the Articles of Agreement in December 1945. The IMF was designed to monitor exchange rates and lend reserve currencies to member nations as needed. The IMF today consists of 189 member nations with the stated intent to "foster global monetary cooperation, secure financial stability, facilitate international trade, promote high employment and sustainable economic growth, and reduce poverty around the world."

The Bretton Woods Agreement was formally dissolved during the years between 1968 and 1973. There were too many dollars chasing too many goods and services around the world which led to fast-rising inflation rates, weakening foreign currency rates, and concerns over the increasing price of gold that was tied to the dollar. President Richard Nixon called for a temporary suspension of the dollar's link to the gold standard system, and foreign governments started to let their currencies float to other pegged items besides the dollar or gold. Shortly thereafter, the Bretton Woods system ceased to exist.

The Petrodollar

Bankers, currency traders, investors, and central banks all do not seem to like how inflation can severely diminish the purchasing power of the dollar. Between the mid-1940s and early 1970s, the U.S. flooded the world with dollars after the passage of the Bretton Woods Agreement. Some nations would only accept payments in the form of dollars instead of their own currency because it was so highly regarded. Even though the dollar was a "fiat currency"[2] that was backed by nothing after being issued by the Federal Reserve, it was partly backed by gold as a de facto "reserve currency" under the Bretton Woods Agreement. The more dollars that were spent worldwide, the more dollars that were printed, and the dollar's purchasing power plunged after inflation rapidly increased.

The deficit in trade spending rose each year after Americans bought more foreign goods than foreigners who purchased American goods. France

---

[2] Fiat currency is money that a government has declared to be legal tender, but it is not backed by a physical commodity. The value of fiat money is derived from the relationship between supply and demand rather than the value of the material that the money is made of.

became so concerned about the weakening dollar that they pulled all of their gold that was stored with the Fed in New York in 1967. Four years later in 1971, President Nixon made it difficult for any member nation to convert their dollars into gold.

In the early 1970s, President Nixon sent his Secretary of State, Henry Kissinger, over to Saudi Arabia with a new financial scheme that was intended to benefit both nations.
The ruling House of Saud was offered a deal that consisted of the following key elements:

1. America's strong military would guarantee protection of Saudi Arabia and all of its oil fields.

2. The U.S. would agree to sell the Saudis any weapons needed for protection from other nearby nations in the Middle East.

3. The U.S. would make sure that the ruling Saudi family remained in power for as long as the newly coined "Petrodollar" ("oil for dollars") program remained in effect.

In exchange for military protection, the Saudis would agree to complete all of their oil sales with U.S. dollars. Additionally, the Saudis would agree to take their oil profits and invest them in U.S. Treasuries. No gold would be needed to purchase oil from the Saudis, the largest oil producer in the world at the time. Many nations around the world were obliged to build up a fairly large supply of dollars on the fixed-currency exchange to buy the much-needed oil from the Saudis after the Petrodollar system formally began in 1974. At this point, the Petrodollar ruled the financial world more so than any other currency pegged to gold, silver, or some other item of value.

Credit Cards

Physical cash and coins began to merge with "plastic money" after the introduction of America's first credit card. Frank X. McNamara, the owner of a small loan company in New York, came up with the brilliant idea in the early 1950s to offer a new form of credit called a "charge plate" that could be used by customers at local restaurants in the New York region. Because the card was primarily designed to be used at local restaurants, the original name was *The Diners Club Card*. As high demand and positive word spread around town, more businesses flocked to sign up for the new credit card program such as companies associated with department stores and hotels.

With better access to credit, consumers spent more at these retail stores and restaurants. The local economy was boosted and consumers were happy to eat and shop at better places than they were used to before the introduction of plastic money. Financial companies -- *American Express* and *Carte Blanche* -- would later purchase the *Diners Club Card* before expanding it around the nation and the world.

Recent Credit Card Trends

The average non-mortgage consumer debt per consumer at the end of 2016 was reported to be $39,216, per Creditcards.com. Some other financial studies found that the average American consumer with any sort of credit card balance today had close to a $33,000 balance that did not include any automobile, student loan, mortgage, or other type of debt.

As of 2014, the four largest credit-card networks in the United States were Visa, Mastercard, American Express, and Discover. Here are some statistics related to each of these cards:

- Visa: $1.2 trillion in volume spending from holders of 304 million cards in the U.S. and another 545 million credit cards in foreign countries.

- Mastercard: There was $607 billion charged in 2014 on 191 million U.S. cards and 576 million foreign cards.

- American Express: $668 billion was charged on 54.9 million U.S. cards and on 57.3 million foreign cards.

- Discover had a credit purchase volume of $129 billion in 2014.

The 10 largest credit-card issuers in the United States in 2014 had an estimated $671 billion in outstanding loans. Combined, the following 10 financial groups held almost 85% of all outstanding credit-card loan debt out of the more than 5,000 credit card issuers, according to *PaymentsSource*. Or, 4,990 credit card issuers held only 15% of all credit card debt as compared with just 10 banks holding the other 85% of all such debt.

Outstanding Balances by Credit Card Issuer (4th Quarter 2014)*

Financial Institution	Outstanding Loans	Percent of Market
1. Citigroup	$140.7 billion	17.8%
2. JPMorgan	$120.3 billion	15.2%
3. Bank of America	$102.3 billion	13.0%
4. Capital One	$81.0 billion	10.3%
5. American Express	$60.7 billion	7.7%
6. Discover	$55.9 billion	7.1%
7. Synchrony	$39.7 billion	5.0%
8. Wells Fargo	$31.1 billion	3.9%
9. Barclays	$20.7 billion	2.6%
10. U.S. Bancorp	$18.5 billion	2.3%

Microfinance

The origins of "crowdfunding" or "crowd-sharing" programs date back to the beginnings of microfinance (also known as "microcredit") programs. Microfinance is a type of banking service option that is offered to people in low-income groups or others who may be unemployed. These same borrowers with less access to income also have fewer options to credit or financial services. Microfinance was established as a way to offer improved financial options to people in need of small loans for food or the establishment or expansion of their business operations.

In the early years of microfinance, it was more likely that neighbors would contribute very small amounts of money to be pooled as a loan for another neighbor in financial need. Over the years, local banks and private money lending groups would offer these smaller loans with very high annual interest rates and fees in dollar amounts that might vary from $100 to $25,000 or more. With upwards of 50% of the global population supposedly living on less than $2 per day in income, the microfinance boom became quite popular in places like India and other parts of South Asia.

Even though the microfinance lending system is usually thought of as more closely linked with regions in Asia, the first documented microfinance lending business was attributed to the Irish Loan Fund system that was established by Jonathan Swift as a way to improve financial conditions for impoverished Irish citizens as far back as the 18th century.*

In more recent years, the World Bank has reported that upwards of 500 million people have directly or indirectly benefited from some type of microfinance lending program. Some of these small loans are directly targeted to women while others are offered as startup capital for new business ventures. In spite of the fact that many borrowers live well below the poverty line in their respective country, the reported repayment rate for microfinance loans was 98.9% in 2016, per a micro-financing institution named Opportunity International.*

Crowdfunding

Crowdfunding is more like an online version of the microfinance industry or a joint venture-type partnership between multiple parties who share or pool their funds together to help start a new business, or pay for medical bills, college expenses, or some other debt that cannot be paid by an individual. People today are more likely to see some type of a *Go Fund Me* request page on their social media than they may see an actual loan advertisement from a national bank. With these crowdfunding options, friends, family, and strangers can contribute $10, $50, or $100 or more toward a good cause to help out someone in need. The relatively small amounts of capital contributions can add up to thousands or tens of thousands of dollars if enough people fund and share the crowdfunding request with hundreds or thousands of their own friends on social media in a matter of just a few days or so.

Let's take a look below at some of the most pivotal dates in crowdfunding history across the world:*

1700s: The Irish Loan Fund was established by Jonathan Swift to benefit low-income families in rural Ireland.

1800s: More than 300 microfinance programs in Ireland give out small sums of money for relatively short periods of time. During the peak years, upwards of 20% of Irish families used at least one type of microfinance program to borrow funds.

1976: Dr. Mohammad Yunus, one of the original early pioneers of the modern-day microfinance movement, launched a lending program in Bangladesh as a way to offer low-income residents banking opportunities. The first loan was the equivalent of just $27 (U.S.) to 42 women in bamboo villages. Five years later, the program reached 30,000 members.

1983: Dr. Mohammad Yunus' fund later transformed into Grameen Bank. This microlending bank reaches an estimated eight million borrowers with about 97% of the funds going to female-operated businesses.

1997: A British rock band by the name of *Marillon* raised $60,000 online so they could have enough money to fund their tour of U.S. markets.

2005: An online microfinance company named *Kiva* was formed with the intent to offer individual investors the chance to provide small loans to struggling entrepreneurs in poor areas around the world. In its first year of operation, investors who provided this capital to borrowers in many parts of the world earned an overall annual rate of return that was higher than 98%. By comparison, the 2012 returns for the Dow Jones Industrial Average (DJIA) index was less than 7%. More investors began to take notice that this microfinance company had generated annual returns that were almost 91% higher than the Dow Jones index returns.

2006: The first peer-to-peer lending marketplace in the U.S. named *Prosper* was formed.

2006: Michael Sullivan, the founder of *FundaVlog*, was credited with coining or creating the "crowdfunding" term.

2006: Dr. Mohammad Yunus and Grameen Bank won the Nobel Peace Prize for helping so many millions of impoverished people around the world.

2008: The crowdfunding firm, *Indiegogo*, was formed as an online place that enables people to donate funds more easily by removing the middleman (banks or other financial institutions). The lender and the borrower are matched up directly online with the click of a button online.

2008: The crowdfunding firm named *Peerbackers* was founded with the stated intention of raising money online by small donations from a large number of investors as a way to meet a specific funding goal. The firm offers participants rewards or perks in exchange for meeting the financial goals.

2009: The crowdfunding firm *Kickstarter* opened their operations to the public. The goal of the group is to provide a funding platform for creative projects that were supported by friends, fans, and other members of the public in return for rewards.

2010: The highly successful and well-known *Go Fund Me* crowdfunding firm was established on May 10, 2010. Five years later, the original founders of this firm sold their majority stake in the company to Accel Partners and Technology Crossover Ventures for $600 million. Donations to people in need of cash are usually considered "personal gifts" which are not taxed as income in most cases. Some donations made for charitable reasons may be eligible for tax deductions to the person who made the contribution.

Crowdfunding for Real Estate

Crowdfunding programs around the world have loaned an estimated amount as high as $11 trillion or more for business startups, medical bills, and various other types of debt and equity ventures related to technology, stocks, and real estate. In comparison, the outstanding unpaid balances of all residential and commercial mortgage loans in the United States may be smaller in size at somewhere close to $10 trillion. If only a relatively small fraction of this global crowdfunding money starts to invest in real estate in the United States, then it may become the number one source of debt and equity money for the construction and acquisition of residential and commercial real estate properties. If so, conventional banks, REITs (Real Estate Investment Trusts), partnerships, and investment firms on Wall Street may soon be going to crowdfunding firms for their own capital sources.

Since 2012, crowdfunding has expanded to become one of the best lending options for the purchase and financing of residential and commercial real estate. As conventional bank lending tightened up significantly after 2009, borrowers and investors began seeking out private money sources more than ever before. More buyers are realizing that their fastest lending option to purchase a discounted foreclosed home is by way of a reliable crowdfunding source. Real estate agents may soon realize that some of their best buying and selling clients may be multi-million and multi-billion- dollar real estate crowdfunding platforms that own hundreds or thousands of properties.

Real estate agents need to understand that buying and lending trends for real estate are changing faster than ever before due to technological advances that allow investors to literally click on a button from thousands of miles away from the subject property to purchase the home prior to clicking on another button to apply for a mortgage loan. Often, buyers will find the property first before they seek out a real estate agent to draw up the contract. Some polls show that 80% to 90% of people find their property first online before they speak with a licensed agent. With the average American alleged to have an eight second attention span, the typical buyer wants access to properties for sale, capital sources, and a real estate agent who can be reached almost 24/7.

Depending upon the debt or equity structure selected for a specific real estate crowdfunding platform, many investors will place their funds ($1,000 or more in some funds) into a limited liability company (LLC). The crowdfunding investors do not have ownership of the properties acquired by some crowdfunding platforms, but they do gain access to the income for the property on an annual basis by way of a document called an Operating Agreement.

Investors are able to quickly analyze certain properties available for investments by reviewing income and expense reports and photos online in the comfort of their own home. Just like how day trading for stocks became popular in the 1990s after improved access to business channels like CNBC and stock and bond numbers that unfold on their home computer in real time, real estate investors are using crowdfunding and digital money sources to buy and sell real estate without even stepping outside their home to drive by or visit the subject property. Initial funds for crowdfunding platforms or more conventional real estate purchases can be made with wire transfers, online bank account transfers, or some form of digital payment option like *Paypal, Apple Pay,* or *Google Wallet.*

Real estate investors for properties owned or controlled by crowdfunding platforms and individual sellers can be reviewed, purchased, funded, and closed on a person's home computer or smartphone here in the 21st century. There are third-party companies like *FundAmerica, Accredify,* and *Crowdcheck.com* that can confirm within just a few moments that a person is creditworthy and financially qualified enough to invest their funds in some type of property venture. In many ways, these companies are like online versions of escrow, accounting, mortgage underwriting, appraisal, and title companies all rolled into one.

The JOBS Act (Jumpstart Our Business Startups Act) was promoted as a new law that would increase the funding of small businesses and new investment opportunities by easing many of the nation's toughest securities regulations. After the passage of the JOBS Act that was signed into law by President Barack Obama on April 5, 2012, the crowdfunding pools began to reach out to investors seeking capital to purchase and refinance residential and commercial properties. Subsequent amendments to the JOBS Act called Title II, which took effect on September 23, 2013, and Title III - Equity Crowdfunding, which took effect on October 30, 2015, helped make real estate lending and investing more attractive for crowdfunding firms.

Over the past several years, the amount of funds being invested in real estate properties has grown exponentially at compounded rates. In effect, crowdfunding for real estate has eliminated the middleman (banks) and allowed investors to share in much higher profit returns by investing directly with the property owners as an equity partner or as a lender. Instead of receiving net negative returns after taxes and inflation while placing funds in bank's checking or savings accounts (0% to 1% interest, if any), investors are placing their funds with crowdfunding firms that are buying, holding, leasing, or selling properties for some tremendous profits.

Let's review some of the numbers for the real estate crowdfunding industry in the U.S. over the past few years:

1. Between 2013 and 2014, the real estate crowdfunding industry grew by 156%. At the time, it was valued at $1 billion dollars.

2. In 2015, the real estate crowdfunding industry was reported as surpassing $2.5 billion in size.

3. By 2016, the real estate crowdfunding industry grew to a valuation near $3.5 billion. It was not one of the fastest growing branches of the crowdfunding sector.

4. The real estate crowdfunding industry was estimated to be on

pace to reach $5.5 billion by the end of 2017.

5. The World Bank forecasts that the entire crowdfunding industry may be worth $93 billion by 2025.

6. There are many real estate crowdfunding campaigns that vary in size from $50,000 to $50 million or more for individual property purchases or lending opportunities. Some real estate crowdfunding firms focus on the purchase of individual fixer-upper homes at prices between $50,000 and $200,000 each, while other larger funds will invest their capital in the purchase, refinance, or new construction of much larger commercial properties such as high-rise office buildings, one-hundred-plus unit multifamily apartment buildings, or newer hotel properties.

Blockchain Technology and Cryptocurrency Systems

As of 2017, approximately 1% to 2% of all forms of money in the United States are physical currencies (bills or coins). The other 98% to 99% of money types are digital. Rumors abound that physical money may be entirely replaced by digital currency options that will likely include some type of a cryptocurrency option. There are an estimated one thousand or more cryptocurrency choices as compared with about 180 national currencies.

Once cryptocurrency systems become more efficient, investors from all over the world will be able to look at properties in places like California (one of the most preferred states in the nation for foreign investors) will be able to buy a home from their home in China and click their digital funding option to escrow to close the transaction within as short as one day. Real estate agents who are technologically savvy and understand how digital currency systems can be transferred from their national currency system into a more uniform and global cryptocurrency system will probably find a lot of clients from around the world. At this point, all buyers and sellers of properties must complete their transfer disclosure forms, purchase contracts, listing agreements, natural hazard reports, and other addenda. So, agents may not be assisting with finding the properties or helping the buyers find access to third-party capital, but they will be needed for the completion of the real estate contracts.

Some investors in cryptocurrencies like *Bitcoin, Ripple,* and *Ethereum* have earned annual returns of hundreds or thousands of a percent. Some cryptocurrency investors are cashing out of these cryptocurrency investments before the "bubble" bursts and are buying gold, silver, stocks, or real estate with the profits. It is probabe that some wise person will come up with an idea in the near term to transfer cryptocurrency profits into crowdfunding platforms for real estate or California escrow accounts with just one click of his or her smartphone key.

By early December 2017, the peak price of the 2017 year for *Bitcoin* made if officially the most valuable bank on the planet for a short time period after surpassing JPMorgan Chase, Citibank, Bank of America, and Wells Fargo. Yet *Bitcoin* has no actual cash. As such, today's financial markets and banking rules are much different than the past financial markets that so many people had learned about in their earlier years.

Let's take a look below at the Top 10 most valuable cryptocurrency systems to better understand how more money is moving from physical sources into more digital ones:

Cryptocurrency	**Market Cap Size (12/30/17)**
1. Bitcoin	$215,151,764,327
2. Ripple	$90,428,398,425
3. Ethereum	$68,350,596,189
4. Bitcoin Cash	$40,416,228,884
5. Cardano	$16,249,609,970
6. Litecoin	$11,835,757,112
7. IOTA	$8,750,406,056

8. NEM	$8,486,657,999
9. Dash	$7,743,132,188
10. Stellar	$5,684,525,835

* Source: https://coinmarketcap.com/

The total market cap size of the Top 100 cryptocurrencies in the world as of December 30, 2017 was $565,174,886,702 (or just over a half trillion), per coinmarketcap.com. When comparing the half trillion dollar (U.S.) size with the crowdfunding market share around the world that is at least 22 times larger at $11 trillion, the cryptocurrency system may just be in its infancy stages and could potentially grow at a similar pace as the crowdfunding industry over the past 35 years.

If so, then real estate agents may be spending more time on transactions involving digital currency options rather than bank funded loans. Agents can either choose to learn more about these ongoing technological and currency advances or they may be left behind. It's all about the digits, for better or for worse.

Chapter One Summary

- **Money** is defined as "anything commonly accepted by people for the exchange of goods and services." If both parties to a transaction perceive that the item being exchanged has value, then the value is established as long as they have some degree of trust between them.

- **Barter** is a system of exchange where goods and services are directly exchanged between two or more parties for other types of goods or services without using any medium of exchange like money, gold, or silver. Bartering dates as far back as 6000 BC, and was reported to have been introduced by tribes in Mesopotamia (once known as the "cradle of civilization").

- In 700 BC, the Lydians (tribes based in what is now Turkey) would become the first Western culture to make their own coins. Over the years, many different types of coins would be made of gold, silver, or both.

- The barter system in the 21st century still exists by way of some of the best-known company personnel who exchange goods, services, accommodations, content, and time with or without actually owning the items of value that are being exchanged. Modern-day barter examples include Uber, Facebook, Instagram, Netflix, Airbnb, Alibaba, and Ebay.

- Commodity money is a form of money whose value originates from a commodity of which it is made. The commodity money consists of objects that have value in themselves (intrinsic value) in addition to value that is derived in their use as money. The most common types of commodity money used as **media of exchange** include gold, silver, copper, salt, shells, tea, candy, cowries, sugar, wheat, alcohol, and cigarettes.

- Commodity money would later evolve into a type of **representative money** system in which a coin, shell, or paper certificate would represent the underlying commodity that was about to be exchanged. Commodities are classified as **hard commodities** (items that are mined from the ground) and **soft commodities** (farm and ranch items) which include gold, diamonds, rubber and oil (hard commodities) and wheat, sugar, cocoa, fruit, and pork products (soft commodities). Commodities are traded at exchange locations like the Chicago Board of Trade (CBOT), the Chicago Mercantile Exchange (CME), and the New York Board of Trade (NYBOT).

- California derives its main nickname (**"The Golden State"**) from the peak Gold Rush years near the mid-1800s shortly before the region officially became a U.S. state in 1850.

- The Massachusetts Bay Colony issued the first paper money in the British territory that later became the state of Massachusetts on February 3, 1690. The original paper money was called a **bill of credit**. This paper money was used to pay soldiers for their war efforts as the early American colonists battled with British troops while they tried to establish new settlement regions. Later, a new currency system was created that was named the **"continentals"** paper money that would later fail.

- The creation of the U.S. Mint, the federal monetary system, and the U.S. Coinage Act of 1792 would eventually replace other types of currency systems.

- The creation of a bank **"clearinghouse"** system was established sometime in the late 1700s in Great Britain. In the 20th and 21st centuries, banks can present checks to private clearinghouses or to the Federal Reserve System for regional, national, and international check collection.

- The **Bretton Woods Conference** was a United Nations Monetary and Financial Conference that was held in Bretton Woods, New Hampshire in 1944. There were 44 member nations in attendance. From this conference of allied nations near the end of World War II, a new international monetary system was formed that was pegged to a $35 per ounce price of gold that was pegged to the U.S. dollar as the world's **reserve currency**. The **International Monetary Fund** (akin to the world's chief financial monitoring group) was developed out of Bretton Woods.

- In the early 1970s, President Richard Nixon would take the U.S. off the Bretton Woods currency policies that were backed more by gold. Nixon and Henry Kissinger worked together to convert the monetary system to one that was backed by the underlying values of oil barrel prices with nations like Saudi Arabia (the world's largest oil producer at the time). As a result, the **Petrodollar** ("oil for dollars") system arose. Much higher inflation rates would follow as the purchasing value of the dollar weakened, and real estate asset prices in the U.S. would rapidly increase, especially in California.

- Frank X. McNamara, the owner of a small loan company in New York, was given credit for being the first person to come up with the idea for credit cards (or "charge plates"). The first credit card was named *The Diners Club Card* primarily since the card was accepted at local restaurants.

- The concept of **crowdfunding** dates back to Ireland in the 1700s. Today, it is one of the main sources of capital used to purchase and finance both residential and commercial properties after the passage of the original **JOBS Act** and a few subsequent amendments called **Title II** and **Title III**.

- There are an estimated 1,000-plus cryptocurrency choices as compared with about 180 national currencies. Upwards of 99% of all forms of money used in the U.S. today are some type of digital currency system that does not involve actual physical paper bills or coins.

Chapter 1 Quiz

1. What gives money value?
   A. If backed by gold
   B. If backed by silver
   C. If backed by a central bank
   D. People's perceptions

2. A system of exchange where goods and services are directly exchanged between two or more parties is called
   A. Conversion
   B. Barter
   C. 1031-exchange
   D. Sale

3.Which products were thought to be first used in the act of barter?
   A. Money
   B. Food crops
   C. Livestock
   D. Both B and C

4. A form of money that derives its value from an underlying asset or good tied to it is called
   A. Fiat currency
   B. Cryptocurrency
   C. Greenback
   D. Commodity money

5. Gold, silver, diamonds, and oil are types of
   A. Representative money
   B. Soft commodities
   C. Hard commodities
   D. Barter

6. What was the name of the very first paper money issued in the Massachusetts Bay Colony region back in February 1690?
   A. Greenback
   B. Bill of credit
   C. Continentals
   D. Treasury bill

7. Where and approximately when did the first known check clearinghouse type of system originate?
   A. Rome in the early 1500s
   B. Athens in the mid-1600s
   C. Great Britain in the late 1700s
   D. New York City in the late 1800s

8. What is the name of the system used by the Federal Reserve System to read the lines and characters found on checks in the U.S. in more modern times?

    A. ADR

    B. MICR

    C. Check Analysis System (CAS)

    D. Data Mining

9. How many allied member nations were at the Bretton Woods Conference in 1944?

    A. 44

    B. 33

    C. 22

    D. 11

10. What was the original price of gold per ounce that was pegged to the international monetary system established at Bretton Woods?

    A. $25

    B. $35

    C. $45

    D. $55

11. With President Richard Nixon's Petrodollar system, which nation worked the most closely with the U.S. to get this currency system started?

    A. Iran

    B. Iraq

    C. Saudi Arabia

    D. Great Britain

12. What legislation really boosted the crowdfunding for real estate boom?

    A. JOBS Act

    B. Title II of the JOBS Act

    C. Title III of the JOBS Act

    D. All of the above

Answer Key:

1. D	6. B	11. C
2. B	7. C	12. D
3. D	8. B	
4. D	9. A	
5. C	10. B	

CHAPTER 2

THE HISTORY OF BANKING

Overview

Mortgage and consumer lending have rapidly changed over the past few hundred years across the nation. Most real estate buyers will likely qualify for loans from one of the main primary market funding sources that are included within this section of the course. This chapter will cover the main lending sources that are found in the primary lending markets and the various types of loan products that they offer to consumers. To truly understand how the financial markets operate today, we must go back in time to learn about how banks and other financial institutions first got their start as well as their latest operating guidelines today.

The Origins of Banking

The origins of banking go back thousands and thousands of years to Babylon ("the cradle of civilization"), Greece, Turkey, and Rome. Yet there are very few banking or financial institutions that have survived for thousands or even hundreds of years into the 21st century.

While these older financial institutions may have established some core banking methods that still exist today, there are not too many financial institutions besides the Vatican Bank that are still open for business today.

The oldest surviving banks that do still exist today and have survived numerous boom and bust economic cycles in their regions include the following:

1. Banca Monte dei Paschi di Siena: This is the oldest surviving bank in the world. It was formed in Siena, Italy back in 1472. The original name was *The Monte de Pietà* (or *Monte Pio*); and it was originally established to make loans to the poor out of charitable funds. The citizens of Siena put up their income from their land as guarantees against loans for farming and city infrastructure improvements. In modern times, there are several branches throughout Italy.

2. Berenberg Bank: The second oldest bank in the world was founded in 1590 in Hamburg, Germany by Hans and Paul Berenberg. The two Berenberg brothers ran a cloth trading and import/export business. The Hamburg region was one of the main trading centers in Europe that included both German and Dutch citizens who made very good money trading and shipping goods back and forth. The bank was needed to safely store the trader's new-found profits which lead to the bank expanding over the next several hundred years with offices throughout Europe.

3. C. Hoare & Company: This old bank was founded in 1672 in London, England by Sir Richard Hoare. The first symbol used on the sign for this bank was that of a golden bottle instead of a numbered street address because the modern street-numbering system had not been invented yet. At the time, a golden or gilded bottle was a sign of luxury and wealth that was more commonly used by goldsmiths who acted as the precursors to more modern paper currency and banking systems. The first bank almost burned to the ground during World War II, but was saved by a few brave employees. Today, the bank is still completely family-owned and managed by direct descendants of Sir Richard Hoare.

4. The Bank of Scotland: This bank was founded in 1695 in Edinburgh, Scotland. It was the first bank to print its own currency in Scotland in the 17th century. The bank helped local residents set up their own businesses which, in turn, increased its customers' income and net worth. Today, the bank is known as Halifax Bank of Scotland; it is one of the largest banks in the world with offices in many countries.

5. Bank of New York (now Bank of New York Mellon): This is the fifth oldest surviving bank in the world and the number one oldest bank in the United States. It first opened its doors in 1784 in New York City. The bank was established by Alexander Hamilton, one of the founding fathers who served as the very first Treasury Secretary as well as an experienced licensed attorney. Hamilton was also the main author of the Federalist Papers that helped pave the way for the adoption of the U.S. Constitution. Today, most people may be more familiar with the hit musical on Broadway called *Hamilton* about the person featured on the $10 bill than the fact that this man helped form the oldest surviving bank in the United States. The Bank of New York was the very first company that was traded publicly on the New York Stock Exchange when the stock exchange opened for business in 1792.

Temples and Merchant Lenders

Banks have been around as far back as when the first coins and paper bills were minted. One of the main reasons why banks were opened was so that people could have a place to safely store their hard-earned funds. Many banking customers who had enough money set aside went on long trips overseas. Some worked in the shipping business or went on hunting expeditions far away from their home. At those times, instead of leaving their coins, bills, gold, and silver bars just laying around their homes (because home safes did not exist yet), people began placing their funds for safekeeping in the local banks.

Before banks existed in the U.S. and in European nations, many people stored their valuables in nearby temples or other places of worship. These same temples had honest and trustworthy priests and temple workers there almost 24 hours a day who kept a close eye on the stored valuables. There are some historical records from Rome, Egypt, Greece, and Ancient Babylon in the Mesopotamia region that note that some of these temples also loaned money out as well as stored it. Because temples were usually the financial centers for a tribe, town, or city region, they were typically the first places to be robbed or pillaged during wars.

The easiest valuable items for temples to store were gold or silver coins. As opposed to storing a 2,000-pound cattle commodity, a bag of coins could be easily stored in a relatively small space. Local wealthy merchants who bought and sold commodities, jewelry, and other products began to offer storage services for valuables to local townspeople in exchange for a small fee. The merchants began lending coins to local residents with interest to people in need. The largest loans generally came from the temples while the small loans were handled by the wealthy merchants or moneylenders.

The Banking Evolution

It was the early Romans who moved financial-service options from temples to more formalized banking buildings that were located in distinct financial centers. Most banking and lending services moved from temples and wealthy merchants over to these first banks that were built during the Roman Empire. Wealthy merchants, or moneylenders, still played a significant role lending smaller loan amounts to those in need of money for food, clothing, and shelter. The less fortunate citizens of Rome were willing to pay much higher rates and fees to the private moneylenders than they did with the banks. The moneylenders were like today's "loan sharks" that offer private rates and fees much higher than conventional rates and and make it much easier to qualify.

It was Julius Caesar, the leader of the Roman Empire at the time, who changed Roman law shortly after taking power giving the newly formed and powerful banks the right to confiscate land in lieu of loan payments should the borrower default on his loan. This was the earliest known establishment of foreclosure power for banks in world history. The relationship between a creditor/lender and a debtor/borrower was changed forever as a result of granting foreclosure power to the banks. Prior to Caesar's changes to the banking codes, noblemen who owned land were untouchable throughout previous history as they had rights to pass on both debts and assets to their heirs until either the creditor or the debtor's descendants had all passed away.

The Roman Empire eventually collapsed partly due to too much inflation, a weakening currency system, massive government debt that was directly linked to military expenses, and consumers losing faith in their currency system. But the banking institutions set up in Rome survived and expanded across parts of Europe and elsewhere over the next several hundred years.

The papal bankers at the nearby Vatican Bank became more powerful in the ongoing Holy Roman Empire with groups like the Knights of the Temple leading the way during the Crusades. The smaller private moneylenders (or "money changers") who competed with the Catholic Church's banks were denounced and arrested for the violation of **usury** laws that were related to charging borrowers rates and fees that were considered too expensive and unfair.

What were the main items stored by early temple and merchant bankers?

The ruling monarchs that reigned in other nations across Europe began to pay closer attention to the success of banking institutions near Rome and the Vatican. Many of these same kings and queens offered charters and contracts to newly formed banks so they could provide loans to the local villagers or townspeople that originated from the monarch's royal treasury. Generally, it was up to the ruling king or queen to establish the rates and fees for these loans through the local banks. The high profitable returns collected by the monarch's bank loans led them to spend more money on the expansion of their kingdom and on military might. Unfortunately, some ruling monarchs spent too much of their profits and ended up running out of money. Without sufficient amounts of money at their disposal, several monarchs were overthrown and kicked out of their castles.

The acknowledged father of banking and more modern economic theories in America was Adam Smith. Mr. Smith was an 18th-century philosopher who was a major proponent of **laissez-faire** economic policies. Laissez-faire is a French term that literally means "leave alone" or "let you be." It has come to refer to a policy or attitude of letting things take their own course, without interference. Smith's "invisible hand" theory set the foundation for laissez-faire economic philosophy, which claimed that government intervention in the marketplace between private parties was unnecessary. It would be the consumers' changes in their demand for resources, goods, or services that would automatically result in new price adjustments without any additional regulation needs.

Adam Smith believed that the tendency of the free market to regulate itself by means of competition, supply and demand, and self-interest and wealth preservation strategies for each individual was the most effective way for the economy to grow at a healthy pace. Bankers and moneylenders in the American colonies also preferred a self-regulated economy that was free from too much government regulation. As a result, the earliest financial institutions in the American territories were able to limit the state's involvement in the management and supervision of their banking operations. To attract the most customers, every bank and all the moneylenders tried to offer the best services at the lowest prices which set the basis for **free market capitalism**.

Adam Smith's Economic Theories

Adam Smith wrote many of his economic ideas in his book, *Wealth of Nations*, that is still read to this day. One of the most important sections of the book was about the **Theory of Economic Development**. It was a belief in natural laws and that agriculture was the main industry that could make a nation truly wealthy. Below, we discuss the main tenets of his economic theory.

Natural Law: Adam Smith promoted the use of natural law in economic affairs. Smith advocated or pushed for the philosophy of free and independent action without too much government interference. Each individual member of a society who is left alone to pursue his own personal economic activity or financial dream will maximize the output to the best of his own ability. A person's freedom of action will bring about the absolute best for the individual which, in turn, will likely lead to an increase in wealth and progress for a society or nation.

Adam Smith believed that free trade with minimal outside interference from competition or government actions were the best approach. Smith also asserted that natural laws are far superior to state or federal laws. It was Smith's argument that man-made or statutory laws could never be perfect and beneficial to a society as a whole. Smith claimed that nature's laws that exist more freely were more just and moral than man-made legislation.

Smith's economic theory was based on the Laissez-faire principle that required that the state should not impose too many restrictions on the freedom of an individual for both their personal and business activities. The economic development theory was built upon the ideals of saving money, division of labor, and a much wider access to markets near the individual.

Smith was heavily influenced by the 18th century doctrine of natural law, which said "there is a set of rules or rights of justice and perhaps even of morality in general which are, or may be known by, all men by the help either of reason or of a moral sense, and which possess an authority superior to that of such commands of human sovereigns and such customary legal and moral regulations as may contravene them."[3] Smith's economic theory allowed for the producers of goods and services to produce as much as they were able to at the time, earn as much income as possible, and save a great deal of money for their families. This economic theory was originally used as one of the main pillars supporting the promotion of free market capitalism.

Production Function: Adam Smith thought that there were three main factors behind production - labor, capital, and land. "The annual labour of every nation is the fund which originally supplies it with all the necessaries and conveniences of life which it annually consumes, and which consist always either in the immediate produce of that labour, or in what is purchased with that produce from other nations," as Adam Smith once said. Smith valued labor and hard work over the land supply because land was fixed and did not change much. But the increase of

---

[3]   O.H. Taylor, Economics and Liberalism, Collected Papers, Cambridge (1955), p. 423.

labor and technological improvements for productivity could lead to the increase of capital or food crops for farmers and other business owners.

Division of Labor: Smith wrote that the rate of economic growth would be determined by the size of the productive labor and the productivity of that labor. The productivity of labor is partly based upon the available supply of workers and the efficiency of their technological systems selected for their work. The division of labor is made more efficient by dividing workers into smaller groups that can be more easily managed. Each smaller group, in turn, can focus on specializing on certain skills that can be repeated over and over at a faster pace. The automobile and home building industries would later follow Smith's division of labor proposals with their creation of assembly lines of workers who handled fewer tasks like adding wheels to a new car or electrical wiring to a new home.

Adam Smith's three main benefits that were associated with the division of labor theory included:

1. the increase of dexterity for workers;
2. reducing the amount of time required to produce the commodity; and
3. the invention of more efficient and reliable machines and equipment.

Capital Accumulation: An efficient and organized labor force will create more products for consumers and more wealth for the workers and the business owners. "Any increase in capital stock in a country generally leads to more than a proportionate increase in output on account of a continually growing division of labour," said Smith.

Smith explained that "Investments are made because the capitalists want to earn profits on them. When a country develops and its capital stock expands, the rate of profit declines. The increasing competition among capitalists raises wages and tends to lower profits." Smith believed that farmers, producers, and businessmen were the main "agents of growth" for the economy. It would primarily be free trade and competition that would expand the size of the market and the overall economy.

From Adam Smith's perspective, the true root base for increased economic growth for a state or nation would start with the expansion of farming and ranch businesses. As their production and revenues increase in size, he believed that it would expand outward to improve the demand and profit margins for other businesses.

Alexander Hamilton & The First Bank

Sadly, Smith's economic theories did not work out so well for many American banks in the earliest years of their existence. The average life of an American bank back then was just five years. Many of the bank loans were defaulted upon by borrowers who later skipped town, and the bank loans or notes would effectively become worthless. Banks that were state-chartered institutions could only issue loans against any gold and silver coins that they had in reserve. Since bank robberies were common back then, the gunmen would get away with most or all of the silver and gold coins that were once located safely in the bank's main vault. The combination of a high rate of bank-loan defaults and depleted cash reserves after bank robberies led to many banks imploding after a relatively short existence.

Alexander Hamilton, the very first Secretary of the Treasury, made it his priority to improve the banking system and reduce the heavy debt burden that was related to the Revolutionary War. Shortly after Hamilton took office, he said "The debt of the United States … was the price of liberty." One of Hamilton's first acts in his role as Treasury Secretary was to create a more efficient revenue system that was based on custom duties associated with the import and export of goods and excise taxes.

Foreign nations began to respect Hamilton's methods to reduce the budget deficit as the confidence in the newly-formed American government and financial systems started to increase.

Hamilton introduced plans for the establishment of the First Bank of the United States in 1791 as a way to improve faith and confidence in the national banking system. The First Bank was designed to be the very first financial agent of the U.S. Treasury Department. While Adam Smith preached "less government intervention" in the economy, Hamilton felt that the government had to get involved with banks and the overall economy in order to boost it, reduce fraud, and improve access to funds and business opportunities for more citizens. The First Bank was jointly owned by the government and private stockholders.

The First Bank was set up as a depository for public funds and helped assist the federal government with its financial transactions. The First Bank issued its own paper currency that was later collected from citizens when they paid their taxes and debts owed to the federal government. The government, in turn, would use the tax revenue to pay off its own debts that were linked to past wars and government expansions as more territory was declared part of the new American nation.

The national bank would accept member bank notes at par (or face value that was based upon the initial offering of the security). This was very fair for member banks at the time because so many of their bank notes decreased in value after the issuance of their notes. This was due to factors such as high default rates from their banking customers. Market value due to lower demand and higher supply of bank notes or most other types of assets was usually much lower than the original par value during recessionary economic time periods.

The First Bank's purchase of notes from banks would help add much needed new or fresh capital to the member banks. The banks, in turn, would back their notes by purchasing Treasury securities (or bonds) that were backed by the "full faith" of the federal government. The ability to buy and sell notes and bonds for both member banks and the federal government helped to create a **liquid market** that improved access to capital for consumers and government officials. In many ways, this was somewhat like the first version of a secondary market for member banks.

It was Alexander Hamilton who first introduced plans for the creation of the United States Mint for the printing of paper currency and the production of coins (or "coinage"). Initially, Hamilton wanted the Mint to be a part of the Treasury Department. However, Thomas Jefferson, the Secretary of State, argued with Hamilton and demanded that the Mint be a structural part of the State Department. It was Jefferson who won this battle over control of the Mint as it was formally established in 1792 within the State Department. Five years later in 1797, the Mint became an independent agency before later being transferred to Hamilton's first choice at the Treasury Department.

As time moved forward, more depositors would demand the repayment of their state bank notes in the form of gold instead of paper currency. This was partly due to the fact that a high percentage of banking customers had more faith in the ongoing value of gold than in the latest paper currency option. The demand for gold repayment was so high at some state banks that they ran out of adequate capital reserves. Without the money and gold reserves to backup their notes and allow them sufficient funds to buy government securities from the First Bank and Treasury Department, several state banks were forced out of business.

The banking laws frustrated so many bankers that they opposed the renewal of the First Bank's charter in 1811. Shortly thereafter, the First Bank ceased to exist as they shut down for business just like so many state banks. This pivotal event in American banking history could have led to the complete collapse of the entire banking system had not significant changes been made to the financial markets over the next several years.

The Second Bank

Six years after the early demise of the First Bank of the United States, the Second Bank of the United States opened for business in January 1817. The War of 1812 (1812 - 1815) -- a conflict between the United States, Great Britain, and their respective allies -- had depleted cash, gold, and silver reserves for the federal government. The excessive spending related to military expenses led to a massive buildup in debt for the government. The higher debt levels and increased printing of new currency caused inflation levels to spike quite high within the period of just a few years. Subsequently, the faith and confidence levels in the credit and borrowing status for the Treasury Department were perhaps at all-time lows.

The Second Bank was offered a much longer charter for its operations over the next 19 years and it expired in 1836. The Second Bank's primary role was to handle the federal government's revenue deposits from tax collections and other financial sources. Banks chartered in individual states still had serious conflicts with the Second Bank just like they did with the First Bank partly since the state-chartered banks believed that the national bank held too much power and control over the state banks. Politicians who represented their local state bankers in Washington, D.C. fought to break up the Second Bank as well.

President Andrew Jackson strongly opposed the renewal of the charter for the Second Bank. In fact, one of his main platforms for the presidential election was to abolish it. Jackson's main nemesis who he argued with over this national bank issue was Nicholas Biddle, a politician, financier, and president of the Second Bank. Jackson also believed that gold and silver were the only true monies. He maintained that the Second Bank and the Treasury Department were colluding to produce too much paper currency and that that was leading to skyrocketing annual inflation rates. He believed those rates were harming consumers who were losing their purchasing power to buy basic items such as food and clothing at more reasonable prices.

In September 1833, President Jackson issued an executive order that ended the deposit of government funds into the Bank of the United States. Instead of placing government funds with the national bank, the deposits would be scattered around and deposited into multiple state-chartered banks. Most of the first banks selected were owned or controlled by Jackson's fellow Democratic-party allies. In later years, other state-chartered banks were chosen that were run by Jackson's political opponents.

Free Banking Era (1837 - 1863)

In the years prior to 1837, a bank charter could only be granted by a specific legislative act. In 1837, the **Michigan Act** was passed in the same state that allowed banks to qualify for a state charter if they could meet the minimal criteria without having to receive additional approval from the state legislature. A "free banking system" was born after the passage of the Michigan Act that promoted the growth of banking with "less government interference" as Adam Smith had built many of his economic theories on in the past. The states were more focused on minimizing banking fraud than slowing down the creation of new banks that generated more revenues for the state's personal treasury departments.

The state of New York soon followed with its own version of "free banking policy" and other states jumped on the bandwagon shortly thereafter. The "free banks" that were chartered by individual states had much less regulation than any federally-chartered financial institutions. The state banks could issue bank notes against **specie** (gold and silver coins). The free banks were in charge of their own regulation of minimum-reserve requirements, floating interest rates to be paid and charged to customers, and what types of loans and deposit options would be offered to the general public. The success of free banking spread almost nationwide as word got out about how much easier it was for banking officials to operate on a daily basis. Between 1840 and 1863, the vast majority of banking business conducted in America was completed by state-chartered banking institutions.

Just like with "EZ Doc" and subprime loans, the pendulum swung from loans that were "too hard" to qualify for back over to loans that were almost "too easy" to obtain with these "free bank" institutions. "Free banks" were a bit too lax with their loan-underwriting qualification processes that included loans being offered to borrowers with little or no valid security, credit, or collateral to secure the loan. Many banks scrambled to make loans to new clients primarily as a way to generate more fees for the banks' employees and shareholders. Investors started to lose confidence in the value of state-bank notes, especially if they heard rumors that the same banks had minimal to no cash or gold reserves in place as a form of collateral to better secure the bank notes they issued. Over several years, more and more state-chartered banks ran out of assets and closed down their operations.

National Bank Act

After so many state-chartered banks went out of business after following more lax or lenient "free banking" guidelines, several states tightened up their charter approval process and increased their supervision and regulations of member banks. Congress worked to address the problems of the "Free Banking" era by passing the **National Banking Acts of 1863 and 1864 (the "National Banking Act")**. The **United States National Banking System** was created as a result of the passage of these National Banking Acts.

The National Banking Act encouraged the development of a more solid national currency that was backed by bank holdings of U.S. Treasury securities. The acts established the **Office of the Comptroller of the Currency** under the direction and guidance of the U.S. Department of the Treasury. The Comptroller's office was given the authorization to examine, supervise, and regulate nationally chartered banks. This law made federally-chartered banks appear more financially stable than state-chartered banks. Shortly thereafter, a larger share of bank deposits were moved from state-chartered banks over to federally-chartered banks.

The passage of the National Banking Act was also enacted as a way to end the **greenback** paper currency that had been in existence to help finance the North's side of the battle in the American Civil War. The federal government started to tax any and all state bank notes (also referred to as "bills of credit" or "scrip") at a standard tax rate of 10%. The state-chartered banks had much success with their **demand deposit accounts** (or checking account) by the 1880s, and generated a high percentage of revenue from their customer's checking account fees. The intent of this taxation was to force, or strongly encourage, state-chartered banks to become nationally-chartered banks. The birth of the **"dual banking system"** arose from a bank's choice to become a state or federally-chartered financial institution.

Bimetallism

Bimetallism was a political movement near the end of the 19th century that advocated the use of silver as a main core monetary standard in addition to gold. Under economic theories and currency pricing systems, both gold and silver are viewed as valuable monetary commodities that have a price ratio that is fixed by law.

Farmers supported bimetallism because they believed that is was inflationary and would help them pay off their debts much faster with money that had lost some of its purchasing power. Congress had ended silver's role as a major form of currency in 1973, except for small coins that still contained silver. Silver miners loved the concept because it would increase the value of their silver holdings.

Larger Merchant Banks

In the early years of the 20th century, the larger **merchant banks** picked up duties once played by First Bank and others operating in the national banking system over a century or two ago. Merchant banks, especially ones based in New York City, Philadelphia, and Boston, offered consumer loans to individuals and much larger corporate finance loans to businesses. Some of the most powerful and influential merchant banks were run by J.P. Morgan and Goldman Sachs.

A high percentage of their early profits originated from commissions earned from the sale of bonds in Europe more so than in America. The more profit the merchant banks earned from the sale of bonds and other financial products, the more money they had at their disposal to lend to local residents.

J.P. Morgan - Mr. Monopoly

J.P. Morgan was perhaps the best-known merchant banker in New York during the late 19th and early 20th centuries. Morgan was connected to wealthy financial sources in London that specifically included the City of London Financial District (the most powerful financial center in the world). Morgan also had tremendous political clout and connections to local and national political figures. It was Morgan and Company that created U.S. Steel, AT&T, International Harvester, General Electric, and near monopolies in both the railroad and shipping industries.

John Pierpont Morgan was born into a wealthy New England family on April 17, 1837. One of his maternal relatives, James Pierpont (1659 -- 1714), was one of the main founders of Yale University. J.P.'s paternal grandfather was a founder of the then highly-respected Aetna Insurance Company. His father, Junius Spencer Morgan (1813 -- 1890), ran a successful dry-goods food company before later becoming a partner in a London-based merchant banking firm. With the generations of influence and connections in the fields of banking and the retail sector, J.P. Morgan was fortunate to have a head start on his competition as he headed into the banking business himself in the 1850s.

In 1871, Morgan formed a partnership with a Philadelphia banker named Anthony Drexel. By 1895, their firm was reorganized as J.P. Morgan & Company. This company would be the predecessor of one of the most powerful financial institutions on the planet in the 21st century called JPMorgan Chase.

Morgan had so many near monopolies or total monopolies where he controlled the vast majority of the business in a certain sector like transportation that the "Mr. Monopoly" character for the famous board game based upon real estate transactions is based on J.P. Morgan himself. Morgan used various trusts that he owned or controlled more anonymously as creative ways to get around existing antitrust laws that prohibited one person from having too much ownership interest in one or more business sectors.

Morgan was trying to avoid violating the **Sherman Antitrust Act (15 U.S.C. §§ 1 -- 7)** that was passed by Congress in 1890 under the presidency of Benjamin Harrison. The Sherman Act allowed certain business activities to operate competitively with other similar businesses while not allowing them to pick up too much market share. The Sherman Act recommended that the federal government has the right to investigate and pursue individuals and trusts that were deemed powerful cartels or monopolistic groups in their marketplaces. It was thought by many historians that the Sherman Antitrust Act was passed specifically to go after J.P. Morgan.

15 U.S.C. § 2 - Monopolizing trade a felony; penalty

"Every person who shall monopolize, or attempt to monopolize, or combine or conspire with any other person or persons, to monopolize any part of the trade or commerce among the several States, or with foreign nations, shall be deemed guilty of a felony, and, on conviction thereof, shall be punished by fine not exceeding $100,000,000 if a corporation, or, if any other person, $1,000,000, or by imprisonment not exceeding 10 years, or by both said punishments, in the discretion of the court." 26 Stat. 209 §2, (July 2, 1890); *69 Stat, 282; Pub. L. 93–528,* § 3 (July 7, 1955); , *88 Stat. 1708*; Pub. L. 101–588, § 4(b), (Nov. 16, 1990; 104 Stat. 2880; *Pub. L. 108–237, Title II,* § 215(b); 118 Stat. 668 Dec. 21, (1974 to June 22, 2004).

The merchant banks based in the larger cities like New York catered primarily to the wealthier clients who lived near their banks. These same banks did not need to advertise very often and they rarely lent money to the working class or "common" people. There were many allegations of racism against these merchant banks that seemed to favor making loans to Anglo-Americans of European descent. It would be the local private money lenders who would eventually offer loans to consumers in need of capital instead of the larger merchant banks.

The Bank Panic of 1907

The Bank Panic of 1907 was the first financial crisis in the 20th century. The financial losses were almost as significant during the 1907 crisis for many individuals and businesses as during the worst years of the Great Depression (1929 -- 1939). In prior decades and centuries, the economy had experienced wild swings from expansionary to contractionary and everything in between. The Bank Panic was the final proverbial "straw" that led to much more regulation and supervision of banks and the financial markets. It would be the catalyst for the formation of the Federal Reserve (the "Fed") several years later as a way to bring some sort of stability and uniformity to the national banking system.

State-chartered trust companies competed with federally-chartered banks for many years in the larger metropolitan areas like New York City and Boston. Specifically, the trust companies were aggressively pursuing new deposits for savings accounts from customers who previously had their funds placed with the larger merchant banks.

Trust companies were not part of the national payments system for checks and other types of financial instruments that were run through the check clearing system used by banks. Partly because trusts did not offer many checking services, they had fewer fees collected from their depositors to store as cash reserves. Per a study released by the Fed, trusts maintained an average of only close to 5% of cash reserves to deposits (or $5,000 in cash reserves set aside for every $100,000 in deposits). National banks, on the other hand, maintained an average cash reserve to deposit ratio closer to 25% (or $25,000 in cash reserves for every $100,000 in deposits).

One of the main risk exposures for trust companies was that trust deposits were demandable in cash from banking customers. If too many customers asked for their money back on any given day, the trust company was susceptible to bank runs just like banks would be in later years during the depths of the Great Depression. (Perhaps you've seen the movie It's a Wonderful Life?)

Unfortunately, trust companies were actively involved with investments loaned to brokerage firms on Wall Street and elsewhere that were related to some fairly risky securities and equity investments. Trust companies did not require collateral for those loans given to brokerage firms. Some of the short-term loans had to be repaid at the end of the same day they were loaned.

The brokers on Wall Street used their trust funds to purchase securities for themselves or their clients, and then would use these same investments as a collateral for another type of "call loan" (an overnight loan used to make stock purchases from federally-chartered banks). Once the call loan was paid back, the stockbrokers could pay back the trust companies on the same or following day.

It was necessary for the stockbrokers and equity firms on Wall Street and other locations to use loans provided by trust companies at the time because it was illegal for federally-chartered loans to be offered to anyone in the form of an "uncollateralized loan," i.e., a loan with no valid collateral backing. Additionally, the law prohibited federally-chartered banks from guaranteeing the payment of checks written by brokers on their accounts without sufficient funds in the account. The extra cash infusion that was loaned to the investment banks trading stocks and bonds provided kind of a capital float that would make the trades balance out each day while increasing their liquidity or access to cash.

Once the runs on trust company deposits increased after more customers demanded their cash back due to concerns about the stability of the financial markets, the trust companies were not able to offer new loans to the investment banks on Wall Street. Without access to new cash sources from the trust companies, the stock brokerage firms could not make their trades. With fewer trades, the value of stocks began to rapidly decline after more sales than purchases became the norm for numerous stocks. It was a downward financial descent for both the trust companies and firms on Wall Street since they were so closely tied to one another.

On October 16, 1907, two wealthy investors named F. Augustus Heinze and Charles W. Morse both suffered huge financial losses in their failed attempt to grab the majority control and ownership interests in the stock of United Copper. The failed attempt to corner the copper market had caused many customers associated with the financial institutions tied to Heinze and Morse to run to their banks and demand all of the money out of it at once.

Several days later, the New York Clearing House made a statement to the public that the banks associated with Heinze like the Mercantile National Bank had been examined and designated as still solvent and financially strong in an attempt to calm depositors. Both Heinze and Morse were forced out as managers of the Mercantile National Bank along with the rest of their fellow managers. The New York Clearing House then offered to guarantee the bank loans issued by Mercantile with their own clearinghouse loan certificates.

The main financial troubles would soon spread from the federally-chartered banks to one of the largest trust companies in New York called Knickerbocker Trust and to other smaller trust companies. The president of Knickerbocker was a man named Charles T. Barney. Mr. Barney was a close business associate of Morse, and it was later claimed that Knickerbocker played a prominent role in the attempt to corner the copper market.

Once news spread about Knickerbocker on October 18, 1907, customers ran to their offices to demand their cash withdrawals due to fears that the trust company might collapse and they would lose all of their hard-earned deposits. The nearby National Bank of Commerce offered to extend credit to Knickerbocker Trust as a way to cover those significant cash withdrawals in such a short period of time. The same National Bank requested an emergency loan from the New York Clearing House on behalf of Knickerbocker Trust on Monday, October 21st. Yet this loan request was denied because trust companies were not allowed to be members of the clearing-house system or qualify for any loans.

In a near panic after the denial of an emergency loan from the New York Clearing House, a request for aid was sent to J.P. Morgan. Morgan then asked Benjamin Strong, a vice president at Bankers Trust who would later become the first head of the Federal Reserve Bank of New York, to go out and examine Knickerbocker Trust's accounting records to find out if it was creditworthy and financially secure. After Mr. Strong could not confirm whether or not Knickerbocker was financially sound even after reviewing its financial books, partly due to its complex model of investments, Morgan refused to assist Knickerbocker.

On the same day, Knickerbocker's Board of Trustees dismissed Barney from his office as president of the firm solely on the basis of his close connections to Morse and the copper scandal. Shortly thereafter, the National Bank of Commerce announced that it would no longer act as the clearing agent or lender for Knickerbocker after learning about the outing of their friend Barney as leader of the company. Once word hit the street about Knickerbocker's latest challenges, the run on bank funds intensified as almost $8 million in total cash was withdrawn from Knickerbocker during just a few days' time.

Knickerbocker then shut down the trust company in an attempt to stop the massive withdrawal of funds. The suspension of business operations for Knickerbocker would lead to a full scale financial panic in New York City and in other parts of the nation. The run on deposits quickly spread to another large trust company called the Trust Company of America as well as several other smaller trusts.

Investors who held stocks on Wall Street began panicking as well prior to attempting to sell their stocks. Tragically, there were not many buyers with access to cash who could buy stocks even sold at a huge price discount. After J.P. Morgan and his close business associates realized how severe the financial crisis was and that it could get much worse for all of them, Morgan stepped up to provide financial aid as did the New York Clearing House banks.

The financial markets were so spooked at the time that there was an upward spike in the call money interest rates[4] that was shocking to most investors. On the day that Knickerbocker closed down on October 22nd, the annualized call rate shot skyward from 9.5% to 70% before it headed higher to 100% just two days later. Morgan agreed to provide more capital to the New York Stock Exchange along with his friends and business partners so that the stock exchange would not go out of business as well.

Four days later, on October 26th, the New York Clearing House Committee met to form a new managing panel to facilitate the issuance of clearinghouse loan certificates that could be used by financial institutions and customers to gain quicker access to liquid funds. This committee was somewhat of a predecessor to discount window loans from the Federal Reserve System to member banks that were established several years later in 1913. During the Bank Panic of 1907, the New York Clearing House and J.P. Morgan acted like the Federal Reserve and U.S. Treasury while bailing out banks, trust companies, and investment banks on Wall Street that were all close to fully collapsing due to lack of access to cash and credit.

---

4   the interest rate paid on overnight loans on stock collateral offered at the New York Stock Exchange

The Formation of the Federal Reserve

The Bank Panic of 1907 took place before the establishment of the Federal Reserve System, the Federal Deposit Insurance Corporation (FDIC), or the Securities and Exchange Commission (SEC). Each of these financial entities or agencies were designed to bring improved financial stability to the banks and financial markets. Before the central bank called the Federal Reserve (a private entity with a government name), the FDIC, and the SEC were formed, the National Banking Acts had provided some regulatory structure for the day-to-day operations of banks.

However, bank runs were not helped much by legislative acts that were passed decades earlier. Modern day banking evolved from the Bank Panic of 1907 just as the banking system would later change and grow after the Great Depression (1929 - 1939) and the Credit Crisis (2007 and beyond).

One year after the near financial collapse of the U.S. banking and financial system in 1907, Congress passed the Aldrich-Vreeland Act on May 30, 1908 as new legislation designed to assist with future economic and financial crisis situations without having to rely upon the generosity of wealthy individuals to step in and bail out the markets like J.P. Morgan had done. The Aldrich-Vreeland Act provided for the issuance of emergency currency funds while establishing the eighteen-member National Monetary Commission that was chaired by Senator Nelson Aldrich. The group was in charge of determining what changes were necessary to better stabilize the nation's monetary and financial system that specifically had to do with banks and currency markets.

Over the next few years, members of the National Monetary Commission traveled to Europe to learn about how their banks and central bank systems fully operated. In January 1911, Nelson Aldrich offered a plan to Congress in 1912 that called for a new **National Reserve Association**. Many of the ideas for the creation of a new central bank system came from a secret meeting of bankers and politicians on Jekyll Island just off the coast of Georgia. In attendance at the meeting were prominent investment banker Paul Warburg, Treasury official Abram Piatt, Henry Davison, Arthur Shelton, Frank Vanderlip, and a few others. The meeting was so secretive that the attendees could not address one another by their last name partly so that the staff workers in attendance could not share details with their friends and family.

Aldrich's original plan was not well received and was attacked by many politicians who feared that the new proposal to create an independent central bank that was led by U.S. and foreign investors and bankers would give too much power to the bankers while giving too little power to the federal government as it pertained to the management of the nation's banking and financial system. The original plan called for a forty-six member Board to manage the Federal Reserve with only six members directly appointed by the government. But the main person who would be selected to lead the Federal Reserve as chairman would come from a list of just three candidates that were supplied by the bankers' association. Unlike the First and Second Banks of the United States that were run entirely by the federal government, the federal government would have no true valid ownership and management interests in the privately-held (but publicly-named) Federal Reserve.

President Woodrow Wilson did not have a formal banking background, so he solicited advice from Virginia Representative Carter Glass in regard to his opinions about Aldrich's committee plan for the passage of the Federal Reserve Act. Carter Glass would later become the chairman of the House Committee on Banking and Finance. Glass teamed up with the resident expert advisor for the National Monetary Commission named H. Parker Willis when reviewing the Federal Reserve Act proposal. Willis was an acclaimed professor of economics at Washington and Lee University. After going back and forth with their concerns and ideas, Glass and Willis presented their updated proposals for the Federal Reserve Act that President Wilson would later sign in December 1913.

An interesting connection between the Bank Panic of 1907, J.P. Morgan, and the formation of the Federal Reserve took place in 1912 and 1913. J.P. Morgan was the primary financier who funded the construction of the *Titanic* ship. At the time, the ship was claimed to be "unsinkable" and the finest ship anywhere in the world when it set sail on its maiden voyage from Southampton in Great Britain to New York City.

Some of the wealthiest people in the world at the time were onboard the maiden voyage. These prominent individuals and other family members included John Jacob Astor IV (he was claimed to be the wealthiest person on the ship and in the world at the time of the sinking), Benjamin Guggenheim, Molly Brown (the wife of a Colorado mining kingpin who was also nicknamed "the unsinkable Molly Brown" after the ship's sinking), J. Bruce Ismay (the chairman of the White Star Line who first sketched plans for the ship on a dinner napkin in 1907), and the co-owner of *Macy's,* Isidor Strauss and his wife Ida.

Many of the wealthy passengers on the *Titanic* ship were outspoken opponents of the potential Federal Reserve Act that was being shopped around Washington, D.C. as a way to create a new central banking system. J.P. Morgan was scheduled to also be in a room on the *Titanic* ship during its maiden voyage, but somehow had either shown up too late and missed the departure or unexpectedly canceled near the last minute for unknown reasons.

The ship hit an iceberg about 400 miles off of the coast of Newfoundland in the eastern side of Canada and sunk approximately 2.4 miles below the surface of the North Atlantic ocean on April 15th (Tax Day) in 1912. Just 19 months later during the winter or holiday break recess, Congress pushed through the passage of the Federal Reserve Act that President Woodrow Wilson signed on December 23, 1913. The wealthy opponents who did not want the Federal Reserve created had their voices silenced once they went down with the *Titanic*.

Even though J.P. Morgan was the primary funder of the construction of the *Titanic* and was quite fortunate to have accidentally or intentionally missed the ship's tragic maiden and final voyage, he was not so lucky one year later in 1913 while traveling in Rome, Italy. Morgan was found dead due to natural causes in his hotel room on March 31, 1913. At the time of his passing, he was 75 years old and supposedly worth about $118 million. With today's highly inflated dollars, that net worth amount might translate to almost $49 billion.

The Federal Reserve Act led to the formation of America's first central bank, Federal Reserve, that has ruled the U.S. banking system ever since with its management, regulations, and its powers to increase or decrease short-term rates to banks and borrowers. The Federal Reserve also developed various methods to modify bank reserve requirements and add or subtract capital from the economy through the purchase and sale of government securities. The Federal Reserve was created with the intent to stabilize the financial markets and currency system as well as to control annual rates of inflation that could severely destroy the purchasing power of the dollar. Ironically, the value of $1 in 1913 in now worth about 2 cents in 2017, after more than a hundred years of fairly consistent rates of annual inflation.

Chapter Two Summary

- The origins of banking date back several thousand years to Babylon, Greece, Turkey, and Rome. **Banca Monte dei Paschi di Siena** is the oldest surviving bank in the world. It was formed in Siena, Italy back in 1472.

- Before banks were established, many people began storing their valuables in nearby temples or places of worship. These same temples had trustworthy priests and temple workers there almost 24 hours a day who kept a close eye on the valuables. Later, treasurers for royal families started storing and protecting valuables for local townspeople.

- **"Money changers"** became another preferred option for people to store funds and even borrow funds from private "money-changer" individuals who were not usually affiliated with local churches or royal families.

- **Adam Smith**, the famed early American economist, promoted the use of natural law in economic affairs. Smith pushed for the philosophy of free and independent action without too much government interference. Adam Smith thought that there were three main factors behind production - **labor**, **capital**, and **land**.

- **Alexander Hamilton**, the first Secretary of the U.S. Treasury, introduced plans for the establishment of the First Bank of the United States in 1791 as a way to improve faith and confidence in the national banking system. The First Bank would purchase notes from banks while adding new capital sources for the member banks. The banks, in turn, would back their notes by purchasing

Treasury securities that were backed by the "full faith" of the federal government. Eventually, this national banking system would fail and run out of cash and bonds to swap with consumers and government officials.

- Six years after the First Bank of the United States collapsed, the **Second Bank of the United States** opened for business in January 1817 as the nation's top federal charter institution.

- The **Michigan Act** was passed and signed into law in 1837. It allowed banks in Michigan to qualify for a state charter if they could meet minimum qualifying guidelines without have to receive approval from the state or federal legislature. This act eased the qualification process so much for state-chartered banks that it spread across the state and nation as state-chartered banks became the most preferred way to form new banking enterprises.

- Later, many state-chartered banks went out of business partly due to the relatively easy "free banking" guidelines that encouraged several banks to be fairly aggressive with their loan products to customers who would later default. Congress passed the **National Banking Acts of 1863 and 1864** as a way to stabilize that the national banking system.

- The National Banking Act led to the establishment of a more solid national currency that was backed by bank holdings of U.S. Treasury securities. The act established the **Office of the Comptroller of the Currency**. The National Bank Act also found a way to end the **greenback** paper currency that had been in existence to help finance the North's side of the battle in the American Civil War.

- **Bimetallism** was a political movement near the end of the 19th century that advocated the use of silver as a main core monetary standard in addition to gold. These two types of commodities made up the core of many types of currency systems for hundreds of years in the U.S. and thousands of years around the world.

- The **Bank Panic of 1907** (the first big financial panic of the 20th century) was one of the main reasons for the formation of the Federal Reserve several years later in 1913 as a way to bring some sort of stability and uniformity to the national banking system as led by people like J.P. Morgan. The establishment of the **Federal Deposit Insurance Corporation (FDIC)** and the **Securities and Exchange Commission (SEC)** later followed in the 1930s.

- President Woodrow Wilson signed the **Federal Reserve Act** in 1913 that later paved the way for the formation of the Federal Reserve. The entity then became the most powerful financial entity in the United States that directly impacts the access to capital for consumers and banks on a daily basis.

Chapter 2 Quiz

1. Which region of the world has the world's oldest surviving bank as of 2018?
   A. Iraq
   B. Athens, Greece
   C. Rome, Italy
   D. Siena, Italy

2. Who was one of the main founders of the Bank of New York (now called Bank of New York Mellon)?
   A. J.P. Morgan
   B. John D. Rockefeller
   C. Alexander Hamilton
   D. Andrew Carnegie

3. What were the main items stored by early temple and merchant bankers?
   A. Paper bills
   B. Gold coins
   C. Silver coins
   D. Both B and C

4. Which economist or philosopher promoted the concept of "laissez-faire" and "invisible hand" theories which claimed that less government intervention in the marketplace was a good thing?
   A. Henry Moore
   B. Adam Smith
   C. John Maynard Keynes
   D. John Bright

5. What was the name of the original federal bank that was formed in the United States?
   A. First Bank
   B. Federal Reserve
   C. U.S. Treasury
   D. U.S. Bank

6. The ability to buy and sell notes and bonds for both member banks and the federal government that improved access to capital for consumers and government officials is called a more ____.
   A. Equitable market
   B. Debtor state
   C. Liquid market
   D. Leveraged market

7. What legislation made it much easier to create state-chartered banks with less federal-government regulation and supervision than in years past?
    A. National Coinage Act
    B. Michigan Act
    C. New York Banking Charter Act
    D. Regulation B

8. What law did Congress pass to address the "free banking" era related to the lax state-chartered bank guidelines and the subsequent large number of bank closures?
    A. Federal Reserve Act
    B. Second Bank Act
    C. National Banking Acts
    D. Fair Credit Act

9. What legislative act was passed by Congress in 1890 to eliminate a person (J.P. Morgan, for example) or company's monopolistic control over one or more business sectors?
    A. Federal Reserve Act
    B. Anti-Monopoly Control Act
    C. Sherman Antitrust Act
    D. Fair Lending Act

10. What types of lenders were the most negatively impacted by the Bank Panic of 1907 in New York City?
    A. Insurance companies
    B. Equity funds
    C. State-chartered trust companies
    D. Federally-chartered commercial banks

11. What person or entity was given the most credit for bailing out the financial system during the Bank Panic of 1907?

    A. Federal Reserve

    B. J.P. Morgan

    C. New York Clearing House

    D. Both B and C

12. What federal agency was created after the passage of the National Banking Act?

    A. Office of the Comptroller of the Currency

    B. Securities and Exchange Commission

    C. Federal Reserve

    D. Treasury Department

Answer Key:

1. D	6. C	11. D
2. C	7. B	12. A
3. D	8. C	
4. B	9. C	
5. A	10. C	

CHAPTER 3

THE FEDERAL RESERVE & EARLY 20TH CENTURY

Overview

The financial markets and overall U.S. economy changed significantly in the first few decades of the 20th century. As capital, transportation systems, communications, and entertainment sectors became much easier to access for more Americans, the nation changed from a rural majority to a more urban majority after so many people flocked from their rural homes or farms to the booming northeastern metropolitan cities such as New York City, Boston, and Philadelphia.

The introduction of the Federal Reserve as the nation's new central bank also changed the way that money was loaned to both member banks and to consumers, for better or worse. Regardless, the changes in the creation of money and loan opportunities allowed many Americans to enjoy a more prosperous and fun-filled life through much of the first few decades of the 20th century as readers will learn in this chapter.

The Federal Reserve

A German immigrant and wealthy financier named Paul Warburg was one of the main people to draft the Federal Reserve Act that was later signed into law by President Woodrow Wilson in December 1913. The stated intent of the formation of the Federal Reserve was to bring more stability to the national banking system after years of previously failed attempts such as the First Bank of the United States and the Second Bank of the United States many years earlier.

Which man's signature led to the passage of the Federal Reserve Act?

Alexander Hamilton, the first Treasury Secretary, believed that a national banking system would help stabilize the nation's credit and debt systems while boosting the overall economy. Hamilton also felt that some sort of a core central bank power was an absolute priority for America to exercise their new republic's constitutional powers. A major hurdle for lawmakers back in Hamilton's days when the nation's First Bank began was that there were disputes between the commercial banking centers in the North (Boston, New York, and Philadelphia) and farmers and ranchers in the more agricultural South, who believed that a central banking system would be more favorable to the bankers in the northeastern states.

After the early demise and full collapse of the First Bank and Second Bank systems, federal lawmakers thought that the Federal Reserve was the management system that would lead America into more prosperity while protecting the financial markets from too much inflation, a weakening dollar, skyrocketing interest rates, and the threat of more failed banks and other types of financial institutions. Without a central bank in charge of all other private banks nationwide in the 18th and

19th centuries and early years in the 20th century, the supply of dollars was tied to the private banks' holdings of government bonds. This system worked fairly well until there were bank runs when both customers and banks were in desperate need of cash.

Without a centrally-managed government banking system to ease financial fears (by taking certain emergency actions when the demand for money exceeded the available supply at the time), there was no structure in place that allowed a central government the right to print more cash on demand in a relatively short time period. The financial markets were not elastic, fluid, or able to quickly adjust to the latest economic conditions when banks were running out of money due to customers' fears and cash demands. The Bank of Panic of 1907 ended up being perhaps the primary reason why a new central banking system finally would be permanently established several years later.

Another reason offered for the establishment of a central banking system took place in San Francisco on April 18, 1906. This day was memorable and destructive because it was the day that a massive 7.8 earthquake hit the city, causing damages estimated at over $500 million dollars (in 1906 dollars, that is) after destroying more than 28,000 buildings and killing more than 3,000 residents.

An additional 250,000 residents were left homeless out of the total 400,000 residents in San Francisco at the time. With the majority of San Francisco's residents unable to live in their homes and so many businesses and banks closed down, many people were not able to gain access to any cash at the local banks for at least a few weeks. The threat of future disasters just like the San Francisco quake of 1906 were offered up as valid potential reasons for setting up a national central banking system as a way to protect customers' deposits in any future earthquakes, destructive fires like *The Great Chicago Fire* that left more than 100,000 homeless, or hurricanes or tornadoes in the southern states.

The Most Powerful Federal Reserve Families and Companies

The year 1913 was the same year that J.P. Morgan died in a hotel room in Rome, Italy and the same year that the Rockefeller Foundation was formed. The House of Morgan was perhaps the most influential financial firm that ruled both Europe and the United States in the 19th and early 20th centuries. It had effectively operated as a quasi-central bank since 1838 when George Peabody founded it.

Once J.P. Morgan passed away, the Rockefeller and Rothschild families were alleged to have picked up much of Morgan's business operations. It was claimed by many financial and economic historians that the Rothschild family had actually controlled and owned most of the House of Morgan in London and J.P. Morgan & Company in the United States. The House of Morgan's prominent clients included the Astors, DuPonts, Guggenheims, Vanderbilts, and Rockefellers. Companies that were financed or launched by Morgan companies included AT&T, General Electric, General Motors, and DuPont (all are still some of the wealthiest corporations on the planet).

Other well-known U.S. companies financed, directly or indirectly, by Rothschild and/or Morgan included Rockefeller's Standard Oil, Andrew Carnegie's U.S. Steel, and Edward Harriman's railroads through affiliate bankers such as Jacob Schiff at Kuhn Loeb. Schiff worked in a financial alliance with the European Rothschilds.

The four most powerful banks (a/k/a "Four Horsemen of Banking") that have direct ownership and management control of the Federal Reserve include Bank of America, JPMorgan Chase, Citigroup, and Wells Fargo. These same financial institutions also own significant shares of the Four Horsemen in Oil (Exxon Mobil, Royal Dutch/Shell, BP Amoco, and Chevron Texaco (formerly Rockefeller's Standard Oil).

The original eight (8) most powerful family names in charge of the formation of the Federal Reserve back in 1913 included these American and European families and/or their affiliate corporations:

- Goldman Sachs
- Rockefellers
- Lehmans
- Kuhn Loebs (the first four groups were based in New York City)

European families or corporations:

- The Rothschilds of Paris and London
- The Warburgs of Hamburg, Germany
- The Lazards of Paris
- The Israel Moses Seifs of Rome

The 10 most influential banks that may own and manage all 12 of the Federal Reserve Bank branches include:

- N.M. Rothschild of London
- Rothschild Bank of Berlin
- Warburg Bank of Hamburg
- Warburg Bank of Amsterdam
- Lehman Brothers of New York*
- Lazard Brothers of Paris
- Kuhn Loeb Bank of New York
- Israel Moses Seif Bank of Italy
- Goldman Sachs of New York
- JPMorgan Chase Bank of New York

* The near-collapse of Lehman Brothers in September 2008 was one of the financial low points for the markets during the worst month for the last Credit Crisis.

Some of the largest individual shareholders in the Federal Reserve over the years have included William Rockefeller, Paul Warburg, Jacob Schiff, and James Stillman. Just as private shareholders usually own stock in community banks, the main central bank called the Federal Reserve is privately-owned and controlled by many of the same shareholders that own banks that offer loans to consumers and mortgage borrowers every day.

The Fed's Monetary Policy

The Federal Reserve is in charge of **monetary policy** here in the United States even more so than Congress, the President, or any other segment of the federal government. The federal government is in charge of **fiscal policy** which is related to the power of taxation and the government's spending decisions that may either increase or decrease the overall economy. When taxes are increased and the government spends less money each year on public works projects like new roads, highways, or schools that can create more jobs, the economy will likely slow down. Conversely, lower taxes and increased national spending will probably boost consumer spending and stimulate the overall economy. Both monetary policy and fiscal policy go hand-in-hand to either increase or decrease the current directions of the national economy up and down.

The Federal Reserve System was created as a two-part structure in 1913. There is a central authority called the Board of Governors based in Washington, D.C., and a decentralized network of 12 Federal Reserve Banks located across the nation.

The 12 districts are located in the regions below:

- 1st District, Boston. Connecticut (excluding Fairfield County), Massachusetts, Maine, New Hampshire, Rhode Island, and Vermont;

- 2nd District, New York. New York State, twelve counties in Northern New Jersey, Fairfield County in Connecticut, Puerto Rico, and the Virgin Islands;

- 3rd District, Philadelphia. Eastern Pennsylvania, Southern New Jersey, and all of Delaware;

- 4th District, Cleveland. Ohio, Western Pennsylvania, Eastern Kentucky, and the northern panhandle of West Virginia;

- 5th District, Richmond. Maryland, Virginia, North Carolina, South Carolina, and most of West Virginia;

- 6th District, Atlanta. Alabama, Florida, Georgia, and parts of Louisiana, Mississippi, and Tennessee;

- 7th District, Chicago. Iowa and most of Illinois, Indiana, Michigan, and Wisconsin;

- 8th District, St. Louis. Arkansas and portions of six other states: Missouri, Mississippi, Tennessee, Kentucky, Indiana, and Illinois;

- 9th District, Minneapolis. Minnesota, Montana, North Dakota, South Dakota, twenty-six counties in Northwestern Wisconsin, and the Upper Peninsula of Michigan;

- 10th District, Kansas City. Colorado, Kansas, Nebraska, Oklahoma, Wyoming, northern New Mexico, and Western Missouri;

- 11th District, Dallas. Texas, northern Louisiana, and southern New Mexico; and

- 12th District, San Francisco. Nine western states--Alaska, Arizona, California, Hawaii, Idaho, Nevada, Oregon, Utah, and Washington-- and American Samoa, Guam, and the Northern Mariana Islands.

* Source: Federal Reserve Bank of Richmond

The Federal Reserve was established with characteristics related to both the private and public sector. The primary ownership interests, control, and management belong to private individuals and financial institutions based in both America and Europe while the Fed derives some of its authority from Congress. The Board of Governors for the Federal Reserve was created as an independent government agency. But the Federal Reserve Banks were formed like private corporations. Member banks hold stock in the Federal Reserve Banks which pay them annual dividends as with many other types of stock or bond investments.

The Federal Reserve has three main functions in its role as the nation's central bank. These functions include the provision and maintenance of an effective payments system, the supervision and regulation of banking operations, and the conducting of monetary policy. The Fed also has annual goals or **"mandates"** that it tries to reach that include: maximum sustainable employment, stable prices, and moderate long-term interest rates.

The Federal Reserve reportedly collects the majority of its income from interest received on U.S. government securities or bonds that it has purchased through **open market operations** and other types of **monetary policy** methods that directly impact consumers and member banks. The three main types of monetary policy tools used by the Federal Reserve to affect consumer spending trends, banks, and the overall economy are:

- the movement of short-term rates for consumers and member banks;
- the reserve requirement rules for banks; and
- open market operations.

The **discount rate** is the interest rate that Reserve Banks charge commercial banks in their districts for short-term loans. These rates complement or assist open market operations in achieving the desired or targeted near-term **federal funds rate** and can improve liquidity (or the improvement of cash access) for commercial banks. The lowering of the discount rate is **expansionary** in that it is likely to boost borrowing demand from banks and their individual and business customers. The raising of the discount rate is viewed as **contractionary** because it may discourage banks and borrowers from lending and spending more expensive funds due to the higher cost of borrowing. The rates are changed by the Board of Governors and the Reserve Banks at their regularly scheduled annual meetings or at emergency sessions as needed.

The **reserve requirements** are the amounts of cash or credit deposits that must be set aside by banks as determined by the Federal Reserve. These reserve or excess funds must be held either in a bank's values or on deposit at a Reserve Bank. An increase in reserve requirements is **expansionary** because it increases the amount of funds in circulation for the banking system that can later be lent out to consumers and businesses. A decrease in reserve requirements, on the other hand, is viewed as **contractionary** because there are fewer dollars available in the banking system to be loaned to individual and business borrowers. The Board of Governors at the Federal Reserve has the sole authority to increase or decrease reserve ratio requirements.

An example of a reserve requirement ratio might be a 5% reserve requirement, which would mean setting aside $50,000 in cash for every

$1 million dollars of customer deposits. Should the Fed decide that the economy is growing too fast with near-record highs for consumer spending, inflation, and bank loan defaults, the Fed may decide to both increase the reserve ratio requirements and the interest rates to slow the borrowing and spending trends. If so, the Fed might raise the reserve requirements from 5% to 10%, for example, and banks would then be required to set aside $100,000 for every $1 million dollars of customer deposits.

The **open market operations** action is the most frequently-used tool by the Federal Reserve to stimulate the economy through the buying and selling of government securities or bonds. The purchase or sale of large amounts of government securities will either expand or contract the money supply. The purchase of securities injects more money into the banking system and stimulates growth while the *sale* of securities decreases the amount of capital for banks and contracts or slows the overall economy. The Fed's regional banks offer electronic payment systems that include **fund transfers** and the **automated clearing house (ACH) system** for quicker access to money or credit.

The **Federal Open Market Committee (FOMC)** is the monetary policymaking body of the Federal Reserve System. The FOMC is comprised of 12 members which include the seven top members of the Board of Governors who meet in Washington, D.C. and other regions, and five (5) of the 12 Reserve Bank presidents who rotate every so often with their appointment to the FOMC. Each year, there are eight (8) scheduled meetings that are held, or about one meeting every six (6) weeks.

Sometimes, the Fed may hold additional "emergency" meetings when there are concerns about the latest direction of the banking and financial markets. A prime example of the Fed holding multiple emergency meetings in addition to their regularly scheduled eight (8) meetings per year was in late 2008 and 2009 as the Credit Crisis worsened. Former Fed Chairman Ben Bernanke even made a statement to a subcommittee meeting before some members of Congress in March 2009 about the fact that the financial system almost collapsed during the last week of September 2008.

The **Federal Funds Rate** is the rate at which a depository institution lends funds maintained at the Federal Reserve to another depository institution overnight. Generally, the most creditworthy institutions will be allowed to borrow and lend overnight funds to each other. This rate is one of the most important interest rates in the nation because it affects monetary and financial conditions that directly impact employment, growth, and inflation.

The Federal Open Market Committee will increase the fed funds rate by decreasing the money supply in the banking system. With less capital available to borrow for banks and consumers, the increased demand for capital that is greater than the available supply of funds will probably move interest rates higher. Higher rates may reduce or cool inflation levels during times when the Fed thinks that the national economy is growing too fast. During recessionary or stagnant economic times when unemployment rates are higher, the Fed may set targeted fed fund rates at their meetings that are lower than current rates that will hopefully boost the economy after spending and borrowing increase.

Banks and other depository institutions will maintain accounts at the Federal Reserve as a way to make payments for themselves or on behalf of their banking customers. At the end of each banking day, banks make sure that their amount of funds loaned or set aside meet the latest reserve ratio requirements. Any excess funds can be loaned from one depository bank to another so that the other financial institution can cover any of its balance shortfalls, if needed.

To summarize, the federal funds rate represents the main interest rate for banks to lend to one another when additional funds are needed. In simpler terms, a bank with excess cash, often referred to as excess liquidity, will lend money to another bank that needs to quickly raise its liquidity due to cash or credit shortfalls at the time.

The rate that the borrowing institution agrees to pay to the lending institution is determined by the two banks. The weighted average rate for all of the types of negotiated rates between lending and borrowing banks is called the **effective federal funds rate**. The effective federal funds rate is determined by both market demand between lending and borrowing banks and is influenced by the Federal Reserve through its open market operation actions that are put into effect to either expand or contract the economy.

Federal Reserve Note

A $1, $5, $10, $20, $50, and $100 bill are legally defined as "Federal Reserve Notes" (or United States banknotes) as opposed to a true dollar bill. These are the main physical banknotes that are currently in circulation in the country. These banknotes are denominated in U.S. dollars, and are printed by the United States Bureau of Engraving and Printing on paper made by Crane & Company in Dalton, Massachusetts.

The Federal Reserve Note was authorized by Section 16 of the Federal Reserve Act of 1913. The banknotes are issued to the Federal Reserve Banks by decision of the Board of Governors of the Federal Reserve System. The banknotes are placed into circulation by the Federal Reserve Banks at which time they become liabilities of the Federal Reserve Banks and financial obligations of the United States taxpayers. Or, money is created as a form of "debt" that is to eventually to be repaid with interest to the governing central bank more so than to the U.S. Treasury.

Currently, the largest physical banknote being produced today is the $100 bill. Many years ago, there were much larger banknotes in $500, $1,000, and even $10,000 increments that were in circulation. Some of these older large bills are still around, but most people probably will not see them at their local grocery store.

Listed below are charts of the types and distribution (by percentage) of physical banknotes in circulation in 2016 (per the Federal Reserve):

Year	$1	$2	$5	$10	$20	$50	$100
2016	11.7	1.2	2.8	1.9	8.9	1.7	11.5

Older bills with face amounts of $500, $1,000, $5,000, and $10,000 bills that were still in circulation in 2016 and not destroyed represented just 0.0004% of all bills used in the national economy in 2016. The total amount of all banknotes produced in 2016 that were in circulation represented 39.8% of all banknotes used in the national economy.

The rest of the banknotes still being used in 2016 were older banknotes produced in earlier years. The Federal Reserve has said that the average lifespan of a $100 bill is 15 years, a $20 lasts for 7.7 years, a $1 bill lasts for an average of 6 years, and a $5 lasts for just 4.9 years.

The two types of money in a **fractional reserve banking system** are currency issued by the Federal Reserve and bank deposits at commercial banks. Central bank money can be created by banknotes, coins, and electronic money. As of 2017, 98% to 99% of all types of money created is created digitally on a computer screen or some other display method.

A **fractional reserve banking system** is one in which only a small fraction of bank deposits are set aside in the form of actual cash on hand in a bank branch's vault that is available for daily withdrawal by customers. Some financial analysts claim that most bank branches keep less than 1% of all customer deposits on hand in the form of hard cash in their vaults. Should there ever be a bank run at a small bank branch, they could run out of cash fairly soon. Banks may loan up to 10 or more times their actual bank deposits as loans to new customers thanks to credits given to them by the fractional reserve banking system and from the Federal Reserve. For example, a bank with $10 million in customer deposits may lend out 10 times that deposit amount (or $100 million) to other banking customers for loans related to credit cards, automobiles, small businesses, construction, and real estate purchases.

The Roaring Twenties

The 1920s was one of the most prosperous decades of the past few hundred years in America. This was the very first decade when more Americans lived in cities than on farms. The total wealth for the entire nation more than doubled between 1920 and 1929. This newfound wealth turned America more into a "consumer society" than at any point in the nation's previous history.

Thanks to the power of advertising many of the same products on radios and in newspapers in larger metropolitan cities like New York City, Boston, and Philadelphia, American consumers began purchasing many of the same consumer goods and services that they heard about on the radio or read about in the newspapers. Americans also listened to much of the same music and news, and began using the same slang when speaking to one another.

Women became more independent in the 1920s as evidenced by their "flapper" look that consisted of bobbed hair and shorter skirts, smoking cigarettes, and drinking alcohol, while being more sexually free than in previous generations. Women also started to work in their own careers more in the 1920s. Thanks to the advance of the *Women's Suffrage* movement and the passage of the 19th Amendment, women gained more rights, including the right to vote. More women than ever before were working in white-collar jobs that afforded them the opportunity to live more freely and spend more of their hard-earned dollars on consumer goods and services.

The novel, *The Great Gatsby*, made references to the elaborate parties at mansions on Long Island or in the Hamptons in New York State, which attracted hundreds of people from New York City and other areas. There, they could show off their newfound wealth accumulated from a booming stock market.

Prohibition in the United States was a nationwide constitutional ban on the production, transportation, and sale of all types of alcoholic beverages during the 1920s to the early 1930s. Yet, people still held large parties in private homes like the *Gatsby* mansion and celebrated their increasing stock wealth while drinking illegal alcoholic beverages.

It was the 18th Amendment to the U.S. Constitution, ratified in 1919, that had banned the production and sale of "intoxicating liquors" in the United States. On January 16, 1920, the federal Volstead Act closed every single bar, saloon, and tavern in the country. From that point forward, it was illegal to sell any type of "intoxication beverages" with alcohol levels greater than 0.5%. An underground bar scene and economy grew from this Prohibition as seen in old films at illegal "speakeasies" (slang for underground bars or clubs) that were controlled by some bootleggers or mobsters like the Chicago gangster named Al Capone.

Both men and women purchased consumer goods like home appliances such as electric refrigerators and large radios that could be listened to in the living room with the rest of the family. The very first commercial radio station in the nation was Pittsburgh's KDKA station that hit the airwaves in 1920. Just three years later, there were more than 500 radio stations across the nation.

Near the end of the 1920s, there were an estimated 12 million households that had some type of radio. Additionally, about 75% of all Americans went to a movie theater every week on average by the end of the booming 1920s.

Alongside the advancement of the communications and entertainment industries, the transportation sector was just getting started with the automobile assembly line designed by Ford Motor Company. Cars could now be mass produced faster than ever before at Ford at much lower costs.

The lower costs to produce the cars could then be passed on to consumers as seen with the popular Ford Model T car that was priced at just $260 in 1924. By 1929, 20% of Americans had their own car. Businesses like gas or service stations, motels, and small grocery markets began to spring up alongside the roads filled with new cars to accommodate all of the new drivers on the American roads.

Here are some of the key statistics that compare the start of the 1920s with the end of the bullish or prosperous decade just before the Great Depression turned the economy upside down:

- Population in 1920: 105.7 million
- Population in 1930: 122.8 million

The very first U.S. Census Bureau year when the urban population surpassed the rural population: 1920

- Percentage of homes with electricity in 1920: 35%
- Percentage of homes with electricity in 1930: 68%

- Percentage of farms with electricity in 1920: 2%
- Percentage of farms with electricity in 1929: 9%

- Average per capita income for all Americans in 1929: $750
- Average per capita income for American farmers in 1929: $273

Dow Jones Industrial Average (DJIA) stock numbers

November 1919: 119.62
August 1921: 62.57
September 1929: 381.17
November 1929: 198.69
July 1932: 41.22

The stock market reached peak highs in the later months in 1929 while helping to create approximately 25,000 to 35,000 millionaires in the United States. After the market reached new lows a few years later in 1932, the number of millionaires in the nation was thought to be closer to just 5,000. At the time of the stock market crash in October 1929, less than 1% of all Americans owned stock at the time.

Food prices also crashed for farmers after the fall of 1929. The farm industry represented a major portion of the overall economy back in the

1920s, so the massive price drops for some of their core food crops was financially devastating to farmers throughout the nation. Specifically, two of the main crops for farmers, wheat and cotton, had horrific price drops as you can see below.

Wholesale Price of Cotton

1920: 42 cents per pound
1921: 10 cents per pound
1932: 5 cents per pound

Wholesale Price of Wheat
1920: 42 cents per pound
1921: 10 cents per pound
1932: 5 cents per pound

* Source: U.S. Census Bureau

The economic boom times of the 1920s would eventually turn to a bust time that would change the way access to money for banks, consumers, and mortgage borrowers was handled when offered by private lenders, community banks, and government-assisted lending programs that would later make the mortgage and overall financial markets much more efficient. From "boom to bust and back to boom" would be the economic trends over the next several decades as readers will learn about in the next few chapters.

Chapter Three Summary

- The most powerful wealthy families behind the formation of the Federal Reserve including J.P. Morgan and the Rockefellers, the Warburgs, the Carnegies, the Rothschilds, the Astors, the DuPonts, the Lazards, and the Harrimans.

- The four most powerful banks (a/k/a "Four Horsemen of Banking") that have direct ownership and management control of the Federal Reserve include Bank of America, JPMorgan Chase, Citigroup, and Wells Fargo.

- Lehman Brothers, Kuhn Loeb Bank, and Goldman Sachs out of New York were reported as some of the most influential banks that assist with the management and operations of all 12 of the Federal Reserve Bank branches. California is located in the Federal Reserve's 12th district region as led by the headquarter branch in San Francisco.

- The Federal Reserve is in charge of **monetary policy** here in the United States. The federal government, by way of Congress and the Treasury, is in charge of **fiscal policy** which is related to the power of taxation and the government's spending decisions.

- The Fed's main monetary policy actions that can increase or decrease the supply of money to the public include: 1) the movement of short-term rates like the Fed Funds Rate; 2) changing the reserve ratio requirements for member banks; and 3) open market operations strategies that involve the buying or selling of government securities.

- The **discount rate** is the interest rate that Reserve Banks charge commercial banks in their districts for short-term loans. The **Federal Funds Rate** is the rate at which a depository institution lends funds maintained at the Federal Reserve to another depository institution overnight.

- The lowering of short-term rates is viewed by economists as **expansionary** since it increases the supply of capital to the markets. If the Fed increases rates and reduces capital access, then this is referred to as **contractionary** (or the tightening of the financial markets).

- The **Federal Open Market Committee (FOMC)** is the monetary policymaking body of the Federal Reserve System. There are 12 members in this committee that include the seven top Board-of-Governors members and a rotating five (5) of the 12 Federal Reserve Bank branch presidents. The Fed typically holds eight (8) scheduled meetings where they vote on topics like increasing or decreasing interest rates approximately once every six (6) weeks.

- Federal Reserve banknotes ($1, $5, $10, $20, $50, and $100 bills) are placed into circulation by the Federal Reserve Banks at which time they become liabilities of the Federal Reserve Banks and financial obligations of U.S. taxpayers. As such, money is created as a form of "debt" that is to eventually to be repaid with interest to the Federal Reserve more so than to the U.S. Treasury.

- The two types of money in a **fractional reserve banking system** include: currency issued by the Federal Reserve and bank deposits at commercial banks. With fractional reserve banking and lending systems, member banks are allowed to set aside a relatively small amount of cash prior to lending out upwards of 10 times the total combined customer deposits in the form of new bank loans for items like credit cards, automobiles, and homes.

- The **Roaring Twenties** (1920s) experienced much newfound wealth for more Americans as the access to affordable money was much easier than ever before. As a result, more people bought consumer goods and services, homes, and stocks until the financial bubble began to burst in 1929 near the start of the Great Depression.

Chapter Three Quiz

1. Which man's signature led to the passage of the Federal Reserve Act?
   A. Paul Warburg
   B. Woodrow Wilson
   C. John D. Rockefeller
   D. Nelson Aldrich

2. Which group is in charge of monetary policy in the United States?
   A. Federal Reserve
   B. Congress
   C. U.S. Treasury
   D. Securities and Exchange Commission

3. Which group is in charge of fiscal policy?
   A. IRS
   B. U.S. Treasury
   C. Congress
   D. Both B and C

4. How many Federal Reserve Bank branches are across the nation?
   A. 10
   B. 12
   C. 14
   D. 15

5. Which Federal Reserve district is where California is located?
   A. 6th
   B. 8th
   C. 12th
   D. 14th

6. What is another name for the Federal Reserve's annual goals that they try to reach that include the best targeted unemployment rates, stable consumer prices, and moderate long-term interest rates?

A. Mandates

B. Directives

C. Guidelines

D. Regulations

7. What is the interest rate that the Federal Reserve charges member banks for short-term loans?

A. LIBOR

B. Fed Funds Rate

C. Discount Rate

D. Swing Rate

8. What is the economic term for the Fed's lowering of short-term rates and the reduction of allowable reserve ratio requirements?

A. Recessionary

B. Expansionary

C. Deflationary

D. Contractionary

9. What is the economic term used to describe times when the Federal Reserve raises short-term interest rates while demanding that member banks increase their reserve ratio requirements?

A. Inflationary

B. Contractionary

C. Reflationary

D. Disinflation

10. Which answer below is **not** an open market operations strategy used by the Federal Reserve?
    A. Changing reserve ratio requirements for banks
    B. Moving short-term interest rates up or down
    C. Raising the tax percentage rates
    D. Buying and selling government securities from the financial markets

11. Which percentage rate for all U.S. money in circulation in modern times is actually physical, i.e., in paper bills and coins?
    A. 1% to 2%
    B. 25% - 27%
    C. 33% - 35%
    D. 82% - 84%

12. What is the term used to describe when banks lend out 10 times or more of their actual cash deposits on hand at their local branch?
    A. Fiat currency
    B. Federal Reserve's leverage system
    C. Derivatives
    D. Fractional reserve banking system

Answer Key:

1. B	6. A	11. A
2. A	7. C	12. D
3. D	8. B	
4. B	9. B	
5. C	10. C	

CHAPTER 4

GREAT DEPRESSION & GOVERNMENT FINANCING

Overview

The Great Depression (1929 - 1939) was a major catalyst for changing financial markets in the United States and in many other nations around the world. In this chapter, we will explore the causes and outcomes related to the Great Depression, and the solutions presented by the federal government to boost confidence once again in the financial markets. Government-assisted forms of financing by way of FHA, VA, USDA, and customer and bank guarantees through the FDIC and other government-sponsored programs played a prominent role in the growth of the financial and real estate sectors dating back to the Great Depression era as will be covered in this section of the course.

The Great Depression - A Short History

The Bank Panic of 1907 was just a warm-up for the next major economic downturn time period to hit the United States beginning in the late 1920's. While the Bank Panic of 1907 lasted only a relatively short period of time, the Great Depression (1929 - 1939) lasted 10 years. Millions of investors were wiped out in the stock market and lost their jobs, homes, and sometimes even their families. Consumer spending fell to record low levels at the time while few investors had access to capital to make new investments to expand their businesses or to purchase stocks, bonds, or real estate even at discounted prices.

Almost every "boom" and "bust" cycle over the past 100 plus years began with access to relatively easy and affordable types of money ("boom" or positive economic cycle) followed by the tightening of credit access and higher interest rates ("bust" or negative economic cycle). The Great Depression, the bust that followed the Roaring Twenties boom, was perhaps the best example of a booming and busting economic cycle pattern that went from peak highs to lows shortly thereafter.

The Great Depression was the longest and most severe economic depression ever experienced by the industrialized Western world. Although it began in the United States, the economic chaos and destruction would later spread to many other regions worldwide, especially in Europe. Japan and Latin America were not hit as hard as the U.S. and Europe during the depths of the economic downturn. There were drastic declines in output for many key business sectors, unemployment numbers reached as high as 25% nationwide, and asset deflation became the norm for stocks, bonds, and real estate due to the fact that there were more sellers than buyers with access to cash or credit at the time.

America's economy was tied to many other Western nations by way of the gold standard, which linked the vast majority of countries in a network of fixed currency exchange rates that were tied to the underlying fluctuating gold prices. The gold markets were blamed by some economic and financial historians as either the main cause of the spreading economic depression or as the potential solution to save the worsening financial markets.

Shortly after the Roaring Twenties economic boom was near its peak, the Great Depression officially began as just an ordinary recession in the summer of 1929. Between the top and bottom of the financial markets and overall U.S. economy, industrial production fell 47%, the real gross domestic product (GDP) numbers fell 30%, and the whole price index declined by a staggering 33%.

From the peak to the depths near the bottom of the economic cycles during the Great Depression years, here are some of the numbers that show how far some of the wealthiest economies fell within just a few years:

Nation	Economic Decline (Peak High to Low)
United States	46.8%
United Kingdom	16.2%
Germany	41.8%
France	31.3%
Italy	33.0%
Japan	8.5%
Canada	42.4%
Belgium	30.6%
The Netherlands	37.4%
Sweden	10.3%
Denmark	16.5%
Poland	46.6%
Czechoslovakia	40.4%
Argentina	17.0%

Source: *Britannica*

Most nations that traded with the United States back in the 1930s suffered wholesale price declines of 30% or more between 1929 and 1933. Some of the most significant price declines took place between September 1929 and December 1930 for products such as coffee, silk, cotton, and rubber as these prices fell almost by half.

Herbert Hoover, the 31st president, took office in the same year that first experienced the economic depression. Hoover was in office until 1933 when Franklin D. Roosevelt ("FDR") later replaced him as president. Hoover would be considered the "fall guy" for America's woes by many historians while FDR would later be characterized as the "savior" for creating various job works programs and financial guarantees that boosted the stock, bond, real estate, and job markets shortly after taking office.

One of President Hoover's most controversial decisions was his backing of the **Smoot-Hawley Tariff Act** (June 17, 1930) that raised import duties as a way to supposedly protect American farmers and businesses from international competition. Prior to the passage of Smoot-Hawley, the United States already had one of the highest tariff (or import tax) rates in the world with close to a 20% import tax rates. Once Smoot-Hawley was passed, it doubled tariff rates on imported goods to an incredibly high rate of 40%.

This protectionist mentality that promoted American goods over foreign goods seemed to do more harm than good after fewer people could afford to buy imported goods. Inflation began to increase for both American and foreign products, and unemployment numbers began to worsen after fewer foreign markets would agree to purchase American goods exported to other parts of the world as retaliation for the 40% tariff taxes in the United States. In later years, FDR signed the **Reciprocal Trade Agreements Act** that reduced tariff levels, promoted more equal, fair, and balanced trade, and improved trade and business cooperation with foreign governments.

In October 1929, the stock market crashed with the average value of the 50 leading stocks at the time falling by almost 50% within just two months. By 1932, many stock averages were 25% or less of their peak highs. There was a combination of a 20% to 25% national unemployment rate during certain years combined with salary declines for those fortunate enough to hold a job that fell by somewhere between 40% and 60% for some job sectors.

President Hoover's Financial Stimulus Programs

The year 1932 was perhaps the worst year of them all for the national economy during the depths of the Great Depression. It was best known as the year when bank runs become fairly common as depositors scrambled to pull money out of thousands of banks just before they went out of business. Unemployment reached 25%, the national average income was 50% below that of the peak in 1929 before the economic downturn started, and the stock market values were 75% below its 1929 peak highs. With less access to money, barter became a popular form of payment as people shared food for other household products as a way to survive the economic collapse.

President Hoover pushed for the passage of several key acts that did provide more financial stability in the short and near term for the national economy. Many of Hoover's acts would later be improved upon by FDR after he took office in 1933. These Hoover acts that were passed included the **Reconstruction Finance Corporation (RFC) Act of 1932** and the **Federal Home Loan Bank Act of 1932**.

The purpose of the **Reconstruction Finance Corporation (RFC) Act of 1932** was to provide loans to banks, savings banks, building and loan associations, credit banks, mutual savings banks, industrial banks, and life insurance companies. Loans were also made to financially destitute railroads that were on the verge of collapse. Hoover thought that a safe and sound transportation system for the nation was key to a solid economy.

The **Federal Home Loan Bank Act of 1932** established the Federal Home Loan Bank Board (FHLBB), which charters, supervises, and regulates the federal savings and loans. The act also established the Federal Home Loan Banks (FHLBs) entity that was given the authority to lend to savings and loans to finance home mortgages.

The Gold Standard

Gold has been the most popular choice for currency dating back thousands and thousands of years. Gold was exchanged as coins, bars, and jewelry either by itself or mixed with silver or other metals. California's main nickname, the Golden State, is a reference to the large gold mining deposits first discovered at Sutter's Ranch in 1948 that helped to inspire the Gold Rush and the addition of California as a new state two years later in 1850.

The first modern-day paper currency in the United States was printed by Treasury Secretary Salmon Chase in 1861. Other nations followed with the printing of their own currencies that were usually somehow tied, directly or indirectly, to the fixed or floating value of gold (also referred to as a "gold standard"). The gold standard was a guarantee that the issuing government would later redeem any amount of paper money for its equivalent value in gold. Instead of carrying much heavier gold bars or coins when shopping, consumers could carry the very lightweight paper currency bills in their pockets. Unfortunately, gold prices seemed to drop quite often shortly after another new massive gold discovery site was found by miners such as at Sutter's Ranch or other regions across the world.

One of the stated reasons for the creation of the Federal Reserve in 1913 was "to stabilize gold and currency values" both in the United States and abroad. Before the Fed could attempt to stabilize the gold, currency, and financial markets, World War I broke out between 1914 and 1918. European nations began suspending their national currency links to the underlying gold standard so that these nations at war could print enough new money to pay for their expansion of military operations.

When too much money is printed too quickly, **hyperinflation** is likely to follow as the purchasing power of this printed currency backed by nothing of value buys far fewer goods and services. The rampant skyrocketing inflation becomes more noticeable to us when our basic everyday food items double in price in the period of just days, weeks, or months. After World War I ended in 1918, most nations realized that the gold standard was a better option as they rushed to return to a modified version of a new gold standard.

In spite of the lessons learned during World War I about the dangers of hyperinflation after abandoning the gold standard for a nation's currency, several nations later left the gold standard and printed as much money as possible in an attempt to boost the economy in a more positive direction. After the stock market began to crash in October 1929, more and more investors began trading in currencies and commodities like gold instead of stocks. The demand for gold pushed prices much higher after more people started exchanging their weaking dollars for gold.

The bank runs that worsened in 1932 and 1933 scared many investors away from keeping their money in banks or other financial institutions that they did not trust or have much confidence in during the worst economic years. More people began hoarding gold in their homes because they did not want to leave any valuable assets with banks that might close down after too many depositors demand the withdrawal of funds during bank runs.

Instead of lowering interest rates to boost the national economy during the severe economic downturn, the Federal Reserve kept raising interest rates. The stated reasons made by Fed officials was that they were trying to make the weakening dollar appear more valuable to investors in the U.S. and abroad and the Fed wanted to inspire more people to stay with dollars instead of transferring to gold as their financial safety net. Unfortunately, the cost of doing business became more expensive due to the higher rates, and more businesses were forced into bankruptcy while worsening the already shockingly-low national unemployment figures.

Roosevelt Takes Power

FDR officially became the 32nd President of the United States on March 4, 1933. He held office the longest of any president in U.S. history during 1933 to 1945. On March 5, 1933, after one day in office, FDR launched the **New Deal** and asked Congress to meet with him in a special session a few days later on March 9th. He declared a **national bank holiday** that was originally planned to close all banks from March 5th to March 9th. Later, the national bank holiday was extended until March 13th.

Which program did FDR launch just one day after taking office as President in March 1933?

The **Emergency Banking Relief Act** was signed into law by President Roosevelt on March 9, 1933. The act was a response to the nearly 10,000 U.S. banks that had failed between President Hoover's years in office (1929 -- 1933). Each time a bank failed, its depositors would lose all of their money because the FDIC banking insurance system had not yet been created. The banks that were closed down during the national bank holiday would later reopen after bank examiners deemed them financially sound and not on the verge of running out of cash (or the act known as **disintermediation** when depositors pull funds out of banks prior to investing them directly on their own).

The Emergency Banking Relief Act also expanded presidential powers to deal with a banking crisis, gave the Comptroller of the Currency power to take over any troubled banks on the verge of financial collapse, allowed the Secretary of the Treasury to offer financial assistance to weak banks, and assigned more power to the Federal Reserve to issue emergency currency when needed. This legislation was designed partly so that the Treasury and Federal Reserve were given powers to quickly act to ease up on banks and debtors during economic times when improved access to money at more affordable rates was needed instead of reduced access at higher rates.

FDR claimed that he was concerned about the financial safety of many banks, the frequency and extent of the increasing bank runs from customers who demanded both their dollars and gold holdings, and the rapid decline in the amount of gold reserves at the Federal Reserve Bank of New York. FDR demanded that all U.S. banks turn over their gold deposits to the Federal Reserve instead of to their customers. By the time that banks reopened for business on March 13th, they had turned their gold over to the Federal Reserve and could no longer redeem dollars for gold. In addition, gold could no longer be exported to other nations.

On April 5, 1933, FDR demanded that all Americans turn in their personal holdings of gold in exchange for dollars. If any American disobeyed these presidential orders, they could be arrested for various financial crimes. FDR said that this decision was made to prohibit and outlaw the hoarding of gold and the redemption of gold by other countries. The amount of excess gold collected from banks and from American citizens later led to the creation of the national gold reserves at Fort Knox in the state of Kentucky. Shortly thereafter, the United States held the world's largest supply of gold.

The year 1933 was still a very challenging financial year during the depths of the Great Depression in spite of all of FDR's New Deal plans that were set into motion. The national money supply was still 40% lower than in 1929 near the peak highs. There were upwards of 4,000 commercial bank failures and another 1,700 savings and loans that went out of business in 1933 alone. The FDIC is granted authority to examine almost 8,000 state-chartered banks that were not members of the Federal Reserve Board (FRB) shortly after being established

The **Federal Deposit Insurance Corporation** first began with the power to insure bank accounts up to $2,500 for each depositor in 1933, especially for commercial banks. The next year, the deposit amounts were increased to $5,000 in 1934. The FDIC coverage benefits per account would later increase to these amounts over the next several decades:

FDIC coverage protection

1950: $10,000
1966: $15,000
1969: $20,000
1974: $40,000
1980: $100,000
2008: $250,000

The costs associated with FDIC coverage protection were paid by regular premium payments that were paid by the insured banks. All member banks that were affiliated with the Federal Reserve System were required to insured their deposits using FDIC protection. Nonmember banks not affiliated with the Federal Reserve were permitted to do so if they met the minimal FDIC financial and operation standards.

The FDIC program was so successful in the early years of operation that upwards of 90% of all deposits held at commercial banks were covered by FDIC. Most funds at mutual savings banks were also insured by FDIC.

In later years in the 1980s, federally chartered savings and loan associations created their own deposit insurance program called the **Federal Savings and Loan Insurance Corporation (FSLIC).** Shortly after the collapse of hundreds of large savings and loans in the 1980s and early 90s -- partly due to risky construction and construction loans coupled with the payment of deposit rates that were much higher than loan interest charges that caused a negative annual rate of return for Savings and Loans ("S&Ls") -- the FSLIC insurance program ran out of money after trying to bail out too many S&Ls. Later, the FSLIC fund was dissolved, and the responsibility for insuring S&Ls (also called savings banks and thrifts) was transferred to the FDIC.

FDR's acts granted the **Office of the Comptroller of the Currency (OCC)** the authority to appoint a conservator with the powers of receivership over all national banks that were threatened with suspension or financial insolvency. The **Securities Act of 1933** was enacted and required that all publicly-held corporations file detailed financial disclosure statements.

Requirements to share financial information with the public deprived bankers of their monopoly with respect to financial information that they had been unwilling to share with others outside of their corporate boardrooms.

The Securities Exchange Act of 1934 passed which led to the creation of the **Securities and Exchange Commission** (SEC). This act required that any company with securities that are traded on national exchanges such as on Wall Street or in smaller over-the-counter (OTC) systems to file registration applications and annual reports with the SEC. The stated purpose for investment companies to file their annual registration filings with the SEC was so that both regulators and investors are well aware of the true financial shape of the securities firm.

The **Gold Reserve Act of 1934** was enacted on January 30, 1934. This act prohibited the private ownership of gold except under license granted by the federal government. It was described as *"an act to protect the currency system of the United States, to provide for the better use of the monetary gold stock of the United States, and for other purposes."*

The main part of the Gold Reserve Act included this section below:

> *"SEC. 2. (a) Upon the approval of this Act all right, title, and interest, and every claim of the Federal Reserve Board, of every Federal Reserve hank, and of every Federal Reserve agent, in and to any and all gold coin and gold bullion shall pass to and are hereby vested in the United States; and in payment therefor credits in equivalent amounts in dollars are hereby established in the Treasury*

in the accounts authorized under the sixteenth paragraph of section 16 of the Federal Reserve Act, as heretofore and by this Act amended (U.S.C., title 12, sec. 467). Balances in such accounts shall be payable in gold certificates, which shall be in such form and in such denominations as the Secretary of the Treasury may determine. All gold so transferred, not in the possession of the United States, shall be held in custody for the United States and delivered upon the order of the Secretary of the Treasury; and the Federal Reserve Board, the Federal Reserve banks, and the Federal Reserve agents shall give such instructions and shall take such action as may be necessary to assure that such gold shall be so held and delivered...."

The Gold Reserve Act allowed the government to pay its debt in dollars that were created by the Federal Reserve instead of dollars backed by gold or with gold bars or coins. The act gave FDR the power to devalue the gold dollar by 40%. The main way that FDR was able to do this was to increase the value of gold that had been priced at nearly $20.67 per ounce for the past 100 years to $35 per ounce. The increase in gold prices shot up the government's gold holdings from approximately $4.033 billion to $7.348 billion. The dollar probably declined in value closer to 60% after the gold prices were changed by FDR.

In 1933, the **Glass-Steagall Act** (also known as the Banking Act of 1933) was signed into law as new legislation that was structured to prevent banks from using depositors' funds for risky investments such as in the stock market. The Glass-Steagall Act was named after Senator Carter Glass, a former Treasury Secretary and the founder of the U.S. Federal Reserve System, and Harry Steagall, a prominent member of the House of Representatives and chairman of the House Banking and Currency Committee.

Glass-Steagall gave new powers to the Federal Reserve to regulate retail banks. The act also prohibited banks from selling riskier and more complex securities related to stocks and insurance contracts. And the act was designed with the intent to separate investment banking from retail banking as visualized with an actual glass wall between these investment divisions. Effectively, a regulatory firewall was created between commercial and investment bank activities that were curbed and controlled more by the Federal Reserve and various federal agencies. The intent was to make banks more cautious when investing depositor funds in investments that were once considered too risky and speculative prior to the collapse of several thousand banks nationwide.

The **Federal Deposit Insurance Corporation (FDIC)** was created under authority of the Banking Act of 1933. It was formed to improve customer confidence in the weak national banking system by insuring a certain portion of customer funds in savings and checking accounts for member banks that were eligible for the FDIC coverage benefits in the event of future bank failure. The FDIC later became a permanent government agency after the passage of the **Banking Act of 1935**. Banks that qualified for FDIC insurance benefits after passing the bank examinations suddenly became the banks of choice for depositors who were worried about losing their money. The banks without FDIC coverage would most likely close their business operations at some point in the future due to less demand from banking depositors who were unwilling to risk their funds with potentially financial unstable banks.

Between 1929 and 1933, the total bank failures in the United States resulted in the loss to depositors of about $1.3 billion dollars. The passage of the Banking Act of 1933 (or Glass-Steagall Act) initially funded the FDIC with $289 million in capital that was provided by the U.S. Treasury and the Federal Reserve Board. The act also extends federal oversight to all commercial banks for the first time ever. Banks were prohibited from paying interest on checking accounts and national banks were allowed to branch out statewide in most regions as a result of the passage of the Banking Act.

Franklin Roosevelt's New Deal

During FDR's first 100 days in office, he moved swiftly to change the banking, currency, and financial system. FDR also asked Congress to end Prohibition and make alcohol sales legal once again. A short time later, Congress ratified the 21st Amendment to end national Prohibition laws.

In May 1933, FDR signed the **Tennessee Valley Authority Act** into law as a way to enable the federal government to build new dams along the Tennessee River that both controlled flooding and helped generate new inexpensive hydroelectric power. Congress then passed a bill that gave the federal government the right to pay farmers to **not** produce any new commodities like wheat, tobacco, corn, and dairy products in order to improve prices that had fallen so far in recent years. These government grants to farmers to stop production was a way to increase commodity prices once again that could later improve income levels for farmers and ranchers across the nation.

In June, the **National Industrial Recovery Act** was passed to guarantee that workers had the right to unionize and to demand better wages, rights, and working conditions. The act did suspend some antitrust laws so that a few larger companies could expand their operations while also establishing a federally funded **Public Works Administration**.

The Public Works program was put into effect to lower national unemployment levels with the creation of millions of new jobs for large-scale projects associated with the development of new dams, bridges, hospitals, roads, and schools. The plan was to spend at least $3.3 billion in the first year and a total of $6 billion during the entire public works program in order to boost employment, stabilize purchasing power, improve banks, and help revive the overall national economy.

The **Civilian Conservation Corps (CCC)** was a public work relief program that operated from 1933 to 1942 as part of FDR's programs. Upwards of three million new jobs were created for primarily unemployed and unmarried men between the ages of 18 to 25 (later expanded to 17 to 28 years of age) over the nine years that the CCC program existed. Workers were provided with shelter, clothing, food, and wages of $30 per month that was equal to about $550 in 2015 dollar value. Most workers sent home about $25 of the $30 monthly salary to other family members, and survived on just $5 per month.

In 1935, there were a reported 9,027 state banks and 4,692 national banks, per the FDIC. There were 26 FDIC-insured banks that failed in that same year. The approximate number of banks remained fairly consistent between 1935 and the 1980s.

The Federal Credit Union Act of 1935 was signed into law for the establishment of federal credit unions.

In 1936, there was so much gold being stored at Fort Knox in Kentucky that the U.S. Treasury Department constructed an impregnable storage fortress to hold the gold that is probably safer than most military bases or prisons.

In 1937, the amount of cash and U.S. government securities represented about 52% of banks' assets in the nation. This was more than double the cash and securities proportions held in 1929. An additional 77 FDIC-insured banks failed in 1937 alone.

The **Recession of 1937 - 1938** near the final years of the Great Depression began to worsen more than the prior years of 1935 and 1936 after FDR's New Deal programs had begun to provide some stability to the financial markets. In 1936, FDR began cutting back on some of his national spending and financial-relief programs that had been set up as part of the New Deal. Shortly thereafter, the economy again weakened in 1937 and 1938 until the nation became more stable towards the end of 1939 and the early 1940s. There were another 74 FDIC-insured banks with $69.5 million in assets that failed in 1938 alone.

Some of the best known and most-powerful financial agencies that were created in the 19th and 20th centuries included:

<u>Banking Regulatory Agencies</u>

<u>Agency Codes</u>
OCC = Office of the Comptroller of the Currency
FRB = Federal Reserve Board
FHLBB = Federal Home Loan Bank Board
FDIC = Federal Deposit Insurance Corporation
NCUA = National Credit Union Administration
OTS = Office of Thrift Supervision

Agency	Year Created	Created to Regulate and Supervise:
OCC	1864	State Banks and Savings and Loans
FRB	1913	National Banks
FHLBB	1932	Savings and Loans
FDIC	1933	State Non-member/Chartered Banks
NCUA	1935	All Insured National Credit Unions
OTS	1989	Federal Savings Associations and Mutual Savings Banks

The Birth of Government-Assisted Mortgage Loans

Saving Homes in Foreclosure

Within FDR's first 100 days in office, he helped to establish the **Home Owners' Loan Corporation (HOLC)** in order to help stabilize real estate values that had fallen so dramatically in the first few years of the Great

Depression. Because thousands of banks had run out of cash and closed for business permanently, it was quite challenging to find new mortgage loans to purchase or refinance existing mortgage debt.

The HOLC program was structured to grant long-term mortgage loans to more than one million homeowners who were facing the loss of their property at a daily foreclosure filing rate of almost 1,000 homes a day. The HOLC was able to save approximately 80% of the homes in default for the original property owners. The program really existed for only three years after it opened for business in 1933 prior to later ending its lending program in 1936. The mortgage-relief bailout programs that would follow over the next 80 years really have the HOLC program to thank for the establishment of this financial sector.

The Federal Housing Administration (FHA)

Congress created the Federal Housing Administration (FHA) program in 1934 to develop the new foundation for a national mortgage market. The FHA became part of the Department of Housing and Urban Development's (HUD) Office of Housing in 1965. FHA is the single largest insurer of mortgages in the world. To date, FHA has insured over 47.5 million mortgaged properties against foreclosure risks since its inception in 1934.

Currently, the FHA has almost 4.8 million insured single-family mortgages in its portfolio along with more than 13,000 insured multi-family apartment projects. In recent years, the vast majority of funded residential-purchase loans for owner/occupants were likely to have been backed by FHA insurance.

FHA provides mortgage insurance on loans made directly by FHA-approved lenders throughout the nation. It insures owner-occupied residential loans (one-to-four unit properties) as well as certain much larger commercial properties such as multifamily apartment buildings and even some hospitals.

The percentage of homeownership increased right alongside the introduction and expansion of FHA-insured mortgage programs between the 1930s and the 21st century. The rates of homeownership increased over the next 70-plus years thanks to FHA mortgage opportunities for millions of Americans. We can see that with the increase of homeownership rates at just 40% in the 1930s up to a peak high that reached 69% in 2005 just before the last housing bubble market popped.

Mortgage insurance protects funding lenders from the risk of default. For properties with a first mortgage at 80% loan-to-value (LTV) or higher, the lender will usually require that the borrower obtain some type of mortgage insurance to cover the lender's risk. The lender must be FHA-approved before the bank can offer any FHA financing option to its borrowers.

Many FHA-approved mortgage lenders can obtain FHA mortgage insurance options for loan amounts up to 96.5% of the purchase price or appraised value of the subject property. The FHA loans are typically insured by some combination of an upfront mortgage insurance premium (UFMIP) and annual mutual mortgage insurance (MMI) premiums that are paid monthly. The upfront fees may vary from a lump sum amount ranging from 1% to 2.25% of the loan value, depending upon factors such as the borrower's creditworthiness, the loan size, the term of the loan, and other considerations. The MMI (mutual mortgage insurance) fees may vary from 0% to 1.35% of the loan amount or value range. The FHA has made several changes within recent years to accommodate larger loan sizes, declining borrower FICO credit scores, and other loan issues that can either make it much easier or more difficult for one or more borrowers to qualify.

One of the most popular features of the FHA loan is the fact that only 3.5% cash down payments are required for many of its loan options. What is even more amazing is that most or all of these down payments can be gifted from family, friends, or some non-profit charitable funds that are related to the housing industry. Sellers may be allowed to pay the vast majority of non-recurring (or one-time) closing costs that are associated with the purchase transaction such as loan, escrow, title, and other third-party fees.

FHA loan-limit guidelines have become a bit more confusing in recent years. Regions of the nation and state of California may be designated as "low cost" or "high cost" housing regions or counties. Because California properties are so much higher than the rest of the nation in many coastal county regions, it is more likely that the pricier coastal counties like San Diego, Orange, Los Angeles, Santa Barbara, and San Francisco will be classified as high-cost regions for FHA and for conventional loans that are not insured by a government or private insurance agency.

In prior years, FHA's minimum national loan limit "floor" was set at 65% of the national conforming loan limit. On the highest side of the home-price scale, the maximum national loan limit ceiling for FHA might be 150% of the national conforming limit. In some pricier regions like prime coastal counties in California, there may be higher loan amount exemptions granted that are even above the standard "high cost loan limit" amount.

California FHA Loan Limits by County (2017 numbers)

County	FHA 1-unit limit
Alameda	$636,150
Alpine	$463,450
Amador	$332,350
Butte	$293,250
Calaveras	$373,750
Colusa	$275,665
Contra Costa	$636,150
Del Norte	$275,665

El Dorado	$488,750
Fresno	$281,750
Glenn	$275,665
Humboldt	$327,750
Imperial	$275,665
Inyo	$369,150
Kern	$275,665
Kings	$275,665
Lake	$275,665
Lassen	$275,665
Los Angeles	$636,150
Madera	$275,665
Marin	$636,150
Mariposa	$322,000
Mendocino	$373,750
Merced	$275,665
Modoc	$275,665
Mono	$529,000
Monterey	$575,000
Napa	$636,150
Nevada	$477,250
Orange	$636,150
Placer	$488,750
Plumas	$336,950
Riverside	$379,500
Sacramento	$488,750
San Benito	$636,150
San Bernardino	$379,500
San Diego	$612,950
San Francisco	$636,150
San Joaquin	$362,250
San Luis Obispo	$586,500
San Mateo	$636,150
Santa Barbara	$636,150
Santa Clara	$636,150

Santa Cruz	$636,150
Shasta	$275,665
Sierra	$304,750
Siskiyou	$275,665
Solano	$431,250
Sonoma	$595,700
Stanislaus	$299,000
Sutter	$276,000
Tehama	$275,665
Trinity	$275,665
Tulare	$275,665
Tuolumne	$331,200
Ventura	$636,150
Yolo	$488,750
Yuba	$276,000

Because the FHA loan limit amounts are based upon floating or changing underlying conforming loan amounts and property values, the FHA loan amount limits can increase each year when property values are continuing to move in an upward direction. For example, the new maximum FHA loan limit sizes for certain high cost regions in California may go as high as **$679,650** as of January 1, 2018 for a single-unit property such as a home, condominium, or townhouse. The maximum owner-occupied loan amounts for two, three, and four-unit (duplex, triplex, and fourplex) properties have loan amount ranges as high as **$870,225 for a duplex**, **$1,051,875 for a triplex**, and up to **$1,307,175 for an owner-occupied fourplex building** as of 2018.

Prior to the existence of the FHA, the housing industry was in fairly bad shape. During the depths of the Great Depression, upwards of two million construction workers had lost their jobs. The mortgage loan options offered to those fortunate few who could actually qualify for a home loan from a solvent bank were limited to 50% of the market value for the property (50% loan-to-value) with a loan term spread out over just three to five years prior to ending with an all due and payable balloon payment as the final payment amount. It was not surprising that there were more renters than homeowners (60% renters vs. 40% homeowners) before the formation of the FHA.

Urban Flight to Suburbia

During the 1940s and especially after the end of World War II, the FHA helped to finance military housing and new single-family homes for returning veterans. Due to factors such as the stress of living in large urban centers like New York City, Boston, and Philadelphia, increasing crime, and an increasing birth rate that began peaking in the mid-1940s when the Baby Boom (1946 to 1964) rapidly increased in size, more urban residents wanted to live calmer and more family-oriented lifestyles that could be found in new suburban communities like **Levittown** (Long Island, New York) and **Allentown** in eastern Pennsylvania.

The new roads and highways built after the passage of the public works act by FDR allowed more people to commute from long distances in outlying new suburban regions to their offices in the crowded metropolitan areas. Many of the earliest suburban homes built in places like Levittown were not much larger than the typical 800 square-foot apartment located in New York City.

The suburban homes offered homeowners two, three, and four-bedroom home-plan options that would accommodate the growing size of the typical post-World-War-II family with close to three children per household in the peak Baby Boom years. Many of the suburban homes featured green lawns in the front and backyards, white picket fences, and community swimming pools and parks for the children to play in nearby.

One of the most appealing features of new suburban homes in Levittown was the price that was just under $8,000 on average. The $8,000 price was near the maximum allowable loan limit for both the FHA and VA mortgage loans offered by the Department of Veterans Affairs with anywhere between 0% to 3.5% down for VA and FHA loans, respectively.

Both FHA and VA provided insured or guaranteed loans to more than 11 million homeowners in the years following World War II. The 41,000 mile interstate highway program that was funded by some of President Roosevelt's public works programs or local tax subsidies helped to speed up the commute between suburbia and the busier metropolitan regions where most of the jobs were still located.

VA Mortgages

A VA loan is a home mortgage loan that is partially guaranteed by the U.S. Department of Veterans Affairs (VA). The loan is issued by qualified lenders that are approved by the VA. Originally, the VA mortgage was designed to offer long-term mortgage financing options for military personnel who were returning from lengthy battles during World War II and other conflicts.

Eligible veterans who could supply a copy of a **Certificate of Eligibility (COE)** form to VA-approved lenders would likely qualify for a 100% loan-to-value mortgage with absolutely no money down to purchase the property. Under the **Servicemen's Readjustment Act** that was passed by Congress back in 1944, the VA was authorized to guarantee a portion of a funded mortgage loan for a home, farm, or business that was originally offered to a qualifying military veteran, active duty personnel member, or to his or her surviving spouse.

Over the history of the VA mortgage program, about 18 million properties have been funded. In 1992, the VA loan-guarantee program was expanded to include Reservists and National Guard personnel who have served honorably for at least six years as part of the enactment of the **Veterans Home Loan Program Amendments of 1992 (Public Law 102 - 547, approved October 29, 1992)**.

Because such a high percentage of VA loans are offered at 100% loan-to-value with no money down, the appraised value of the subject property is critically important to both the funding lender and the VA which guarantees a certain percentage or dollar amount of any defaulted or foreclosed mortgage. As such, an appraiser must be VA-approved first by meeting its rigid guidelines necessary to complete an appraisal on approved VA paperwork forms. This type of special VA appraisal is called a **Certificate of Reasonable Value**.

VA Loan Amount Guarantees

The number of loans that are guaranteed by VA vary depending upon factors such as the size of the loan and the location of the property. Some parts of the state or nation are priced well below the median home average while other regions are priced much higher, especially in many counties in California. Please note that the original lender and/or the current mortgage-loan servicing company is responsible for most of the defaulted loan should the losses exceed the VA loan-guarantee limits in a foreclosure situation.

Let's take a look below at some of the most basic VA guarantee formulas that have been used historically over the years to better understand the dollar amount of the loan that is guaranteed by VA in the event the mortgage borrower may later default and lose the property to foreclosure:

VA Loan Amount	Maximum Guarantee
$45,000 or less	50% of the loan amount
$45,001 - $56,250	$22,500
$56,251 - $144,000	40% of the loan (maximum of $36,000)
$144,000 or more	Amt up to or equal to 25% of county limit

There is absolutely **no** mortgage insurance required for a VA mortgage like there is with an FHA loan. With no mortgage insurance premiums to make that can add an extra $100 to $200 or more per month for FHA loans, the VA borrower will have monthly payments that are lower.

The closing costs, however, can be higher for VA loans as compared with FHA loans. These closing costs can average between 1% and 3% for larger home purchase prices and up to 3% to 5% for less expensive loans. The seller or lender can provide credits towards the VA buyer's closing costs that cover most of the total combined closing costs. However, the closing costs cannot be financed in the loan. If the financing of closing costs were allowed, it would bring the closing loan-to-value ratio well above the already high 100% LTV range.

Maximum Loan Guarantees for Single-Unit Homes in California (2018)

The amount of a VA loan is not capped or limited like a ceiling loan amount as you have with the FHA loans or conforming loan amounts.

Rather, the maximum amount of the loan that will be guaranteed by the VA may vary from relatively small dollar amounts near $25,000 up to as high as $679,650 in some of the pricier high-cost county regions in California and other states. Borrowers who wish to obtain loan amounts above the highest maximum loan amounts for VA mortgages generally need to put 25% cash down for the amounts higher than the maximum amounts. For example, a requested loan of $779,650 (or $100,000 above the maximum loan amount) in an expensive California region would require a down payment of $25,000 (or 25% of the additional $100,000 amount).

Listed below are the VA maximum loan amount guarantees for some of the more expensive counties in California as of 2017:

CA	ALAMEDA	$679,650
CA	ALPINE	$463,450
CA	CONTRA COSTA	$679,650
CA	EL DORADO	$517,500
CA	LOS ANGELES	$679,650
CA	MARIN	$679,650
CA	MONO	$529,000
CA	MONTEREY	$615,250
CA	NAPA	$679,650

CA	NEVADA	$477,250
CA	ORANGE	$679,650
CA	PLACER	$517,500
CA	SACRAMENTO	$517,500
CA	SAN BENITO	$679,650
CA	SAN DIEGO	$649,750
CA	SAN FRANCISCO	$679,650
CA	SAN LUIS OBISPO	$615,250
CA	SAN MATEO	$679,650
CA	SANTA BARBARA	$625,500
CA	SANTA CLARA	$679,650
CA	SANTA CRUZ	$679,650
CA	SOLANO	$460,000
CA	SONOMA	$648,600
CA	VENTURA	$672,750

The Bretton Woods Agreement, Weakening Dollars, and Real Estate

Wars, military personnel, the value of the dollar, and the real estate boom years were seemingly all tied together in the 1940s. In 1944, when the VA loan program was established, the dollar was established as the world's premiere currency thanks to the passage of the Bretton Woods agreement. When the Great Depression officially ended in 1939, more countries went back to the modified gold standard. Gold was pegged at $35 per ounce then, which made U.S. real-estate options more attractive.

World War II (1939 to 1945) caused military spending to rapidly increase for many nations based in Europe and Asia, as well as for the United States. As a result of the escalating military spending for the largest war in world history at the time, inflation and currency devaluation soon followed for many nations involved in the war efforts. Bretton Woods and VA mortgage-loan products made single-family home investments a wise choice due to the zero dollar purchase options with weakening dollars that could grow rapidly in value if pegged to home prices that typically exceeded annual inflation rates. Bretton Woods also opened the door for several of these 44 member nations to invest funds in land, homes, and commercial properties in the United States. The surging foreign investment interests in American real estate caused prices to soar across the nation.

Partly due to so many weak economies and much physical destruction in various European nations, the Bretton Woods Agreement was signed into law between the 44 member nations that would set the precedent for the establishment of the dollar as the world's preeminent or most-distinguished currency in the world that was backed by gold. It also allowed more money to flow into new real estate development projects in Europe as part of the rebuilding efforts after years of destruction from the war. As such, real estate construction projects were completed at a rapid pace in both the U.S. and Europe thanks to the passage of Bretton Woods.

The 44 nations in attendance at Bretton Woods conference held in Bretton Woods, New Hampshire in 1944 were:

Australia	Iceland
Belgium	Iran
Bolivia	Iraq
Brazil	Liberia
British Raj[5]	Luxembourg
Canada	Mexico
Chile	Netherlands
Republic of China	New Zealand
Colombia	Nicaragua
Costa Rica	Norway
Cuba	Panama
Czechoslovakia	Paraguay
Dominican Republic	Peru
Ecuador	Philippines
Egypt	Poland
El Salvador	South Africa
Ethiopia	Soviet Union
France	United Kingdom
Greece	United States
Guatemala	Uruguay
Haiti	Venezuela
Honduras	Yugoslavia

The **World Bank** and the **International Monetary Fund (IMF)** were two new global powers that were set up as a result of Bretton Woods to monitor the new global financial system. America was truly the dominant power behind the World Bank, IMF, and the new global currency system. In addition, the United States was the only country of the original 44 member nations that still had the ability to print dollars. Many of these same dollars would then flow back into the financial markets prior to

---

[5]   India, when it was ruled by the British until 1947.

being loaned out to borrowers who were flocking to purchase new real estate properties.

Chapter Four Summary

- While the Bank Panic of 1907 only lasted a short period of time, the Great Depression (1929 - 1939) lasted 10 years. Between the top and bottom of the U.S. economy, industrial production fell 47%, the real gross domestic product (GDP) numbers fell 30%, unemployment reached 25%, key stock values dropped 75%, and the whole price index declined by a whopping 33%.

- President Herbert Hoover, in the early years of The Great Depression, signed the **Reconstruction Finance Corporation (RFC) Act of 1932** and the **Federal Home Loan Bank Act of 1932** as potential ways to stabilize the banking system and overall financial markets. Yet these new policies did not help to improve the financial markets or stabilize the fragile stock and real estate markets.

- Franklin D. Roosevelt (FDR) officially became the 32nd President of the United States on March 4, 1933. The following day on March 5th, FDR launched the **New Deal** program that involved a series of government-assistance and bailout strategies such as **public works assistance** programs like the **CCC (Civilian Conservation Corps)** that created millions of new jobs for young Americans that involved the building of new parks, streets, libraries, and highways.

- The **Emergency Banking Relief Act** was signed into law by President Roosevelt on March 9, 1933 in order to provide financial solutions for the nearly 10,000 banks that had collapsed across the nation. The years 1932 and 1933 were two of the worst ever for **bank runs** as customers scrambled to literally run to their bank and pull out cash before the bank went out of business with no

FDIC insurance in place at the time to cover the depositors' financial losses.

- The creation of the **Federal Deposit Insurance Corporation (FDIC)** in 1933 started with a $2,500 insurance-ceiling limit per account. Since most depositors had less than this amount in a bank at any given time, the FDIC fund began to restore some confidence in the safety of the banking system. In 2008, this FDIC limit would be increased 100 times the original amount up to $250,000 per account.

- In 1933, the **Glass-Steagall Act** (also known as the Banking Act of 1933) was signed into law to prevent banks from using depositors' funds for risky investments such as in the stock market or in complex insurance investments.

- President Franklin Roosevelt established the **Home Owners' Loan Corporation (HOLC)** within a few months of taking office in order to help stabilize real estate values. The HOLC program granted long-term mortgage loans to more than one million homeowners who were facing the loss of their property at a foreclosure rate of almost 1,000 homes every day. About 80% of these delinquent mortgage loans were saved by the HOLC program.

- Congress formed the **Federal Housing Administration (FHA)** program in 1934 to develop the new foundation for a national mortgage market. The FHA is the single largest insurer of mortgage loans in the world today. To date, upwards of 47.5 million mortgages have been insured by the FHA. Loans up to 96.5% loan-to-value ratio that are insured by the FHA are the most popular types of owner-occupied residential loan products these days.

- A **VA loan** is a home loan that is partially guaranteed by the **U.S. Department of Veterans Affairs (VA)**. There are no monthly mortgage insurance premiums to pay like with FHA loan products in spite of the 100% loan-to-value mortgage products offered to qualified military personnel. To qualify for a no-money-down loan, the borrower applicant must present a **Certificate of Eligibility** form to a VA-approved mortgage lender.

Chapter Four Quiz

1. What negative economic event was used as the basis or main argument for the passage of the Federal Reserve Act so that the banking system and financial markets would not suffer so much future turbulence, high rates of inflation, or a weakening dollar?
   A. The collapse of First Bank
   B. The collapse of Second Bank
   C. The Bank Panic of 1907
   D. The Great Depression

2. Between the peak and depths of the U.S. economy during the first few years of the Great Depression, approximately how far did overall industrial production rates drop?
   A. 25%
   B. 32%
   C. 47%
   D. 68%

3. What was the name of President Hoover's signed legislation and failed program that raised import duties on consumer goods as a way to protect American farmers and businesses from international competition during the early Great Depression years?
   A. Hoover Goods Tax Act
   B. Smoot-Hawley Tariff Act
   C. Sherman Antitrust Act
   D. Import Tax Act

4. What program did Franklin D. Roosevelt launch just one day after taking office as President in March 1933?
   A. Tax Relief Act
   B. Wall Street Reform Act
   C. Gold Confiscation Act
   D. New Deal

5. What is the approximate number of banks that failed in the U.S. between 1929 and 1933?
   A. 14,000
   B. 10,000
   C. 5,500
   D. 1,100

6. What was the maximum amount that the newly formed Federal Deposit Insurance Corporation (FDIC) would insure for each bank account?
   A. $500
   B. $1,000
   C. $1,500
   D. $2,500

7. What was the maximum FDIC coverage limit for bank accounts in the U.S. as of 2018?
   A. $250,000
   B. $150,000
   C. $100,000
   D. $10,000

8. What act was signed into law as new legislation structured to prevent banks from using depositors' funds for risky investments such as in the stock market or complex insurance funds back in 1933?
    A. National Banking Act
    B. Bank Fraud Act
    C. Dodd-Frank Act
    D. Glass-Steagall Act

9. What act created the Federal Deposit Insurance Corporation?
    A. Banking Act of 1933
    B. FDIC Act
    C. Federal Reserve Act
    D. SEC Act

10. What public works assistance program created a few million new jobs for young American workers as part of President Roosevelt's New Deal program?
    A. New Jobs Program
    B. Civilian Conservation Corps
    C. National Employment Act
    D. Employment Reserves Program

11. What program during the Great Depression was established to help stabilize property values and save homes from foreclosure?
    A. Roosevelt Bailout Program
    B. Home Owners' Loan Corporation
    C. National Mortgage Relief
    D. Financial Assistance Program

12. Which entity is the largest insurer of mortgages in the world?
    A. FDIC
    B. FHA
    C. VA
    D. SEC

Answer Key:

1. C	6. D	11. B
2. C	7. A	12. B
3. B	8. D	
4. D	9. A	
5. B	10. B	

CHAPTER 5

PRIMARY LENDERS

Overview

The root definition of a **primary lender** has changed more than ever before as readers will learn in this chapter. The evolution of banking grew from royal families' treasuries to goldsmiths to commercial banks, and then to more-sophisticated types of private and public lending sources that did not actually collect any customer deposits prior to making their loans. The new funding sources came from insurance companies, equity capital, derivatives contracts, crowdfunding platforms, and other money sources that effectively eliminated the middleman (or banks) so that the wealth could be shared at higher-percentage rates with the direct investors. Non-bank lenders are approving and funding mortgage loans much faster than commercial banks which makes it more appealing to borrowers, buyers, property sellers, and real estate agents since, as we all know, "time is money!"

Commercial Banks in The Early Years

The modern version of U.S. commercial banks dates back more to the banking system in England in the 17th century than to any other older banking region, like Mesopotamia, Rome, Greece, or Turkey. British banking began when British merchants and sailors deposited their funds with some type of treasurer that was affiliated with a local king or queen at the time. After much of this wealth magically "disappeared" from the royal coffers or treasury, the merchants sought out the assistance of the local goldsmiths who had very large and secure safes at their disposal that could be used to store gold, silver, coins, and paper assets such as banknotes, promissory notes, and mortgages.

After some time had passed, the goldsmiths noticed a trend that was more common than not with their customers related to their deposit and withdrawal habits. Often, the goldsmith's customers would take out only a portion of their deposited funds on an as-needed basis. The customers did not want to carry around all of their stored valuables partly because robberies took place on almost a daily basis in some crowded urban areas. As a result, most of the goldsmiths' customers left the majority of their deposited funds in the safes under the goldsmiths' care.

The goldsmiths were already charging storage fees to hold their customers' assets. Yet they were also thinking up new ways to generate more revenue streams. The best idea that many goldsmiths could come up with was the loaning out of excess reserves to other customers. Goldsmiths went from being just "storage suppliers" (or "money holders") to bankers (or "money lenders") who could earn much higher rates of return by using their customers' own assets to lend out to other customers without risking any of the goldsmiths' own funds in the process.

The commercial banks that opened for business in the 19th century were for-profit business firms that were usually structured as joint-stock type companies. The vast majority of commercial banks that operated in the late 1800s obtained corporate charters from their respective state legislatures. Commercial banks, savings banks, insurance companies, and other financial institutions helped the nation grow by channeling savings wealth to new business entrepreneurs by way of various types of personal and business loans.

Commercial banks essentially acted like financial intermediaries in that they pooled the savings wealth collected from a large number of depositors in the nearby town or city before the same banks loaned out the deposits as loans to other banking customers. On the bank's balance sheet or accounting statement, they would list their borrowed wealth from depositors as a **liability** while listing the loan payments received from other banking customers who borrowed the funds for some type of loan as an **asset**. If the bank paid a 5% annual interest rate to savings account holders and charged 7% to other customers for a loan request, the net difference between the savings and loan rates was the bank's profit (7% - 5% = 2% annual profit) in addition to other one-time bank fees.

Most commercial banks in the late 18th and early 19th centuries owned assets such as gold and silver coins, bars, or bullion that was also referred to as "specie" back in those early banking days. Banks held the notes and deposits of other banks, public securities, commercial paper, and mortgages secured by land, homes, or small commercial buildings. Any creditors of commercial banks would be paid by way of the gold or silver holdings or with the notes or deposits from other banks. Commercial banks also owned federal or private securities such as government bonds or corporate stock shares in their financial portfolios.

Some of the bank assets were described as "discount loans" in that they were collateralized by commercial paper (i.e., promissory notes (or IOUs for debt) or bills of exchange) that were discounted at the bank by borrowers. For example, a $1,000 promissory note that was payable to the bank by an individual or corporate entity would be discounted to a $900 note prior to being sold off to another customer. The bank would discount the note $100 in order to receive $900 in cash today instead of waiting another year or two to receive the full-face amount of the $1,000 note.

Most commercial banks would create their initial wealth that then allowed them banks to purchase assets after issuing several types of liabilities. Most of the earliest commercial banks were joint-stock companies that issued equities ("stock") in some type of initial public offering (IPO). The stock shares were not fully redeemable for cash at a later date, so stock investors who held bank stocks in their investment portfolio could only sell their shares to other investors in the secondary "stock" market. The bank's "capital stock" that consisted of irredeemable shares made up usually the most wealth for the commercial bank's balance sheet.

Banking customers with other types of commercial-bank liabilities such as banknotes and checking deposits could request money (or money-like financial instruments) when redeeming their claims against the bank almost any banking day of the week. Usually, these commercial banks were open four, five, or six hours between Monday and Friday or Saturday. The customer could "cash out" their funds by showing up in person to physically withdraw the money in banknotes or coins, or by writing a check to a third party against the customer's checking account balance. An older banknote was somewhat like an engraved promissory note that was similar to a Federal Reserve note and was payable to the bearer who possessed it at the time of cash-redemption request.

Commercial banks would issue stock shares to customers in exchange for their financial assets. These same financial assets (coins, banknotes, gold, silver, promissory notes, mortgages) would then then be held on deposit by the bank or loaned out to other investors. Banks also hoped that customers who had purchased stock shares would later place more deposits into the bank's savings and checking accounts. These banknotes, deposits, and coins would transfer from person-to-person and bank-to-bank while growing in size, with interest payments that would eventually create more wealth for the commercial banks.

Modern-Day Commercial Banks

Today's most successful commercial banks make much of their money from offering loans to customers and then collecting interest income. The most common types of loans that a commercial bank will make to their customers are automobile, business, and personal loans in addition to some residential and commercial-mortgage loans (purchase, refinance, and construction).

The main source of capital that commercial banks have to work with usually originates from their customers' checking accounts, savings accounts, money market funds, and certificates of deposit (CDs). Each customer who deposits his or her funds into one of these short or long-term bank accounts is effectively lending money to the bank. In exchange for placing funds into the commercial bank, the depositor will usually receive some type of interest rate. In recent years, the interest rates might vary between 0% for personal or business checking accounts to 0.5% to 1.5% for savings accounts due to rates being near all-time lows.

Today's commercial banks earn much of their income by the spread between the amount of interest paid to customers for their deposits and the interest that the bank earns on loans. This spread that should hopefully be positive for a bank is known as the **net interest income**. An example of a net interest income spread between a savings rate paid out and interest income received from a loan is as follows:

A banking customer places $100,000 into a commercial bank for a one-year savings account that pays 2%. The bank pays the customer just $2,000 in interest over the next 12 months.

Another banking customer needs a one-year construction loan to complete a major remodel on their 35-year old home that is in desperate need of repair and modernization with new bathrooms, a kitchen with updated appliances, and flooring throughout the home. Because the loan request is a riskier second mortgage behind the owner's $127,000 first mortgage, the bank offers this equity line (or HELOC - home equity line of credit) at a rate of 10% that is all due and payable in 12 months. There are two six-month extension options available to the borrower to extend the line of credit out from 12 months to 18 or 24 months, if needed. The interest payments collected by the bank over the next 12 months will be equal to $10,000 (10% of $100,000).

The net interest income spread for just the $100,000 for the bank that is deposited and loaned out as a line of credit for a construction remodel is equal to an $8,000 profit ($10,000 - $2,000). In addition, the bank might have charged extra loan-processing or mortgage-underwriting fees for the equity line of credit that can be counted as additional profit for the bank. The bank may also charge a 1% loan origination fee ($1,000) for the $100,000-equity line, so the bank's true profit margins are $9,000 or more.

Largest Commercial Banks

Listed below are the Top 50 largest banks in the world as compiled by S&P Global Market Intelligence as of 2017:

Bank Name	Total Assets (Billions)
1. Industrial and Commercial Bank of China	$3,473.09
2. China Construction Bank Corporation	$3,016.45
3. Agricultural Bank of China	$2,815.92
4. Mitsubishi UFJ Financial Group	$2,626.29

5. Bank of China	$2,611.43
6. JPMorgan Chase & Co.	$2,500.00
7. HSBC Holdings PLC	$2,374.15
8. BNP Paribas	$2,189.27
9. Bank of America	$2,187.70
10. Wells Fargo & Co.	$1,930.12
11. Crédit Agricole	$1,816.97
12. Citigroup Inc.	$1,790.68
13. Mizuho Financial Group	$1,752.19
14. Deutsche Bank	$1,675.69
15. Sumitomo Mitsui Financial Group	$1,648.66
16. Barclays PLC	$1,495.84
17. Société Générale	$1,453.91
18. Banco Santander	$1,413.68
19. Groupe BPCE	$1,302.72
20. Bank of Communications	$1,209.18
21. Postal Savings Bank of China	$1,189.38
22. Lloyds Banking Group	$1,010.12
23. Royal Bank of Scotland Group	$ 986.48
24. Norinchukin Bank	$ 981.10
25. Toronto-Dominion Bank	$ 928.69
26. UBS	$ 920.11
27. Royal Bank of Canada	$ 892.43
28. ING Group	$ 891.25
29. Industrial Bank (China)	$ 872.10
30. UniCredit	$ 863.48
31. Goldman Sachs	$ 860.17
32. China Merchants Bank	$ 855.07
33. China CITIC Bank	$ 854.54
34. China Minsheng Bank	$ 848.39
35. Shanghai Pudong Development Bank	$ 842.83
36. Morgan Stanley	$ 814.35
37. Crédit Mutuel	$ 807.21
38. Credit Suisse	$ 806.79
39. Banco Bilbao Vizcaya Argentaria	$ 771.84

40. Intesa Sanpaolo	$764.71
41. Commonwealth Bank	$703.33
42. Australia and New Zealand Banking Group	$700.24
43. Rabobank	$698.79
44. Scotiabank	$680.24
45. Nordea	$649.29
46. Standard Chartered	$646.69
47. Westpac	$642.33
48. National Australia Bank	$595.19
49. China Everbright Bank	$578.46
50. DZ Bank	$537.28

Banks by Country

Rank	Nation	Number of Banks (Top 100 by Assets)
1	China	18
2	United States	12
3	Japan	8
4	France	6
4	United Kingdom	6
6	Canada	5
6	Germany	5
6	Spain	5
9	Australia	4
9	Brazil	4
9	South Korea	4
9	Sweden	4
13	Italy	3
13	Netherlands	3
13	Singapore	3
16	Belgium	2
16	Switzerland	2
18	Austria	1
18	Denmark	1
18	India	1
18	Norway	1
18	Russia	1
18	Taiwan	1

Fractional Reserve Lending

To understand how commercial banks leverage their customers' savings deposits, one must learn about the concept of **fractional reserve lending** (also known as **fractional reserve banking**). This lending option is partly related to the Federal Reserve's reserve ratio requirement which requires that banks set aside 1%, 5%, or 10% of their deposited funds as a financial safety net that could not be loaned out. These funds were either literally stored in the bank's vault or at the closest Federal Reserve bank district headquarters such as the Federal Reserve Bank of San Francisco for banks located in California.

Some banking analysts have claimed that most small bank branches actually keep the bulk of their available cash for customers in their ATM machines because their bank vaults contain under 1% of all deposited funds instead of the more typical 3%, 5%, or 10% reserve-ratio requirement. While it seems reasonable that banks should set aside some cash reserves in the event that there is a run on deposits by banking customers in need of some quick cash due to natural disasters, job losses, or economic downturns, the fractional reserve lending system is truly the exact opposite of reserve-ratio requirements in spite of their similar names.

Banks will borrow funds from their depositors (savings and checking accounts) before later lending out those same deposited funds to other banking customers in need of a loan for the purchase of a home, automobile, or to start up a new business. Banks will make money by charging borrowers more for a loan (at a much higher rate of interest) than they will pay out to the bank customers for the use of their money. If the banks did not lend out their available funds over and above the reserve-ratio requirements, the banking customers might have to pay additional fees for safekeeping services to store their money like customers had to do with goldsmiths in the 18th and 19th centuries.

Fractional-reserve lending allows banks to create more money "out of thin air" (or by digital credits on a computer system) by loaning out deposited funds creatively at a rate that may be equal to 10 or more times the amount of cash deposits. For example, a larger bank with $500 million dollars in deposited funds may be required to set aside upwards of 10% of this amount to meet their reserve-ratio requirements.

$$\$500,000,000 \times 10\% = \$50,000,000$$

However, the simplest way to explain how fractional-reserve lending works for banks with the same cash deposits of $500,000,000, you divide by 10% instead of multiply in order to figure out how many loans can be created out of the $500 million dollars in deposited funds.

$500,000,000/.10 (or 10%) = $5,000,000,000 (or $5 billion)

To confuse matters, the fractional-reserve banking system is said by many economists to use the "multiplier effect" as the deposited amounts are divided as opposed to being multiplied. The "multiplier" is a reference to how the bank's customer funds are multiplied in much larger amounts before they are later loaned out to other customers and banks.

Money can compound and grow in magnitudes of 10 or more times in a relatively short time period. For example, a $100,000 loan with ABC Bank can grow to ten times the size, up to $1 million or more, after it is deposited, loaned out, redeposited, loaned out again, and deposited and loaned out several times more between customers and banks all over town, the state, or the nation.

The leveraging of assets can be a great thing during prosperous economic times when home prices are increasing consistently by 3%, 5%, 7%, or 10% per year. However, the leveraging of assets and mortgage debt can be absolutely horrific for borrowers and lending banks when prices are plunging downward and foreclosure rates are reaching all-time record highs as they did between 2007 and 2011.

Commercial Banks & Derivatives

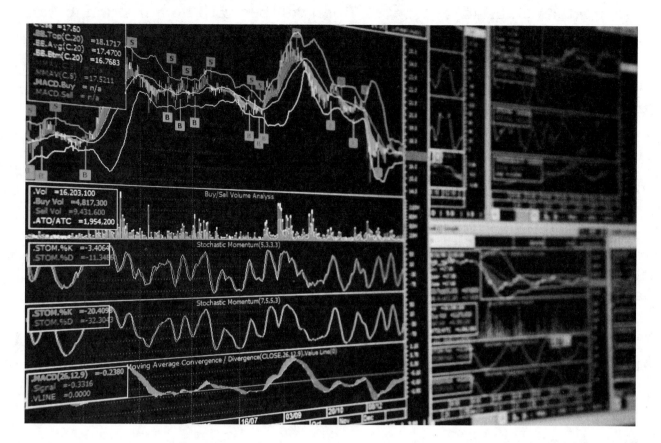

Fractional reserve lending was just one way that commercial banks and other common types of primary lenders creatively increased the size of their wealth. Another way that banks and investors increased the size of their investment portfolio was by way of something called a **derivatives** investment. Generally, the word "derivative" is associated with something that gets its value from another item or underlying asset. Even though this is a real estate and finance course, readers should understand at least the basics in regard to complex securities investments that have directly affected the real estate and banking industry more so than possibly any other external factor.

A **derivative** is a type of security instrument that is dependent upon the underlying value of one or more assets tied to it. In many ways, it is a hybrid of a financial and insurance contract in which two or more parties will be betting on the future direction of an underlying financial contract.

To really simplify these complex derivatives investments, they can be described as akin to a type of financial bet on the direction of an underlying asset. Unlike a casino bet in Las Vegas where the person can lose their entire amount of chips placed on the roulette table, an investment in a derivatives contract can be leveraged the wrong way if the losses are severe enough that can be magnified 10, 20, or 50+ times the original amount of the investment. If the investment in the derivatives contract was $2 billion and the losses could be compounded or magnified by 20 times the original investment amount, the losses might exceed $40 billion ($2 billion x 20).

One of the more popular types of securities instruments was the **interest-rate option derivative** contract used by most of the world's largest commercial banks. With the interest-rate option contract, a bank would be betting on the future direction of an interest rate. If the investor made the correct bet on the future interest rate trends either up or down, the investor could earn a positive leverage return that was as high as 10, 20, or 50-plus times the amount of the original bet, depending upon how complex and creative their bet structure was at the time.

One of the best examples for real estate agents to learn about the risks associated with interest-rate options involve the bankruptcy filing for the entire county of Orange in California in December 1994. At the time, it was the largest county bankruptcy filing in U.S. history with stated losses of nearly $2 billion. The county had to issue more than $1 billion in bonds at higher interest rates to try to raise much-needed capital from investors to cover the county's losses. At a repayment rate averaging $68 million per year in interest and a total principal and interest amount of $1.5 billion, it took 22 years to finally pay off the bond debt by July 1, 2017.

Robert Citron, the former County Treasurer, had agreed to invest a significant amount of county funds with Merrill Lynch in interest-rate option derivatives. Citron later publicly stated that he did not really understand how financially risky that interest-rate option derivative investments were after agreeing to make the investments. Since interest-rate options were so new at the time, there were probably very few people who truly understood how financially devastating the interest-rate option investment could be if the financial bet was made the wrong way. Yet Citron was sentenced to a year in prison and hit with a $100,000 fine in 1996 for making these risky bets with Orange County taxpayer funds.

In 1993 and early 1994, 30-year mortgage rates were near lows not seen in the previous 30 years. Merrill Lynch, the world's largest stock brokerage firm at the time of its collapse in September 2008, had approached Citron with an investment plan that could generate higher annual yields for the county with a new investment strategy. It was claimed that Merrill Lynch thought that interest rates were much more likely to keep moving **lower** instead of higher in the near future. So, an interest-rate option contract was offered to the county of Orange that was effectively a glorified bet that interest rates would keep moving downward. Sadly for Orange County, the Federal Reserve decided to raise interest rates **six times** in 1994.

The Fed Funds Rate for 1994

Fed's Meeting Date	New Rate
February 4	3.25%
March 22	3.50%
April 18	3.75%
May 17	4.25%
August 16	4.75%
November 15	5.50%

The $1,500-plus Trillion Derivatives Market

The county of Orange's financial bust of $2 billion was rather tiny in comparison to the amount of outstanding derivatives held by large commercial banks and investment firms around the world. While no financial analyst can be quite sure of the exact amount of outstanding derivatives due to their complex nature and design, the estimate ranges vary from $1,500 trillion to as high as $3,000 trillion worldwide.

The once-conservative banks had switched from safe investments to rather complex derivatives "bets" that had odds potentially much worse than any casino in Vegas. Unlike a regular bet at a casino where the losses are equal to the amount of funds bet, the investor can lose up to 10 or 20 times the original funds if they bet on the wrong direction of underlying financial instruments such as interest rates, currency valuations, and bond market trends. Banks only increased their bet amounts in derivatives investments even **after** the financial markets almost collapsed in 2008 and the same banks received billions of dollars of bailout funds.

The collapse of the derivatives market in 2007 and 2008 was really the main catalyst for the Credit Crisis rather than too many delinquent subprime mortgage loans as suggested by some financial analysts. In fact, the total number of all defaulted subprime mortgage loans in default that may or may not have eventually gone all the way to foreclosure represented less than 1% of all delinquent assets that caused the financial markets to "freeze up" at the time in September 2008.

The worst point loss for the Dow Jones index took place on Tuesday, September 29th, 2008 when the market fell 777 points (an unlucky number that is normally lucky on slot machines, ironically). This was also the same day that former Federal Reserve Chairman Ben Bernanke described as the day that the financial system almost collapsed worldwide. Interestingly, that date was also the date of the latest quarterly derivatives exchange at the Bank for International Settlements (BIS) (www.bis.org) in Basel, Switzerland that had many more sellers than buyers at this auction.

The most powerful bank in the world that governs and regulates all central banks worldwide (including the Federal Reserve) is the Bank for International Settlements. It is also the same financial institution that handles the bulk of derivatives exchange sales that are tied to assets like subprime mortgages, interest rates, mortgage securities (or pieces of billions of dollars of pooled mortgages), currency values, and residential and commercial properties. Because there were few buyers interested in purchasing derivatives at the BIS derivatives auction sale, the financial markets "froze up" and almost collapsed.

As you can see below, the size of the derivatives market worldwide absolutely dwarfed all other asset categories and estimated dollar amounts in the fall of 2008 and early 2009.

Asset Size	Dollar Amount (in trillions)
Annual U.S. Gross National Product	14.2
Entire U.S. money supply	15.0
U.S. stock markets combined	16.0
All U.S. residential real estate combined	23.0
All world's stock markets combined	50.0
All real estate on the planet combined	75.0
All stock and bond markets on Earth	100.00
All derivatives held in the global market	1,500.00

Source: *Creative Real Estate Magazine*

The total combined value of all assets listed in the chart above that do not include the massive derivatives numbers add up to $193.2 trillion. The $1,500 trillion dollar derivatives is almost 7.77 times larger than the value of our nation's GDP (Gross Domestic Product), money supply, and the combined value of all U.S. and global assets that include all stocks, bonds, and real estate. The 777-point loss for the Dow Jones Industrial Average on September 29, 2008 was just a starting point for the changes that were soon coming for the banking and real estate markets due to the derivatives market being so much larger than most global assets.

In 2009, the websites RunToGold.com and CreditContradiction.com reported these numbers for derivatives, stocks, bonds, currencies, and other assets:

Derivatives:	**$1,600 trillion**
Shadow Derivatives	$800 trillion
Reported Derivatives	$683 trillion
Unfunded Government Liabilities	$250 trillion
Miscellaneous Assets:	**$125 trillion**
Private Business	$10 trillion
Commercial Real Estate	$30 trillion
Residential Real Estate	$80 trillion
Non-Monetary Commodities	$4 trillion
Securitized Debt/Stocks:	**$100 trillion**
Corporate and Municipal Bonds	$25 trillion
World Listed Stocks	$51 trillion
U.S. Listed Stocks	$15 trillion
Broad Currency Illusions:	**$65 trillion**
World Treasury Bills/Government Bonds	$15.5 trillion
U.S. Debt/Treasury Bills	$11 trillion
Physical Currency:	**$4 trillion**
Physical notes (e.g., foreign currencies, etc.)	$2 trillion
Federal Reserve Notes (U.S.)	$800 billion
Power Money:	**150,000 tons**
Gold and Silver	$2 - $4 trillion

Collapsing Financial Markets and California Property Values

In spite of the investment bankers blaming subprime mortgages for busting the financial market system in 2008, it was more of the restricted access to capital options that were busting the real estate markets. This was especially true in the state of California. Some housing analysts suggested that 80% of all purchase money loans that were jumbo in size (more than $417,000 loan amounts at the time) in pricier Southern California regions in the years between 2000 and 2006 were some form of an "EZ Doc" mortgage loan with no formal income verification (or asset verification in some loans) that was most likely an adjustable-rate mortgage (i.e., an option pay ARM with a 1% to 1.5% start rate amortized over 30 or 40 years for the lowest payment options).

Many property owners also held concurrent home equity lines of credit as a second loan behind their first mortgages so that they could make housing repairs or upgrades or pay off some credit card bills, business loans, or student loans.

The easy money credit options to get into and out of properties in California and other places made property values steadily rise between 2000 and 2007 in many housing markets. Once lenders began to eliminate the access to "EZ Doc" subprime mortgage loans that allowed borrowers with lower FICO credit scores in the 500 and 600 ranges to borrow money, then many borrowers were unable to refinance their adjustable rate loans or pull additional funds from their homes because they could not qualify for "full doc" bank loans that required higher (700-plus FICO credit scores) and income verification with W2s or tax returns.

After the adjustable monthly payments on these mortgage loans doubled or tripled due to the Federal Reserve raising short-term rates a whopping seventeen (17) times between 2004 and 2006, homeowners could not find fixed-rate loans that they could qualify for to refinance for lower payment options. With the subprime and EZ Doc loans disappearing on a larger scale in 2006 and 2007, the number of foreclosure rates skyrocketed, especially in California. The more foreclosures within a neighborhood, the farther that home prices might fall if those were the only available sales comparables for the homeowners who were trying to sell or refinance their homes. The rising interest rate environment combined with fewer mortgage options and increasing foreclosure trends made a troubled housing market get worse over the next few years.

Let's take a closer look below for the increasing numbers of foreclosure (or Notice-of-Default) filings in California between the third quarter of 2007 when the Credit Crisis officially started and the second quarter of 2009 when property values were near their recent low points:

Time Period	Notice of Default Numbers
3rd Quarter 2007	72,000
4th Quarter 2007	81,000
1st Quarter 2008	114,000
2nd Quarter 2008	121,000
3rd Quarter 2008	95,000
4th Quarter 2008	77,000
1st Quarter 2009	137,000
2nd Quarter 2009	142,000

Source: *Foreclosure Radar*

With foreclosure numbers reaching record highs in California and other parts of the nation, lenders (commercial banks, especially) stopped filing foreclosure notices. Many banks were concerned that their depositors might run to their local bank branch and attempt to pull all of their cash out of their savings accounts. If enough people pulled their money out, then stock prices would drop considerably which could lead to large layoffs in banking operations and huge salary reductions for both the staff and the chief banking executives.

There were probably several million properties that did not have filed foreclosure notices against the delinquent properties. In some cases, banks would wait one, two, three, or even five years before starting the foreclosure process instead the usual 60 days or so after a homeowner had missed a payment or two. The properties with the much larger mortgage loan amounts of one to ten million dollars for residential properties or commercial properties may have been delayed the most because the banks did not want to acknowledge these serious losses on their balance sheets.

The biggest risk for banks was if they had too much bad debt listed on their publicly-filed income and expense reports related to potential triggers being called in the bank's derivatives holdings. Many financial contracts that were agreed to by parties in a derivatives contract were tied to both underlying pools of millions or billions of dollars of subprime credit or Alt-A credit (effectively A- or B credit grades) mortgages and the financial strength of the lender "guaranteeing" the mortgage pool that was sold to another investor. Several derivatives contracts had clauses that required that the mortgage pool seller (or original lender) with a declining financial net worth would be forced to buy back the previously sold mortgage pools since they did not have enough financial strength to "guarantee" the other party's risk in the future event of a massive default.

Because so many large banks were running low on cash, they could not afford to buy back pools of billions of dollars of delinquent mortgages. As a result, several of the largest well-known banks did not file foreclosure on delinquent mortgages for several years. At a later date, many lenders offered their borrowers some type of a **"cash for keys"** program in which the lender would literally give the delinquent homeowner anywhere from $2,000 to $25,000 or more to just walk away from the home, sign a grant deed or quitclaim deed back to the lender, and hand back the keys to the lender without the lender being required to file a formal foreclosure notice.

Savings Banks

A savings bank is a financial institution that operates primarily with the intent to accept savings deposits in exchange for the payment of interest to customers on those deposits . The very first savings bank to open in Europe was perhaps the **Emparungsklasse** bank in Hamburg, Germany in 1778. One year later in 1799, the first savings bank in England opened for business that was later followed by **postal savings banks** in 1861. A postal savings system was a place where people without access to safes or banks could use post office locations to save their money, especially people of lower income.

As the word of the success of savings banks spread around Europe and later in America, savings banks began popping up in these locations:

Year	City or Town	Country
1798	Tottenham	United Kingdom
1810	Ruthwell	Scotland
1816	Kilkenny	Ireland
1818	Paris	France
1822	Padua	Italy
1825	Tournai	Belgium
1838	Madrid	Spain
1844	Lisbon	Portugal
1853	Luxembourg City	Luxembourg

U.S. Savings Banks

The first chartered savings bank in the United States was the **Provident Institution for Savings** in Boston that was established on December 13, 1816. The **Philadelphia Savings Fund Society** started operating in the same year, but it did not officially incorporate until 1819. Savings banks were later incorporated in Baltimore, Maryland and in Salem, Massachusetts. In 1819, savings banks opened for business in Hartford,

Providence, Newport (Rhode Island), and in New York City.

A savings bank organization can be state or federally-chartered or regulated. Over the past few centuries, there have been a number of different names used to identify a savings bank that include:

- Building and Loan
- Thrift
- Savings and Loan

In the classic holiday film *It's a Wonderful Life,* George Bailey (played by Jimmy Stewart) ran the local Bailey Building and Loan. The local townspeople would place their hard-earned funds into the bank and then it loaned the excess funds to other customers in need of funds to buy their first home. When most people think about a savings bank, they usually think about a financial institution that offers higher rates for longer-term savings deposits and for long-term mortgage loans used to buy properties.

The types of savings account options available from many savings banks today might include:

- Basic short-term savings accounts for consumers
- Online savings accounts
- Money market accounts
- Certificates of deposit (CDs)
- Commercial loans
- Checking accounts with and without interest
- A **pledge account** (a large savings account) that is offered up by the customer as collateral for a new loan
- Specialty accounts (children's, student, and business accounts)

The savings and loan industry reached their peak years in the 1980s and early 1990s. When short-term interest rates averaged in the low to high double-digit rate ranges, long-term CD rates at savings banks were some of the best and safest investment options for banking customers anywhere with 10% and 12%-plus savings deposit returns. The customers' funds were fully insured by the governing FSLIC (Federal Savings and Loan Insurance Corporation) agency that was considered as financially sound as the FDIC at the time.

The deregulation of the savings and loan industry began after former President Jimmy Carter signed the **Depository Institutions Deregulation and Monetary Control Act** on March 31, 1980. The passage of the act was intended to ease regulation guidelines for savings banks so that they could offer more savings and investment options for their banking customers and shareholders. In addition, the act was meant to improve the control of monetary policy for the Federal Reserve. However, the act ended up encouraging savings banks to get involved in more risky and speculative construction and business loans while the Fed seemed to lose some of their control and effective management options while supervising these new banking activities.

Title II of the deregulation act was known as the **Depository Institutions Deregulation Act of 1980**. This section phased out the restriction on the maximum ceiling rates that a savings bank could pay their banking customers for their deposits. To ensure an orderly transition from longer-term savings rate options, the lifting of the savings rate ceiling lasted for the next six years (1980 - 1986). The main problem for savings banks was that inflation and interest rates were peaking in the 1979 and 1980, so their depositors were able to lock into long-term savings rates that eventually would exceed 12% in annual interest payments. Over the next few years, rates would head downward and savings banks would be collected lower interest rates for their loans than they paid out to customers for their savings deposits. As a result, these savings banks had **net losses** between the amount paid to and collected from their customers.

The savings banks in the 1980s began to aggressively offer real estate loans for construction projects, land acquisitions, and high-rise office buildings that were especially located in Texas and California. Brand new high-rise buildings started to sprout from the ground in places like Dallas during the oil and real-estate-boom years in the 1980s as partly glorified by the old television series called *Dallas*.

The **Savings and Loan Crisis** got so bad in the 1980s and 1990s that 1,043 out of the 3,234 savings and loans that were formed in the years between 1986 to 1995 ended up failing. FSLIC would eventually run out of capital and become just as insolvent as the savings banks that they were trying to save. Many years later, the FDIC would take over the ownership and management of FSLIC while being in charge of most state and federally-chartered banking institutions nationwide.

In 1989, a taxpayer bailout measure called the **Financial Institutions Reform, Recovery, and Enforcement Act (FIRREA)** was created to provide $50 billion in funds to help the failed savings banks. FIRREA later formed the **Resolution Trust Corporation (RTC)** to assist with the sale or liquidation of billions of dollars of real estate assets at prices that were literally cents on the dollar off their recent peak market highs. Some apartment buildings in Texas were selling to astute investors for less than $1,000 per unit and other very large land deals were selling for just hundreds of dollars.

The Federal Savings and Loan Insurance Corporation (FSLIC) closed or took over 296 savings and loan associations between 1986 and 1989 while the **Resolution Trust Corporation** shut down or took over the operations of an additional 747 savings and loans between 1989 and 1995 that had a book or market value of between $402 and $407 billion. The General Accounting Office would later estimate the losses to be close to $160 billion dollars, including at least $132 billion that were paid by U.S. taxpayers. Almost 50% of all savings banks which had existed as far back as 1970 were no longer in business by 1989.

Credit Unions

Credit unions differ from banks in that they are formed as not-for-profit cooperative organizations that exist to serve their members or shareholders. Each customer who deposits money into their credit union while pooling their funds with other members is effectively buying shares in the cooperative. Any and all income generated by credit unions is used to fund projects and services that benefit the member and nearby community.

Credit unions and banks are similar in regard to how they accept deposits, make loans, and provide a wide array of financial services such as stock, bond, and pension investments. In years past, many credit unions were formed for members who shared similar jobs such as large engineering, defense industry, military personnel (active or retired) or unionized teachers. In more recent years, many credit unions now allow the spouse and children of members employed in the same line of work as well as other community citizens with no affiliation to the main employment organization or their family that may be the hub of the credit union association. **Navy Federal Credit Union (NFCU)** is the largest credit union by asset size with over 300 branches near military bases across the nation.

Let's review the history of the credit union over the past few hundred years around the world:

1849: Friedrich Raiffeisen, the founder of rural credit unions, started his first credit society in southern Germany.

1864: Friedrich Raiffeisen formed the first rural cooperative lending institution or rural credit union in the world.

1900: Alphonse Desjardins imported the credit union formation from Europe to Canada with the establishment of *Caisse d'epargne Desjardins* in Lévis, Quebec in eastern Canada. This establishment was the forerunner of current credit unions in North America.

1909: Alphonse Desjardins created the first credit union in the United States in the state of New Hampshire. The very first credit union law was passed in Massachusetts with assistance from Alphonse Desjardins and Edward Filene. The **Massachusetts Credit Union Act of 1909** was the first comprehensive credit union law in the nation; it would later serve as a model for the **Federal Credit Union Act of 1934 (FCU Act)**.

1934: President Franklin D. Roosevelt signed the FCU Act which authorized federally-chartered credit unions to operate in all 50 states. The Federal Credit Union Division was placed under the Farm Credit Administration program.

1942: The federal supervision of all federal credit unions was transferred over to the Federal Deposit Insurance Corporation (FDIC).

1948: The renamed **Bureau of Federal Credit Unions** was moved over to the Federal Security Administration agency for supervision and regulatory control.

1953: J. Dean Gannon is named the director of the Bureau of Federal Credit Unions before it is moved under the direction of the brand new agency called the **Department of Health, Education, and Welfare**.

1970-1979: The number of assets in credit unions across the nation tripled in size.

1977: New laws passed which allow credit unions to begin offering new services like the issuance of share certificates and mortgage loans.

1985: Credit unions that are insured by the **NCUSIF** (National Credit Union Share Insurance Fund - the credit union's version of FDIC) were now backed by the "full faith and credit of the United States government," which provided extra security to credit union members.

1998: The **Credit Union Membership Access Act of 1998 (HR 1151)** was signed into law by President Bill Clinton. The law restored membership flexibility for credit union members while making it much easier for more people to join and place their funds with credit unions.

2010: President Barack Obama signed into law the **Dodd-Frank Wall Street Reform and Consumer Protection Act ("Dodd-Frank Act")** in an attempt to bail out financial institutions around the nation after the Credit Crisis worsened. Section 335 of the Dodd-Frank Act amended the FCU (Federal Credit Union) Act to make permanent the standard maximum share insurance (SMSIA) amount of up to $250,000 per account just like with commercial banking account insurance limits. Savings, checking, certificate accounts, and certain retirement accounts such as an IRA (Individual Retirement Account) fund are federally insured up to $250,000 per member per federally insured credit union.

Source: *Mycreditunion.gov*

Which insurance fund protects credit union deposits for the banking customers?

Life Insurance Companies

The first mutual fire insurance company in the U.S. named the **Philadelphia Contributionship for the Insurance of Houses from Loss by Fire** was alleged to have been established by Benjamin Franklin and a few of his associates in 1752. A group of Presbyterian churches later founded the very first life insurance company in the U.S. in the late 1760s. The insurance fund was formed and named the **Corporation for Relief of Poor and Distressed Widows and Children of Presbyterian Ministers**. Later, Episcopalian priests established their own similar life insurance fund in 1769. Prior to the Civil War, the lives of slaves were insured for their owners.

Life insurance companies are some of the largest providers of mortgage capital for commercial real estate properties. These insurance groups especially like to make loans on Class A-type high-rise office buildings in prime downtown metropolitan regions, mid-size to much larger regional retail shopping malls with hundreds of tenants, and 100-plus unit multi-family apartment buildings.

Most life insurance funds are paid monthly or by annual premium payments made by their insured clients for several years or decades. The life insurance companies, in turn, invest these life insurance payments into longer term commercial mortgages that generate higher annual returns than the insurance company pays out to their insured clients or heirs at the time of passing of the named insured. The difference between the amount of funds paid out to a named insured and the interest collected from commercial property mortgages becomes the net profit for the insurance company.

In 2014, an estimated 180 million Americans carried some form of life insurance. In that same year, over 900 life insurance companies reported a total of nearly $147 billion worth of collected direct premiums paid by their customers. To insurance companies, one of the safest and most consistent investment opportunities to grow and compound these billions of dollars worth of insurance premiums is to place it into a commercial property at a loan-to-value range somewhere below 65% or 70% of the value and amortized over a term of 5, 7, 10, or up to 25 years.

The largest life insurance funds in the nation that offer the most commercial mortgage loans and/or equity participation options with shared ownership interests include the following companies:

MetLife: In 2015, this company was listed as the biggest life insurance company in the U.S. with the collection of $11.3 billion in annual premiums which represented 7.66% of the overall market share.

Northwestern Mutual: Northwestern collected more than $9.5 billion in annual insurance premiums in 2014 that equated was equal to almost 6.5% of the American market.

New York Life: This insurance firm wrote almost $8.2 billion in life insurance premiums in 2014, which represented almost 5.6% of the national market.

Prudential: In 2014, Prudential earned more than $7.7 billion in annual premiums (5.3% of the overall market).

Lincoln National: Lincoln reported $6.44 billion in written life insurance premiums in 2014 (4.4% of the total market share).

MassMutual: In 2014, MassMutual reported nearly $5.6 billion in earned written life insurance premiums, which represented 3.8% of the overall market share.

John Hancock: This firm wrote over $4.7 billion in insurance premiums in 2014 (3.2% of the U.S. market).

Transamerica: In 2014, they collected $4.38 billion in life insurance premiums, which was responsible for about 3% of the national market share.

Pension Companies

Pension funds, both U.S. and and foreign-based, provide capital for residential development tracts that may consist of thousands of homes in a community, retail shopping malls, industrial warehouse projects, high-rise office buildings, and mixed-use properties all around the world. The oldest pension program that was created in world history might have taken place in Ancient Rome when soldiers were guaranteed lifetime income after they retired by the ruling monarchs or government authority in charge at the time. Some historians make the claim that when Rome began running out of money to pay their army's underfunded pension plans, which was partly due to the combination of skyrocketing inflation and a weakening currency system, that was perhaps the main reason why Rome fell.

The very first pension or retirement plan that was established in the U.S. dates back to the American Revolution when the Continental Congress would reward surviving soldiers with income for life (a/k/a a "pension"). The pension plan was offered by the federal government in the Civil War and every major U.S. war since.

The first business or corporate pension plan offered in the U.S. was formed by the American Express Company in 1875. Eligible employee participants in the pension plan were required to spend 20 years working there, reach the age of 60, and be recommended for retirement by a company manager and approved by a committee along with the board of directors. The lucky few workers who qualified for an annual pension fund were entitled to receive up to half of their annual salary in their retirement years up to a maximum of $500, per the Bureau of Labor Statistics.

Near the start of the 20th century, banks and railroad companies started to offer more attractive pension plan options to their loyal employees. Other larger well-known companies began offering pension plans such as US Steel, AT&T, Standard Oil, Eastman Kodak, General Electric, and Goodyear. All of these companies (that still exist today) established their pension plans before 1930.

The **Internal Revenue Act of 1921** made pension plans more appealing for businesses and workers by exempting contributions made to employee pensions from federal corporation income tax. By the 1940s, organized labor unions got more interested in pension plans for their members as they pushed employers to offer more pension plan options for their workers. By 1950, nearly 10 million Americans, or almost 25% of the adult workforce, had a pension account. Ten years later in 1960, almost 50% of the national workforce in the private sector had some type of a pension fund in place.

After several pension plans began to fail across the nation in the early 1970s partly due to some risky investments, the federal government passed the **Employee Retirement Income Security Act (ERISA)** in 1974. The new law made pension plans safer and more secure by establishing better legal participations, accounting, and disclosure-requirement standards. The **Pension Benefit Guaranty Corporation** was created as a result of the passage of ERISA which was similar to a type of FDIC insurance program for retirement accounts. Defined benefit plans that were based upon some form of a percentage of salary or fixed dollar amount and defined contribution plans like 401(k) plans allow employees and employers to contribute towards the individual worker's future retirement account balances. These private investment and retirement accounts were to be supplemental to Social Security benefits received by most Americans in their retirement years.

There are trillions and trillions of dollars in retirement accounts worldwide that are in need of generating high consistent rates of returns in places like real estate, stocks, and bonds that aren't considered to be "too risky" for retirees who can't afford to lose this monthly income in the later years. Many of these same private and government pension funds are some of the wealthiest lenders and landlords in America today.

Three hundred of the largest pension funds in the world now account for over 43% of all global pension assets, per a report entitled *Pensions & Investments/Willis Towers Watson 300 Analysis* for 2016. The reported total assets under management (AUM) for these 300 global funds were estimated to be valued at close to $15.7 trillion (U.S.). An estimated 44.1% of all assets of the Top 300 pension firms were based in North America.

The Government Pension Investment Fund of Japan was rated as the largest pension plan in the world with more than $1.2 trillion in assets by the end of December 2016. This fund was more than 39% larger than the second-ranked fund in the world named the Government Pension Fund of Norway. Japanese investors, both private and public, have acquired or made loans on billions of dollars of real estate in just the state of California alone over the past decade or so. Funds from China also actively purchase properties up and down the state of California. The odds are fairly high that a real estate agent in the state will work on at least one transaction in their career that has a domestic or foreign pension plan involved, directly or indirectly, as a lender or property owner.

Most of the top pension funds in the world have more managed assets under their control than the world's largest commercial banks or investment banks. Listed below are the top 10 wealthiest pension funds on the planet as of 2016:

Rank	Fund Name / Nation	Total Assets
1	Government Pension Investment (Japan)	$1.237 trillion
2	Government Pension Fund (Norway)	$ 893 billion
3	Federal Retirement Thrift (U.S.)	$ 485 billion
4	National Pension (South Korea)	$ 462 billion
5	ABP (Netherlands)	$ 404 billion
6	National Social Security (China)	$ 348 billion
7	California Public Employees (U.S.)	$ 306 billion
8	Canada Pension (Canada)	$ 235 billion
9	Central Provident Fund (Singapore)	$ 227 billion
10	PFZW (Netherlands)	$ 196 billion

Other types of private investment groups that pool investors' funds (hundreds or thousands) to purchase real estate or act as a lender include limited partnerships, crowdfunding platforms for real estate, and **REITs** (Real Estate Investment Trusts). Each of these funding groups will have a minimum investment requirement and a net worth requirement for their investors before they are allowed to invest with the groups.

Chapter Five Summary

- Many of the commercial banks that operated in the 19th century were for-profit business firms that were structured as joint-stock type companies. Most of the commercial banks in the late 1800s received corporate charters from their state legislatures.

- Commercial banks issued stock shares to customers in exchange for their financial assets. These financial assets (coins, banknotes, gold, silver, promissory notes, mortgages) were then held on deposit by the bank or loaned out to other investors as **liabilities**.

- **Net interest income** is the amount of interest spread or gains that a commercial bank earns on the difference between what they charge customers for loans and what the bank earns from interest on loans given to bank clients.

- Of the 100 largest banks in the world, 18 are in China while 12 are in the U.S. (e.g., JP Morgan Chase, Bank of America, Wells Fargo, and Citigroup). As of 2017, the world's largest commercial bank was the Industrial and Commercial Bank of China with $3.473 billion (U.S.) in assets.

- A **derivative** is a type of security instrument that is dependent upon the underlying value of one or more assets tied to it. A derivative is like a hybrid of a financial and insurance contract in which two or more parties will be betting on the future directions of an underlying financial contract such as those related to interest-rate movements like the LIBOR index.

- It was the "freezing" of the derivatives market ($1,500 to $3,000 trillion valuation range) in September 2008 that caused the Credit Crisis to significantly worsen. The total estimated value of all subprime mortgages in default at the time were estimated to represent only less than 1% of all bad debt that was hurting banks and the overall financial markets at the time.

- A **savings bank** (also known as a building and loan, savings and loan, or thrift over the years) is a financial institution that accepts savings deposits in exchange for the payment of interest on those deposits to customers. Banks with access to longer-term savings deposits will then lend the money out to home mortgage borrowers.

- The **Savings and Loan Crisis** worsened in the 1980s and 1990s after years of "too flexible" lending policies that 1,043 out of the 3,234 savings and loans that were formed in the years between 1986 to 1995 ended up failing. The main insurance fund called FSLIC (Federal Savings and Loan Insurance Corporation) later ran out of cash after trying to bail out so many insolvent Savings and Loans. The FDIC fund then stepped up to take control and ownership of FSLIC.

- The **Resolution Trust Corporation** was formed to assist with the discounted sale of residential and commercial real estate properties in order to provide some financial relief for these savings institutions and their depositors.

- A **credit union** differs from a bank in that it is formed as a not-for-profit cooperative organization that exists to serve its members or shareholders. Often, the credit union members work in the same employment industry such as teachers, military personnel, or engineers.

- **Life insurance companies** are some of the largest providers of mortgage capital for commercial real estate properties, especially prime office buildings, retail shopping malls, and large multi-family apartment buildings.

- Three hundred of the largest pension funds in the world today account for over 43% of all global pension assets in amounts up to $15.7 trillion. They are some of the biggest investors or lenders in real estate properties in California and the rest of the nation.

Chapter Five Quiz

1. What financial group collects most of its funds from its customers' checking accounts, savings accounts, money market funds, and certificates of deposit (CDs) prior to later lending the funds out to other customers?

    A. Equity firms

    B. Commercial banks

    C. Hedge funds

    D. Crowdfunding platforms for real estate

2. The spread between the amount of interest paid to customers for their deposits and the interest that the bank earns on loans is called ____.

    A. Effective gross return

    B. Cap rate

    C. Net interest income

    D. Annual recovery rate

3. What nation has the highest number of commercial banks in the top 100 for the world as it relates to asset size in recent times?

    A. U.S.

    B. China

    C. Japan

    D. Great Britain

4. A type of hybrid financial and insurance security instrument that is dependent upon the underlying value of one or more assets tied to it is called a ____.

    A. Mortgage

    B. Trust Deed

    C. Derivative

    D. Promissory Note

5. Which quarter and year had the highest foreclosure rates in California?
    A. 4th Quarter 2007
    B. 2nd Quarter 2008
    C. 1st Quarter 2009
    D. 3rd Quarter 2011

6. What was the first chartered savings bank in the U.S.?
    A. Provident Institution for Savings in Boston
    B. First Bank
    C. Philadelphia Savings
    D. New York Building and Loan

7. What taxpayer bailout measure was passed to provide upwards of $50 billion dollars' worth of funds for failed savings banks in 1989?
    A. FSLIC
    B. FIRREA
    C. RTC
    D. Banking Act of 1989

8. Which insurance fund protects credit union deposits for the banking customers?
    A. FDIC
    B. FSLIC
    C. NCUSIF
    D. CUI

9. As of 2014, what was the estimated number of Americans who carried some form of life insurance?
    A. 35 million
    B. 52 million
    C. 70 million
    D. 180 million

10. What is the preferred type of property for life insurance companies to finance over the long term?
    A. Single-family homes
    B. Land
    C. Office buildings
    D. Small retail strip centers

11. What was the estimated value range of the world's supply of derivatives back when the financial markets "froze" up in the fall of 2008?
    A. $100 billion
    B. $575 billion
    C. $1.2 trillion
    D. $1,500 trillion plus

12. What was the approximate percentage of savings and loans that were formed between the years 1986 and 1995 that would eventually end up failing?
    A. 5%
    B. 11%
    C. 22%
    D. 33%

Answer Key:

1. B	6. A	11. D
2. C	7. B	12. D
3. B	8. C	
4. C	9. D	
5. C	10. C	

CHAPTER 6

BAILING OUT BANKS AND THE FINANCIAL SYSTEM

Overview

This chapter discusses details regarding why and how the financial markets crumbled and many of the largest banks, investment firms, and insurance companies had to be bailed out. The markets experienced significant value declines due to their combination of trillions of dollars' worth of derivatives investments and billions of dollars' worth of subprime and Alt-A mortgage losses. Out of these ashes of financial destruction, there arose new government agencies and modified lending and real estate guidelines that changed the mortgage and real estate professions tremendously over the past decade as readers will learn in this chapter.

Banks and Derivatives

The Office of the Comptroller of the Currency (OCC) released a report in early 2017 that made note of the fact that the top 25 largest banks in the U.S. have exposure, directly or indirectly, to 222 trillion dollars of some type of a derivative contract (e.g., an option, futures contract, swap, or some other securities instrument) held in their portfolio. As a comparison, the value of all outstanding residential and commercial mortgages nationally are somewhere within the $10 to $12 trillion range. That would make the value of derivatives contracts potentially 22 times larger than all open mortgages across the United States. If true, then many commercial banks today operate more like securities investment firms than commercial mortgage lenders.

Let's review the total combined asset size and derivatives exposures for some of the best known commercial banks and investment firms in the United States:

Citigroup
Total Assets: $1,792,077,000,000 (or just under 1.8 trillion dollars)
Total Derivatives Exposure: $47,092,584,000,000 ($47 trillion plus)

JPMorgan Chase
Total Assets: $2,490,972,000,000 (just under 2.5 trillion dollars)
Total Derivatives Exposure: $46,992,293,000,000 (almost 47 trillion)

Goldman Sachs
Total Assets: $860,185,000,00 (over $860 billion dollars)
Total Derivatives Exposure: $41,227,878,000,000 ($41 trillion plus)

Bank of America
Total Assets: $2,189,266,000,000 ($2.1 trillion plus)
Total Derivatives Exposure: $33,132,582,000,000 (more than $33 trillion)

Morgan Stanley
Total Assets: $814,949,000,000 (more than $814 billion dollars)
Total Derivatives Exposure: $28,569,553,000,000 ($28 trillion plus)

Wells Fargo
Total Assets: $1,930,115,000,000 (more than $1.9 trillion dollars)
Total Derivatives Exposure: $7,098,952,000,000 (more than $7 trillion)

Source: OCC

One of the best known financial experts in U.S. and world history is Warren Buffet, the main principal in the multi-billion dollar *Berkshire Hathaway* investment firm. Buffett is also one of the wealthiest in the world. In a letter to his shareholders back in 2003, he referred to risky derivatives investments as **"financial weapons of mass destruction."**

Mr. Buffett wrote these prophetic words of wisdom several years before the derivatives markets "froze up" and almost collapsed the financial and real estate markets in the U.S. beginning in 2007 and 2008:

"The derivatives genie is now well out of the bottle, and these instruments will almost certainly multiply in variety and number until some event makes their toxicity clear. Central banks and governments have so far found no effective way to control, or even monitor, the risks posed by these contracts. ***In my view, derivatives are financial weapons of mass destruction, carrying dangers that, while now latent, are potentially lethal****."*

The **Emergency Economic Stabilization Act of 2008** was enacted on October 3, 2008 shortly after the financial system almost collapsed. It was signed into law by President George W. Bush. The law was described as being related to the bailout of banks tied to the "subprime mortgage crisis." Yet it was really more of a bailout of banks, firms on Wall Street, insurance groups, and even large automobile firms that had been exposed to risky derivatives contracts that were tied to subprime mortgages, interest rate movements, various currencies around the world, credit card and automobile securities, and other types of complex securities instruments that few people really understood back then or even today.

Most Americans do not realize that the FDIC (Federal Deposit Insurance Corporation) was bailed out fairly silently and secretly shortly after Washington Mutual Bank (the largest bank in U.S. history to ever collapse) went out of business near the end of September in 2008. That was the most tumultuous and financially devastating month in the United States since the official start of the Great Depression in October 1929. Earlier in September 2008, Lehman Brothers, Bear Stearns, Merrill Lynch (the world's largest brokerage firm at the time with upwards of $2.2 trillion in client assets being managed by 15,000 brokers), and AIG had all collapsed or almost collapsed prior to being bailed out by the federal government and/or another investment firm or commercial bank.

What was the largest banking collapse in U.S. history back in September 2008?

The bank runs on a massive scale reminiscent of the Great Depression's worst years in the early 1930s that impacted thousands of U.S. banks were averted in the fall of 2008 after the U.S. Treasury and Federal Reserve were forced to step up and provide funds to keep the FDIC solvent and afloat. Without FDIC insurance money in place to protect depositors' funds in weak banks, then more people would have run to the banks to pull cash out of their savings accounts. Before Washington Mutual went out of business, it reported in its 2007 filings with the SEC (Securities and Exchange Commission) that it held close to $328 billion in assets. The next year in 2008, the FDIC reported before the markets almost collapsed that it had only about $40 billion in cash reserves available to bail out banks and other federally-insured financial institutions.

The main sections of the Emergency Economic Stabilization Act (EESA) that offered relief for financial, insurance, legal, and investment institutions as well as some indirect financial relief for troubled homeowners who could no longer afford their mortgage payments included the following main sections of the EESA act.

Section 101. Purchases of Troubled Assets

This section authorized the former Treasury Secretary named Hank Paulson (a former CEO at Goldman Sachs) to established a **Troubled Asset Relief Program (TARP)** to purchase troubled assets from financial institutions. The Treasury Department was given the power to establish an **Office of Financial Stability** to implement and enforce TARP guidelines in consultation with the Board of Governors of the Federal Reserve System, the Comptroller of the Currency, the FDIC, the Director of the Office of Thrift Supervision and the Secretary of Housing and Urban Development.

Section 102. Insurance of Troubled Assets

The Treasury Secretary was required to set up some type of insurance program to guarantee or improve the odds of the repayment of TARP funds at a later date. The risk-based premiums for such insurance guarantees related to TARP would be required to be sufficient enough to cover the financial losses. The Secretary was required to report to Congress with the status of these loan guarantees that were almost the equivalent of an FHA-type program for $700 billion plus in loans. Over the next few years, the bailout loans increased to several trillion dollars as more banks and businesses ran out of cash.

Section 104. Financial Stability Oversight Board

The authority to establish the **Financial Stability Oversight Board** under this section was granted. The board was given the power to review and make recommendations in regard to this authority over individual financial institutions and the overall U.S. financial markets. The board was required to ensure that the policies set forth by the Treasury Secretary and his associates protect U.S. taxpayers and are in the economic best interests of the nation.

The key members on this new oversight board included the Chairman of the Board of Governors of the Federal Reserve System, the Treasury Secretary, the Director of the Federal Home Finance Agency, the Chairman of the Securities and Exchange Commission, and the Secretary of the Department of Housing and Urban Development (HUD).

Section 106. Rights; Management; Sale of Troubled Assets; Revenues and Sale Proceed

This section assigns the right to the Treasury Secretary to exercise authority under this act at any given time. The Secretary is granted the power and authority to manage troubled assets and negotiate the terms and conditions related to the future disposition or sale of the troubled assets like large multi-billion dollar mortgage pools and large commercial properties or packages of hundreds or thousands of foreclosed homes. The profit from the sale of any of these troubled assets will then be required to pay down the national debt.

Section 109. Foreclosure Mitigation Efforts

Any mortgages or mortgage-backed securities that are purchased through the TARP program must have some sort of a plan to mitigate or minimize future foreclosure numbers while encouraging mortgage loan servicing companies to modify their delinquent mortgages with homeowners through loan-relief programs such as **Hope for Homeowners**. The Treasury Secretary is allowed to use loan guarantees and credit enhancements to reduce the number of residential foreclosures across the nation.

Section 110. Assistance to Homeowners

This section makes it a requirement for entities that hold mortgages and mortgage-backed securities such as the Federal Housing Finance Agency, the FDIC, and the Federal Reserve to develop their own plans to reduce foreclosure numbers. Each of these federal or financial agencies must work with mortgage-loan servicers in order to encourage loan modifications or work out plans that allow homeowners to stay in the properties while reducing the losses to taxpayers.

Section 116. Oversight and Audits

This section requires the Comptroller General of the United States to conduct a thorough ongoing oversight or investigative analysis of the activities and performance of the TARP program prior to later reporting to Congress every 60 days thereafter. TARP must establish and maintain an effective system of internal controls related to their own accounting audits as a way to better protect against even worse losses for taxpayers.

Section 122. Increase in the Statutory Limit on the Public Debt

The federal debt ceiling was raised from $10 trillion to $11.3 trillion in order to cover this TARP program. As of 2017, the national debt ceiling has almost doubled to almost $20 trillion dollars partly due to nearly 10 years of bailing out large commercial banks and the rest of the financial markets.

The **Emergency Economic Stabilization Act of 2008** was the first of many financial bailout strategies taken by President Obama, Congress, the U.S. Treasury, and the Federal Reserve in an attempt to unfreeze the financial markets. This act authorized the U.S. Treasury to spend up to $700 billion dollars to purchase distressed assets, especially mortgage-backed securities, and supply banks with much needed cash so that they were able to keep their doors open for business. Unfortunately, there wasn't one listed homeowner anywhere on the list of the original 976 recipients of the approximately $626 billion that was first distributed out of the $700 billion bailout fund.

Many of the loan recipients had absolutely nothing to do with "subprime mortgages" or the commercial banking sector as noted by some of these top 10 loan recipients below:

Name	Business or Agency Type	Amount
Fannie Mae	Secondary Market Investor	$116,149,000,000
Freddie Mac	Secondary Market Investor	$71,336,000,000
AIG	Insurance Company	$67,835,000,000
General Motors	Automobile Company	$50,744,648,329
Bank of America	Commercial Bank	$45,000,000,000
Citigroup	Commercial Bank	$45,000,000,000
JPMorgan Chase	Commercial Bank	$25,000,000,000
Wells Fargo	Commercial Bank	$25,000,000,000
GMAC	Financial Services Co.	$16,290,000,000
Chrysler	Automobile Company	$10,748,284,222

There were 49 companies bailed out with loan amounts exceeding $1 billion each that also included (highest amounts from top to bottom ranging from $10 billion down to $1 billion):

Goldman Sachs
Morgan Stanley
PNC Financial Services
U.S. Bancorp
SunTrust
Ocwen Loan Servicing, LLC
Capital One Financial Corp.
Regions Financial Corp.
Wellington Management Legacy Securities PPIF Master Fund, LP
Fifth Third Bancorp
Hartford Financial Services
American Express
AG GECC PPIF Master Fund, L.P.
AllianceBernstein Legacy Securities Master Fund L.P.

BB&T

Bank of New York Mellon

Wells Fargo Bank, NA (second bailout)

JPMorgan Chase subsidiaries (second bailout)

KeyCorp

CalHFA Mortgage Assistance Corporation

CIT Group

Comerica Incorporated

Bank of America subsidiaries (including Countrywide - second bailout)

State Street

RLJH Western Asset Public/Private Master Fund, L.P.

Invesco Legacy Securities Master Fund, L.P.

Marshall & Ilsley

Oaktree PPIP Fund, L.P.

Blackrock PPIF, L.P.

Northern Trust

Chrysler Financial Services (second bailout)

Marathon Legacy Securities Public-Private Investment Partnership, L.P.

Zions Bancorp

Huntington Bancshares

Discover Financial Services

Select Portfolio Servicing

Nationstar Mortgage, LLC

Florida Housing Finance Corporation

Source: https://projects.propublica.org/bailout/list

Commercial banks that were bailed out by the federal government and Federal Reserve after 2008 sadly did not use the majority of funds to make new loans or modified loan structures to their banking customers. No, most banks used the funds to cover their financial losses related to their risky derivatives investments and to pay their chief banking executives higher salaries and bonuses for not leaving the troubled financial institutions to take jobs elsewhere.

Listed below are some prime examples of well-known commercial banks bailed out shortly after the near implosion of the financial markets in the fall of 2008 and their bonuses paid out to their employees and executives in spite of overall company losses:

Citigroup: The New York-based commercial bank received $45 billion in total government bailout loans and federal guarantees to protect the bank against potential financial losses associated with hundreds of billions of dollars from risky derivatives investments. In exchange for the $45 billion emergency loans, the federal government took 33% ownership interests in Citigroup. Citigroup rewarded 738 employees with bonuses of at least $1 million dollars each by the end of 2008 in spite of the bank losing $18.7 billion the year before. The total amount of bonuses paid out to employees at Citigroup reached $5.33 billion in 2008 alone.

JPMorgan Chase: This global financial institution that has been rated as one of the top 3 financial institutions on the planet at various points received $25 billion in TARP (Troubled Asset Relief Program) funds. JPMorgan awarded bonuses of at least $1 million to 1,626 employees a few months after receiving the bailout money. More than 200 employees collected bonuses in excess of $3 million each.

Bank of America: This American institution that was originally named the *Bank of Italy* when it first opened for business in San Francisco received $45 billion in TARP funds. Bank of America used some of the funds to acquire Merrill Lynch, the world's largest stock brokerage firm that almost collapsed in mid-September 2008, and Countrywide Mortgage, one of the largest mortgage lenders in both California and the rest of the nation. Bank of America paid out $3.3 billion in bonuses to their employees, which included 172 banking personnel taking home over $1 million in bonus money each. Merrill Lynch, indirectly through the BofA bailout funds, paid out $3.6 billion in bonuses (696 employees received more than $1 million each) in late 2008 even though the firm had lost $30.48 billion for the year.

Bank of America Buys Countrywide Mortgage

Countrywide Mortgage was founded in Calabasas, California by David Loeb and Angelo Mozilo in 1969. In 2003, there was an article in *Fortune Magazine* entitled "Meet the 23,000% Stock" that was about how Countrywide's stock was "the best stock market performance of any financial services company in the Fortune 500" over the previous 20 years. Shareholders who had invested just $1,000 in 1982 would have seen the stock compound to more than $230,000 by 2003.

Countrywide was on track to fund more than $400 billion in home loans and earn more than $2.4 billion in net profit in the same year, according to *Fortune.* At the time, Countrywide's profit margins were reported as higher than that of the Disney Company and McDonald's. Angelo Mozilo, the CEO at Countrywide, took home almost $33 million dollars in total compensation in 2003 alone.

Investors on Wall Street seem to love Mozilo and Countrywide. The investment bankers flocked to Countrywide to purchase its mortgage-backed securities (also known as "collateralized debt obligations" or C.D.O.s) that were written as primarily "EZ Doc" and adjustable-rate mortgage (ARM) loans with starting payment rates as low as 1% and with loan terms up to 40 years. Angelo Mozilo was so beloved by many investment bankers on Wall Street that his mortgage pools were snatched up fairly quickly at the highest prices possible. Countrywide became possibly the number one supplier of mortgage-backed securities for Wall Street investors in spite of a relatively small number of borrowers actually applying with "full doc" loans with verified income and assets and "A" grade (720-plus FICO credit scores) creditworthy borrowers.

A high percentage of the Countrywide mortgage loans had a **negative amortization** option if the borrowers continued to pay the minimum monthly payment. The lifetime payment cap for the original mortgage principal amount issued by Countrywide was anywhere from 110% to

125% for its loans. This meant that the highest amount of unpaid deferred interest (or "negative amortization") could grow, for a $100,000 loan, either $110,000 (110% LTV), $115,000 (115% LTV), or $125,000 (125% LTV). Once the deferred unpaid interest was added onto the original principal amount and it reached the maximum loan-amount ceiling, the loan would recast and the monthly payments would adjust upwards so that the borrower had to pay at least interest only payments on the higher loan amount. Often, a borrower's monthly payment would double in size from $1,000 per month (1% monthly payment rate with a 40-year payment term) to $2,000 or more (interest only payment (index + margin = 7% or more) over a 30-year term).

In 2004, Countrywide edged out Wells Fargo Bank to become America's largest lender. Countrywide operated their wholesale mortgage lending division under a d/b/a ("doing business as") name called **America's Wholesale Lender** partly since they were number one in loan volume. In 2005, *Fortune* placed Countrywide on its list of "Most Admired Companies," and *Barron's* financial magazine named Angelo Mozilo one of the 30 best C.E.O.s (chief executive officer) in the world. In 2006, the *American Banker* publication presented Mozilo with a lifetime-achievement award. In 2007 and 2008, the bubble burst for Mozilo, Countrywide, and the financial and housing markets.

In January 2008, the former Bank of America C.E.O., Ken Lewis, announced that the bank would be purchasing Countrywide Mortgage. Lewis seemed excited at the chance to merge Countrywide's ailing subprime and "EZ Doc" business with Bank of America's more traditional home-lending division that focused more on 30-year fixed rate mortgages for homeowners. Lewis said that there was a real opportunity for Bank of America to soon become the number one overall home-mortgage lender in the nation after the acquisition of the former number one overall national mortgage lender.

Ken Lewis had a long-standing personal and financial relationship with Angelo Mozilo that dated back a few decades. Interestingly, it was Ken

Lewis who first loaned Angelo Mozilo $75,000 to start Countrywide Mortgage back in 1969. On January 11, 2008, Bank of America announced the acquisition of Countrywide for $4 billion in stock. Six months later, the total purchase would fall to just $2.5 billion by the time the deal closed after a true picture of the severity of overall losses for Countrywide became more apparent.

Hundreds of lawsuits followed against Angelo Mozilo and Countrywide from injured mortgage borrowers who felt defrauded by the firm once known as *America's Wholesale Lender.* Criminal probes from the Department of Justice lead to additional fines that were obligated to be paid by the new Bank of America parent company. By the summer of 2014, the total losses for Bank of America exceeded $52.7 billion as a direct result of its acquisition of Countrywide and the civil and criminal liability exposure and consumer relief (or mortgage modifications or reductions) that followed them.

Guy Cecala, the publisher of *Inside Mortgage Finance,* was quoted as saying this about Bank of America's purchase of the troubled Countrywide firm: "Clearly, it's the worst acquisition in history. No one really appreciated the liability that was going to be associated with large lenders from the past. Bank of America paid for it." In the first half of 2014, Bank of America had to set aside a whopping $10 billion dollars just for legal expenses to fight court battles associated with the Countrywide acquisition.

What was really ironic and hypocritical about Bank of America's purchase of Countrywide (the biggest subprime lender in America) was that BofA had exited the business of higher-priced subprime mortgage loans themselves in 2001 because it considered the marketplace too risky for the company and its shareholders. In the fall of 2007, Bank of America stopped offering mortgage loans to brokers through its national wholesale lending division because it considered loans originated from licensed mortgage brokers to be a "toxic waste" for BoA due to allegations such as fraud. Yet several months later in January 2008, Bank of

America acquired the largest subprime lender in America that was later described as potentially the "worst financial investment" in U.S. banking history.

The Growth of Non-Bank Loans

Amazingly, many banks took the bailout funds and purchased even more derivatives investments that generated much higher rates of return than loans to their banking customers. As a result of the frustration of finding bank loans from commercial banks, more and more customers sought out alternative non-bank lenders that could easily be found on the internet.

Mortgage lending has shifted dramatically since the official start of the Credit Crisis back in the summer of 2007. The top 10 largest commercial banks had several million mortgage loans in some stage of the foreclosure process between the peak default years of 2007 and 2011. Some financial analysts claimed that California alone had several million foreclosures that took place during that time. The other "bubble" states that burst after the last housing market boom also included Nevada, Arizona, Michigan, and Florida.

Many of these commercial banks had made rather large jumbo mortgage loans that routinely were much higher than $1 million, especially in the pricier states like California. Many of these same commercial banks were publicly-traded and had to file updated annual income and expense reports for investors to review as well as for governing agencies like the Securities and Exchange Commission to closely analyze.

A high percentage of the larger residential and commercial mortgage loans that were in default were not reported on a timely basis by these publicly-traded commercial banks partly because the governing board members did not want their stock values to fall too fast or their banking customers to withdraw too much cash in the form of a bank run as we saw during the depths of the Great Depression.

Listed below are snapshots of the top 10 mortgage lenders in 2011 and 2016. Over the span of just five years, the growth of non-bank loans from financial groups that did not take in actual customer deposits in the form of checking or savings accounts grew at a rather impressive pace. The top three banks (JPMorgan Chase, Bank of America, and Wells Fargo) went from funding 50% of all new mortgage loans in 2011 to 21% of all mortgages in 2016. In 2016, six of the top 10 lenders were non-banks. These non-depository financial entities (noted in **bold letters** in the charts below) increased their mortgage market share from 10.9% in 2011 to 17.11% in 2016.

2011 Market Share	
Wells Fargo	24.20%
Bank of America	10.58%
JP Morgan Chase	9.95%
U.S. Bank Home Mort.	4.38%
Citigroup	4.29%
Ally-GMAC	**3.81%**
PHH Mortgage	**3.51%**
Quicken Loans	**2.03%**
Flagstar Bancorp	1.80%
MetLife	**1.60%**

2016 Market Share	
Wells Fargo	12.55%
JPMorgan Chase	5.95%
Quicken Loans	**4.90%**
U.S. Bank Home Mort.	4.12%
Bank of America	4.07%
PennyMac Financial	**3.37%**
Freedom Mortgage	**2.90%**
PHH Mortgage	**2.01%**
Caliber Home Loans	**2.00%**
LoanDepot	**1.89%**

Source: *Mortgage Only*

Boosting Bubbly Markets with Quantitative Easing

The Federal Reserve had established the **Quantitative Easing (Q.E.)** program in November 2008 in an attempt to boost declining asset values that were associated specifically with stocks, bonds, interest rates, mortgages, and real estate properties. To simplify the explanation of the Q.E. program, the Federal Reserve effectively created trillions of dollars "out of thin air" (or by digital credits) to purchase stocks, bonds, and mortgage assets so that the values would inflate once again. To the Fed and the rest of the national economy, the deflated of asset prices can lead to economic depressions like the Great Depression that can last for 10 years or even 20 or 30 years like in Japan since the early 1990s.

Today's financial markets are more globally connected than ever before, so it is understandable why this financial bailout program was duplicated in several nations worldwide. Listed below are some of the key years for the introduction of Quantitative Easing (Q.E.) policies in Japan, the U.S., and portions of Europe in the 21st century.

Quantitative Easing - Japan 2001: The real estate, stock, and bond market bubbles in Japan during the 1990s far exceeded any bubble in California or the rest of the nation during any decade over the past few hundred years. Between the 1950s and late 1980s, Japan experienced its miraculous and infamous "bubble economy" in which both real estate and stock values soared to stratospheric levels. Just like with most bubble markets, the peak high values can eventually go "pop" prior to falling well below their all-time market highs in a short or long period of time.

Some of the most successful businesses in Japan during these boom decades included automobile firms such as Toyota, Nissan, Honda, and Mitsubishi. Japanese industry was ruled by large family-controlled industrial and financial business dynasties that were known as *zaibatsu* (financial clique), which later evolved into *keiretsu* (business conglomerates) in the second half of the 20th century.

Many of these keiretsu groups were organized through a series of interlocked industrial corporations that were connected around one specific Japanese bank. This same core bank provided the primary capital sources to the affiliate industrial corporations that were related to sectors like automobiles and consumer electronics. A prime example of one bank owning and controlling multiple business sectors include Mitsubishi Bank, Mitsubishi Corporation, Mitsubishi Motors, and Mitsubishi Heavy Industries. Many of these financial and business conglomerates were publicly-traded, and many of these affiliate companies and the Japanese government would buy and hold stock shares in order to guarantee long-term price stability and boost overall stock values beginning in the 1950s.

The **Marshall Plan** that the U.S. had implemented after defeating Japan near the end of the Second World War improved the ways that businesses operated as Japanese firms moved from more historically traditional and less effective strategies to newer Western techniques that rapidly increased exports to America and other nations. The Marshall Plan was eventually proven to be successful for Japan because U.S. financial aid was provided to rebuild Japan's economy after two atomic bombs were dropped on Nagasaki and Hiroshima in August 1945.

Industries in Japan gained a competitive edge over their American counterparts by copying Western products, improving their function and design, and then selling them back to the West for much cheaper prices. Although Japan lacked as many natural resources as America, they made up for it by improving their manufacturing methods and product quality for items such as cars and electronics. By the late 1970s, Japan had fine-tuned and advanced their robotic assembly-line techniques to the point that they could build better products at a much faster pace and a cheaper price.

Before there were the global American electronics, computer, and software firms named *Apple, Intel,* and *Google,* the best-known firms seemed to originate from Japan in the 1970s and early 1980s with products such as the Walkman, the VHS recorder, the pocket transistor radio, video games, and advanced stereo systems. The world's first computer game was called "Space War!" and was invented at the Massachusetts Institute of Technology (MIT) back in 1962. In spite of early U.S. origins, the video-game industry was later perfected and dominated by Japanese manufacturers for the next several decades.

Some of the best-known electronics products that Japan exported in the 1970s, 1980s, and 1990s included:

Space Invaders: Developed by Taito in 1978;

Pac-Man: Designed by Namco in 1980;

Family Computer: A home console video-game system built by Nintendo in 1983;

Game Boy: A portable computer game system developed by Nintendo in 1989; and

Sony PlayStation: The most advanced home-computer game system ever designed at the time in 1994.

By the early 1980s, many financial analysts believed that the Japanese firms Sony and Hitachi might one day acquire some of America's most successful firms such as Intel and IBM. Japan was considered the "King of the Global Electronics Industry" by the early 1980s after so many American electronics firms went out of business because they could not compete with Japanese technology or cheaper prices.

Japan's global and financial dominance was so staggeringly impressive that many economists believed that Japan would eventually replace the U.S. as the most powerful economy on the planet. Japan also became the world's number one largest creditor nation primarily thanks to Americans' demands for their goods and services. Additionally, the Japanese people had the world's longest life expectancy partly thanks to newfound wealth for many citizens and a healthier diet than most other areas of the world.

The U.S. national economy was also experiencing tremendous growth during the 1950s to the '80s as suburbia expanded in size. As a result, the growth of financial markets, exported American goods and services around the world, and the U.S. demand for exported Japanese goods increased. The U.S. was the number one largest economy in the world, but Japan was ranked number two.

Japanese conglomerates started to acquire landmark properties and businesses in the United States that included prime California assets such as the Pebble Beach golf course and Columbia Pictures in Hollywood. In addition, the very famous Rockefeller Center in New York was acquired by Japanese investors. Much of this Japanese wealth that was created to purchase and expand businesses and purchase American real estate originated from skyrocketing Nikkei stock values (the equivalent of the main Dow Jones Industrial Average index in the U.S.). The Japanese market eventually peaked in price in 1989 before the bubble popped and the need for Quantitative Easing methods later followed as discussed below.

Nikkei 225 Price History

Price	Trading Date
92.54	January 31, 1950
962.70	February 1, 1960
2,029.41	June 11, 1970
6,737.06	April 7, 1980
38,915.87	December 29, 1989
13,468.46	January 6, 1999
8,701.92	February 14, 2003
7,198.25	March 12, 2009
23,653.82	January 12, 2018

The Japanese Real Estate Bubble Pops

The Imperial Palace near Tokyo, Japan

The only asset bubble that grew larger than the stock bubble of the 1980s in Japan was its real estate bubble. Japanese investors in the 1980s were some of the largest land and commercial-property investors in California as they acquired properties with billions of dollars from their stock and business-exporting wealth. Many California residents and brokers were actually fearful that Japanese nationals would own more of the state than California natives.

At one point near the bubble market peak, the Imperial Palace where the Emperor of Japan lives was claimed to be worth more than all of the real estate and land in California combined.

On a price per square mile comparison, this is quite shocking when comparing the land sizes of the Imperial Palace and the entire golden state.

Land Size Comparisons
Imperial Palace: 1.316 square miles
State of California: 163,696 square miles

Even though California was over 163,694 square miles larger than the Imperial Palace, it was valued at an overall price **lower** than the relatively small 1.3 square-mile headquarters for the Emperor of Japan. Some financial analysts claimed that the Imperial Palace had a peak value in 1989 at close of a whopping $5.1 trillion (U.S.). As a comparison, Japan's GDP (Gross Domestic Product) figures for the entire nation in the same year was $5.3 trillion. In world history as it relates to overvalued properties, there is probably no other more bizarre comparison than the Imperial Palace and California.

By 1991 near the peak of the real estate market in Japan, commercial land prices had risen over 302% as compared to prices in 1985 in the prime Tokyo metropolitan region that included the cities of Yokohama, Nagoya, Kyoto, Osaka, and Kobe. Residential land and industrial land prices jumped over 180% and 162%, respectively, during the same time period. By early 1992, land values began falling at a rapid 19% annual pace for some regions once both the real estate and stock bubbles began bursting.

The overall land prices in 1992 for residential and commercial properties in Tokyo fell to prices last seen five years earlier in 1987. Over the next nine years, land and building values fell to catastrophically low levels as the supply of properties for sale far exceeded the number of available financially creditworthy buyers that was reminiscent of the housing and stock-market bust in the U.S. during the Great Depression (1929 - 1939).

The solution presented by the national government of Japan was Quantitative Easing (Q.E.) in 2001. The birthplace of Q.E. on a massive national scale first took place in Japan as a way to start boosting asset values once again, especially for stocks and real estate. Between 2001 and 2006, the Japanese Central Bank (Bank of Japan - BOJ) flooded the markets with new money in order to create more inflation through the combination of weakening the purchasing power of the Japanese currency (the Yen), and boosting asset values once again.

Even though the U.S. economy was alleged to be three times the size of the Japanese economy during these early 21st century years, Japan supposedly had pumped more money into their own nation than the Federal Reserve and U.S. Treasury had added to the American economy. Between 2001 and 2003, the BOJ increased its monetary base by almost 60%.

Japan continued onward with various Q.E.-type programs over the next several years with these programs that first began near the start of the new millennium:

QE1 - March 2001
QE2 - October 2010
QE3 - April 2013

Over the period of 20 years (from 1993, to 2013) is that the consumer price index (CPI - the main index used to determine national inflation rates) had averaged close to 0% as the markets went from boom to bust. The BOJ maintained its short-term interest rates at close to zero beginning in 1999 up until present day. The U.S. later followed these same Quantitative Easing programs and targeted zero percent interest rate policies that first started in Japan shortly after the U.S. financial and real estate markets began to rapidly descend in a negative direction in the fall of 2008.

Quantitative Easing (1) - United States 2008: The Federal Reserve, America's Central Bank, took notice of the Q.E. policies used in Japan and began to duplicate many of the same strategies in order to boost asset values once again. The large scale purchase of troubled assets and performing assets included billions of dollars of bonds issued by government agencies like Fannie Mae, Freddie Mac, Ginnie Mae, and Sallie Mae as well as private mortgage-backed securities that were available for sale in the market. The bailout of the mortgage-backed securities marketplace that was tied to subprime mortgage loans, Alt-A loans, conforming, jumbo, and other types of conventional loans with Q.E. funds were thought to be needed because there were few other investors willing to take the financial risk to buy up these assets at the time.

Many investors were unwilling to buy millions or billions of dollars of mortgage bonds that were linked to properties that were falling 20%, 30%, and even 50% in value between the worst years of late 2008 and 2011. At the very least, the Fed was trying to stabilize the mortgage and real estate markets by purchasing assets with hundreds of billions of dollars of Q.E. funds. Additionally, the Fed's trillions of dollars of anonymous and publicly-disclosed bailouts -- of prominent banks, insurance companies, and automobile lenders facing near-term financial insolvency and potential bankruptcy -- were used to improve the economy and increase consumer faith in the financial and real estate sectors.

Prior to the implementation of the original Quantitative Easing program in November 2008, the Federal Reserve held somewhere between $700 billion and $800 billion of Treasury notes on its balance sheet. At the time, the Fed primarily invested in relatively safe and secure Treasury notes issued by the federal government. The Fed wasn't known for taking big financial risks with other types of financial instruments secured by residential or commercial mortgages before the start of Q.E. policies.

Shortly after November 2008, the Fed began purchasing about $600 billion in mortgage-backed securities in an attempt to stimulate and boost the mortgage and real estate markets. By March 2009, the Fed held close to $1.75 trillion of bank debt, mortgage-backed securities, and Treasury notes in its portfolio. By June 2010, the Fed's investment portfolio grew to $2.1 trillion. The Fed was purchasing approximately $30 billion per month in two to ten-year Treasury notes every single month to maintain this targeted investment pace.

The Fed tried to stop their Q.E. program around this same time, but asset values began falling yet again. So, the Fed followed with at least two more rounds of Quantitative Easing during these time periods:

QE2 - November 2010: The Fed's announcement of a second round of Quantitative Easing included an additional purchase of $600 billion of Treasury securities between November 2010 and by the end of June 2011.

QE3 - September 2012: The third round of Quantitative Easing was announced on September 13, 2012. The Fed decided to launch a new $40 billion-per-month purchase of mortgage-backed securities as a way to artificially drive mortgage rates to new record lows and a way to inspire more banks to offer new mortgage loans to their borrowers. The Fed also announced that it would likely maintain a **federal-funds rate near zero** "at least through 2015" just like Japan as a way to boost property values again.

This program was also called **ZIRP** (Zero Interest-Rate Policy). On December 12, 2012, the Federal Open Market Committee (FOMC) publicly announced that they had increased their amount of open-ended purchases of mortgage and Treasury notes from $40 billion to as high as $85 billion per month.

Let's take a look below at asset values near the start of QE1 for both stocks and real estate and values over the next 10 years:

Dow Jones Industrial Average	Trading Date
8,443.39	Nov 24, 2008
6,443.27	Mar 6, 2009
9,743.62	July 6, 2010
10,655.30	Oct 3, 2011
12,570.95	Nov 14, 2012
16,086.41	Nov 29, 2013
17,180.84	Dec 15, 2014
17,528.27	Dec 28, 2015
19,216.24	Dec 5, 2016
24,272.35	Nov 30, 2017
26,413.96	Jan 25, 2018

Even with Q.E. money flowing into the markets at **$85 billion per month** from the Federal Reserve, the Dow Jones Industrial Average (DJIA) still hit a low below 6,500 in March 2009.

The DJIA low reached on March 6, 2009 (6,443.27) was 54% lower than its value last reached near the October 9, 2007 market high. As a comparison, the Dow Jones in early January 2018 surpassed 26,400 (or almost 20,000 points higher). Are the stock and real estate markets now too "bubbly" and overvalued?

National Median Home Prices	Month and Year
$191,000	Jan 2008
$177,000	Jan 2009
$165,000	Jan 2010
$156,000	Jan 2011
$151,000	Jan 2012
$155,000	Jan 2013
$165,000	Jan 2014
$172,000	Jan 2015
$182,000	Jan 2016
$194,000	Jan 2017
$205,000	Dec 2017

California Median Home Prices	Month and Year
$465,000	Jan 2008
$371,000	Jan 2009
$335,000	Jan 2010
$323,000	Jan 2011
$304,000	Jan 2012
$333,000	Jan 2013
$397,000	Jan 2014
$424,000	Jan 2015
$454,000	Jan 2016
$487,000	Jan 2017
$520,000	Dec 2017

Source: Zillow Home Value Index

The national economy did not see the price improvements for many prime assets until later in 2009 for stocks and late 2012 or 2013 for real-estate properties even after several years of the Quantitative Easing program. Several financial analysts made the claim that the Federal Reserve became the largest buyer of stocks, bonds, and mortgage pools between late 2008 and through at least 2011. Without the Fed and the U.S. Treasury acting together to boost values again, the stock market values could have fallen to record lows on a percentage basis.

Operation Twist

The Federal Reserve wanted to lower interest rates for mortgage loans so that more home buyers could qualify for larger loan amounts as a way to boost property values. In late 2011 and early 2012, the Fed conducted a monetary-policy strategy called **Operation Twist** that involved the simultaneous purchasing of longer-term bonds and shorter-dated issues it already held in order to drive interest rates lower. This monetary policy name dates back to an old Chubby Checker song and dance craze called "The Twist" that was first used by the Fed back in 1961.

The media also seemed to like the "Operation Twist" name since it provided a type of visual effect that readers or television viewers could imagine when attempting to comprehend how the Treasury yield curve would be twisted and moved downward. If a person visualized a linear upward sloping bond yield curve, this new Fed monetary action was structured to "twist" the end of the yield curve.

When the market interest rates, or yields, increase, the price of a bond will decrease. Conversely, declining bond yields will cause increasing bond prices. The movement of mortgage rates are inverse to bond prices somewhat like the movement of a seesaw on a playground. When one goes up, the other one goes down.

The newer version of "Operation Twist" was established in two main parts. The first version ran from September 2011 through June of 2012 while involving the redeployment of $400 billion of Fed assets. The second part ran from July 2012 through December 2012 with an amount close to $267 billion ($667 billion total).

In December 2012, the Fed announced that it would discontinue the Operation Twist program that had forced 30-year fixed-mortgage rates and their corresponding 10-year Treasury-yield rates to all-time record lows. Declining 10-year Treasuries also lead to declining 30-year mortgage rates since they are tied to one another. Operation Twist was essentially the main financial catalyst that boosted the housing market once again after more borrowers could qualify for much larger loan amounts with 30-year mortgage rates reaching 4% lows.

Let's take a look below at how far mortgage rates have fallen from the official start of the Credit Crisis in 2007 to present day as partly related to the success of the Operation Twist program:

30-Year Fixed Mortgage Rates (Annual Average)	Year
6.34%	2007
6.03%	2008
5.04%	2009
4.69%	2010
4.45%	2011
3.66%	2012
3.98%	2013
4.17%	2014
3.85%	2015
3.65%	2016
3.99%	2017

Source: Freddie Mac

2009 - A Challenging Financial Year

The year 2009 was pivotal in the history of banking, stocks, bonds, and the real estate sector. There were so many multi-billion dollar financial firms on the verge of filing for bankruptcy protection that the federal government and Federal Reserve stepped up to bail them out. Because a large number of these financial firms had investments tied to one another, the implosion of one bank or investment firm could set off a domino-like effect and cause affiliate or associated firms to go under as well.

January: Banks reported losing more than $1 trillion dollars since the beginning of the Subprime Mortgage Crisis in 2007. As a result, banks were forced to raise almost $946 billion in capital to cover their financial losses. An estimated $350 billion of the total $946 billion came from the U.S. Treasury as part of the Bank Bailout. Banks had to hoard their cash to survive instead of making new loans to customers. At this point, more real estate investors and agents began seeking out private money and online non-bank lending sources for capital for their properties.

February: Congress approved the **$787 Billion Dollar Economic Stimulus Package** on February 13th that attempted to boost the economy once again with a combination of tax cuts for individuals and businesses and increased unemployment benefits. Congress also created new jobs in public works programs that were reminiscent of past public works projects offered during the Great Depression. A $2,500 college-tuition tax credit was included along with an $8,000 tax credit for first-time homebuyers, and a sales-tax deduction allowance for new car purchases.

On February 18th, President Barack Obama announced a new $75 billion plan to help stop foreclosures. The **Homeowners Stability Initiative (HSI)** was designed with the intent to help seven to ten million homeowners across the nation avoid foreclosure by either restructuring or refinancing their delinquent loans before the final foreclosure auction date.

March: On March 5th, the Dow Jones stock index fell to 6,594. This closing day number was 53.4% lower than its peak close of 14,164 on October 9, 2007. This staggering point loss was statistically much worse than any other bear market since the month of October 1929 at the start of the Great Depression (until January 2018).

April: The **Making Homes Affordable Program** was launched by President Obama to help more homeowners avoid foreclosure. The **HARP (Homeowners Affordable Refinance Program)** and **HAMP (Home Affordable Modification Program)** were created to assist upwards of 810,000 homeowners in "upside down" situations (mortgage debt exceeds current market value) to refinance their loans and reduce their monthly payments.

July: Foreclosure rates nationwide hit record numbers in the month of July with 360,149 foreclosure filings. California was number one by far in the nation with the largest number of foreclosures of any state. July 2009's foreclosure numbers were 32% higher than July 2008 one year prior as reported by *RealtyTrac*. About 57% of all foreclosures reported nationally were located in just four states: Arizona, California, Nevada, and Florida (also known as "the bubble states").

October: The national unemployment rate reached 10.0% in October 2009. This was the worst national unemployment number since the 1982

recession. An estimated six million jobs were lost in just 12 months dating back to October 2008. A Federal Reserve report showed that lending had fallen by 15% from the nation's four largest banks: Bank of America, Citigroup, Wells Fargo, and JPMorgan Chase.

The U.S. Treasury also reported that these banks had cut back on their lending by $100 billion in a relatively short six-month time period between April 2009 and October 2009. Strangely, the total number of loans made by the big banks that were deemed "too big to fail" when granted hundreds of billions of dollars in bailout funds had fallen 9% between October 2008 and October 2009. Yet the total outstanding balance of loans made had actually increased by 5%, according to the Treasury Department. This meant that banks were making more large loans to wealthy clients (individuals and corporations) as opposed to more loans to homeowners who were struggling to stay afloat.

Chapter Six Summary

- In 2017, the Office of the Comptroller of the Currency (OCC) released a report which found that the top 25 largest banks or investment banks in the U.S. had exposure to $222 trillion of derivatives investments. Citigroup, JP Morgan Chase, Goldman Sachs, and Bank of America were rated as holding the top four largest amounts of derivatives in their portfolios.

- The **Emergency Economic Stabilization Act of 2008** was enacted on October 3, 2008 shortly after the financial system almost collapsed less than a week before. It was signed into law by President George W. Bush.

- The **Emergency Economic Stabilization Act of 2008 (EESA)** called for the establishment of a **Troubled Asset Relief Program (TARP)** that gave more power to the Federal Reserve to purchase assets (stocks, mortgages, bonds) in order to boost values once again with dollar amounts starting at $700 billion prior to later being increased. Directly or indirectly, the Fed would provide trillions of dollars of debt relief for troubled assets and financial institutions.

- The TARP programs also included mortgage relief programs like **Hope for Homeowners** that offered financial assistance to homeowners on the verge of losing their home to foreclosure.

- Fannie Mae and Freddie Mac, America's two largest secondary-market investors, received almost $188 billion combined from TARP in order to stay afloat and open for business.

- Countrywide Mortgage went from being America's largest wholesale mortgage lender to financially insolvent and in need of a bailout by Bank of America and the federal government.

- Between 2011 and 2016, the growth of non-banks for mortgages skyrocketed after so many people began to lose faith in the commercial bank system. Some of the largest online non-bank mortgage lenders who did not receive depositor funds included Quicken Loans, PennyMac Financial, and Freedom Mortgage.

- The Federal Reserve established the **Quantitative Easing (Q.E.)** program back in November 2008 as a way to boost declining asset values that were associated specifically with stocks, bonds, interest rates, mortgages, and real estate properties. For several years, the Fed was purchasing between $40 billion and $85 billion per month in assets using Q.E. funds.

- The Federal Reserve used a monetary policy strategy called **Operation Twist** that involved the simultaneous purchasing of longer term bonds while selling some of the shorter-dated bonds it already held in order to drive interest rates lower beginning in 2011. This strategy was so successful that 30-year fixed mortgage rates reached all-time record lows. The more affordable mortgage rates then allowed a higher number of buyers to purchase homes.

Chapter Six Quiz

1. According to a report released by the Office of the Comptroller of the Currency (OCC) in 2017, what was the reported total dollar amount of derivatives investments held by the top 25 largest banks in the United States?
    A. $750 billion
    B. $1.45 trillion
    C. $43 trillion
    D. $222 trillion

2. What was the largest banking collapse in U.S. history in September 2008?
    A. Countrywide Mortgage
    B. Washington Mutual
    C. IndyMac Bank
    D. Bear Stearns

3. What was the first major financial bailout act signed by President George W. Bush just one week after the financial markets "froze" and the Dow Jones index dropped 777 points in one day?
    A. Emergency Economic Stabilization Act
    B. Dodd-Frank
    C. Consumer Financial Protection Bureau
    D. Wall Street Reform Act

4. What was the original amount of the TARP (Troubled Asset Relief Program) bailout that was set aside to assist near-insolvent banks, other financial firms, and even automobile companies?
    A. $100 billion
    B. $300 billion
    C. $700 billion
    D. $1.6 trillion

5. What group received the largest dollar amount of TARP funds?
    A. JPMorgan Chase
    B. Citigroup
    C. Bank of America
    D. Fannie Mae

6. What bank bailed out and took over the ownership and operations of Countrywide Mortgage (once the largest wholesale mortgage lender in America)?
    A. JP Morgan Chase
    B. Bank of America
    C. New Century Mortgage
    D. Wells Fargo

7. A subprime mortgage loan that can increase in principal size after the borrower chooses to defer unpaid mortgage interest is called____.
    A. Interest only
    B. Partial amortization
    C. Negative amortization
    D. A balloon note

8. What lender had the largest share of the mortgage market in both 2011 and five years later in 2016?
    A. Bank of America
    B. JPMorgan Chase
    C. Citigroup
    D. Wells Fargo

9. The Federal Reserve's program launched in November 2008 that was an attempt to boost declining asset values that were associated with stocks, bonds, mortgages, and real estate was called____.
    A. Operation Twist
    B. Quantitative Easing
    C. TARP
    D. Federal Housing Finance Agency

10. Between 2012 and 2015, the Federal Reserve tried to boost the national economy by keeping the Federal Funds Rate near____.
    A. 0%
    B. 0.5%
    C. 1.0%
    D. 2.0%

11. Near the depths of the market lows in March 2009, how low did the Dow Jones Industrial Average (DJIA) stock index fall?
    A. 6,443
    B. 8,347
    C. 11,972
    D. 14,026

12. In January 2012 (a market low over the past 10 plus years), the median price home in California fell to what amount as compared with December 2017's numbers that reached $520,000?
    A. $435,000
    B. $417,000
    C. $392,000
    D. $304,000

Answer Key:

1. D	6. B	11. A
2. B	7. C	12. D
3. A	8. D	
4. C	9. B	
5. D	10. A	

CHAPTER 7

SECONDARY MARKETS

Overview

In this section, readers will learn about how secondary-market investors provide much-needed capital that directly and indirectly benefits banks, other primary lenders, and banking customers or borrowers. Over the past 80 plus years, the secondary markets have gone from 100% government-backed to more of a primarily private secondary market by way of multi-billion dollar firms on Wall Street and large pension and insurance funds. After the Credit Crisis began worsening and the markets froze up in 2008, the government stepped up to take back the primary ownership and management of the secondary mortgage markets. Through various boom and bust cycles, primary and secondary mortgage-market investors are needed to ensure that the housing markets remain relatively stable as set out in detail below. Some review of previously-discussed concepts and programs is included in this chapter as well.

Fannie Mae

The Federal National Mortgage Association (FNMA) is most commonly referred to as Fannie Mae. It is the best-known secondary market investor that was designed to purchase funded mortgage loans from primary lenders like commercial banks so that lenders had sufficient levels of capital to make more loans to their banking customers. Over the years, Fannie Mae has evolved from a quasi-governmental (or "quasi-private") agency, to one that later became publicly traded with individual shareholders, and then to an entity that was officially bailed out by the federal government during the big Credit Crisis in 2008.

Fannie Mae is a government-sponsored enterprise (GSE) that was originally founded as part of President Franklin D. Roosevelt's **New Deal** plan that was a solution offered to bail out the national economy, which was in the midst of some of the worst years of the Great Depression. The Great Depression (1929-1939) was a financially destructive period of time when both the stock and housing markets were severely impacted. For example, an estimated 20% to 25% of America's outstanding mortgage debt was in default by 1933. That year was perhaps the worst year for bank runs when customers literally ran to their banks to demand to withdraw their entire balance in cash prior to the bank potentially going out of business.

Which government program or legislative act created Fannie Mae?

Americans had lost faith in the banking system and overall financial markets and FDR's New Deal was offered as the main plan to fix the financial markets. It was launched in 1933 shortly after Roosevelt took office and lasted until America officially entered the Second World War in 1942. Three of the main goals of the New Deal plan were:

Economic Recovery: The federal government supplied a great deal of new cash infusion to the banks in an attempt to better stabilize stock and housing prices. The plan was also developed to boost business, industry, and agriculture (farms and ranches), and to provided much-needed capital for state and city governments that were on the verge of financial insolvency themselves.

Job Creation: Upwards of 25% of American adults were unemployed by 1933. A number of new federal agencies were created out of the New Deal to provide millions of new jobs for workers that paid wages that were high enough to assist destitute families struggling to raise enough money just to buy basic items such as bread, soup, and drinkable water. The origin of the phrases "bread line" and "soup kitchen" were literal references to people standing in long lines waiting for food to feed their families. The New Deal also gave more power to workers that included the right to organize in unions.

Public Works Investment: Many of the new jobs created for workers across the nation came about through various public works investment programs. Hundreds of thousands of highways, bridges, schools, libraries, city halls, post offices, parks, homes, and hospitals were built through these New Deal programs. Workers took a great deal of pride in helping rebuild America after years of battling through wars and an economic depression that lasted for years. These programs improved faith and allegiance in the American way of life for millions of U.S. residents and laid the foundation for future federal-assistance programs that still exist in the 21st century.

The best known public-works investment or relief program established out of the New Deal was the **Civilian Conservation Corps (CCC)** program that specifically offered jobs to millions of Americans that were related to various environmental projects across the nation. The CCC was established by an executive order signed by FDR on April 5, 1933. The CCC workers planted more than three billion trees and built shelters and hiking trails in more than 800 parks during its nine years of operation. Today's state and national park system would not exist as we know it without the CCC program.

FDR ran a similar type of environmental conservation program and universal service for young workers in the state of New York back when he was governor. The western states, including California, probably benefited the most from the efforts of the CCC program partly because much of the conservation work took place in the West. The Army transported a few hundred thousand workers out to the western states for these new jobs. By July 1, 1933, over 1,400 working camps had been established for the CCC program. At the time, it was the largest peacetime mobilization in U.S. history.

For people who dreamed of purchasing a new home in America, they first needed some income and a stable, steady job that they could rely on before heading to their local bank for a loan. These CCC programs were instrumental in the creation of jobs that paid young workers -- who were typically between 18 and 25 years of age -- about $30 per month as well as free room and board at one or more work camps for a minimum of six months. The CCC required that each worker send home $22 to $25 of their monthly earnings to help support their families. In many ways, the forced savings requirements inspired many of those families to begin stockpiling enough cash to buy a new home.

The CCC enrolled about three million men across the nation at its peak by August 1935 that included World War I Army veterans, 88,000 Native Americans living on reservations, and experienced foresters and craftsmen. This represented about 5% of the entire national workforce at the time. There were about 2,900 worker camps (free housing and meals) across the nation, with many based in the western states. Once the workers saw firsthand the beauty found in the west as well as the much warmer climate, the migration of millions of families from the eastern states to the western states soon followed. No state would benefit more than California as the years and decades rolled onward.

Once the job market began to stabilize and improve partly thanks to programs associated with FDR's New Deal, the next main focus was to boost the financial system and inspire more Americans to invest and plan for their futures. Fannie Mae was formally established in 1938 by way of updated amendments made to the **National Housing Act** program that was a part of the New Deal plan.

The **Federal Housing Administration (FHA)** program was first developed under the National Housing Act as a way to offer more credit options to lenders and borrowers for home repairs, construction, purchase, and refinancing loans, especially for low and moderate-income families. Fannie Mae, with an initial funding of $1 billion, became the best choice for banks to replenish their capital supply after funding millions of FHA loans across the country for new homebuyers.

Initially, primary lenders like commercial banks and their customers benefited the most from the passage of the National Housing Act and the new FHA program. The Fannie Mae program that passed four years later in 1938 was originally named the National Mortgage Association of Washington. The main intent of this very first secondary-market investment organization was to provide local banks with federal money so that more borrowers could find affordable properties with relatively small down payments.

The main goal of the Fannie Mae program (America's largest secondary-market investor) was to increase the percentage of homeownership nationally. In order to make sure that banks would not run out of cash after approving too many home loans backed by FHA insurance pools, Fannie Mae created a liquid secondary-mortgage market as it specialized in acquiring FHA loans from its affiliated member banks. Shortly after funding the loans, the primary banks would quickly sell off their loans to Fannie Mae. In later years, Fannie Mae then sold off portions of pools or packages of millions or billions of dollars' worth of these mortgages to private and public investment groups so that they would not run out of money themselves.

As discussed earlier in this course, Fannie Mae was later acquired by the **Housing and Home Finance Agency** from the Federal Loan Agency in 1950. A 1954 amendment that was named the **Federal National Mortgage Association Charter Act** converted Fannie Mae into more of a "mixed-ownership corporation" that included both public and private ownership interests. The federal government held the higher-ranking and more valuable controlling stock interests that were deemed "preferred stock" while private investors had the right to invest in the "common stock" that was junior in equity or lien position somewhat like a second mortgage on a home. If Fannie Mae's new corporate structure ever ran out of cash and had to close for business, it would have been the senior preferred-stock shares held by the government that would be paid off first and the common stock investors might end up with zero dollars.

Fannie Mae grew so large in size between 1938 and 1968 that it troubled then President Lyndon Johnson. At the time, President Johnson needed more funds to battle the Vietnam War as he pleaded with Congress to authorize more funds to be released for this military campaign that would last for 19 ½ years. The national budget deficit grew in size so much due to both Fannie Mae and the military conflicts that Johnson decided to take Fannie Mae's massive multi-billion dollar portfolio off of the government's balance sheet. As a result, Fannie Mae was converted in 1968 into a publicly traded company that was owned by investors but still partially guaranteed and backed by the federal government. By 1981, Fannie Mae issued its first mortgage-backed security that Wall Street would later try to duplicate and expand.

The **Housing and Community Development Act of 1992** was signed by President George H.W. Bush as a way to improve access to mortgage capital for more low to moderate-income borrowers. The charters for Fannie Mae and Freddie Mac (discussed earlier and reviewed below) were amended to reflect Congress' view at the time that these two prominent secondary-mortgage market investors "have an affirmative obligation to facilitate the financing of affordable housing for low and moderate-income families in a manner consistent with their overall public purposes, while maintaining a strong financial condition and a reasonable economic return."

The passage of the Housing and Community Act made it a requirement for Fannie Mae and Freddie Mac to meet "affordable housing goals" that were set annually by the Department of Housing and Urban Development (HUD) while being approved by Congress. Initially, Congress wanted the low to moderate-income loan targets to be about 30% of each secondary-market investors' overall investment portfolio in the total number of dwelling units that were financed with mortgages. By 2007, the total number of low to moderate-income mortgage loans held and guaranteed by Fannie Mae and Freddie Mac grew to 55%.

The **National Affordable Housing Act** was enacted in 1990 to protect borrowers from abuse by loan servicers in the secondary market. This is true for both government and private investors who collect monthly mortgage payments. An investor who sells the loan-servicing rights to another company must notify the borrower 15 days before the actual transfer date. The loan servicer does not need the borrower's permission to sell the loan to a new lender or investor. The same service company must notify the homeowner's insurance company that is tied to the loan about the transfer to another loan service company.

Ginnie Mae

The **Government National Mortgage Association (GNMA)** was established in 1968 to promote homeownership by way of government-backed or insured loans. Ginnie Mae was set up and still continues today as a wholly-owned government corporation within the Department of Housing and Urban Development (HUD). Ginnie Mae primarily buys FHA, VA, and the Department of Agriculture's Rural Development loans. It also provides access to capital for urban renewal and affordable-housing projects. Ginnie Mae was the first secondary-market investor to create and guarantee MBS (mortgage-backed securities) products even before Fannie Mae, Freddie Mac, and Wall Street had jumped onto the MBS bandwagon.

Freddie Mac

In 1970, **Freddie Mac (FHLMC - Federal Home Loan Mortgage Corporation)** was created partly as an attempt to end the full monopolization and control of the secondary markets that Fannie Mae had enjoyed over the previous 32 years, and to increase access to new capital for banks and their borrowers. Freddie Mac, one of several government-sponsored enterprises (GSE), was formed as a federally-chartered private corporation that was created by Congress. It would later go completely public in 1989 with stock offerings that would expand its business operations and increase the salaries paid to its top executives.

Freddie Mac was the very first agency or investment group to introduce the mortgage-related security instrument in 1971. It would purchase funded mortgages from primary banks or other lenders prior to repackaging them as mortgage-backed securities (MBS - mortgage loans or securities that are collateralized by cash flows from pools of mortgage loans). Freddie Mac would later sell portions or the entire pooled funds to investors with some type of guarantee to investors that the principal and interest payments would be made on time, regardless of whether or not the original borrowers paid their monthly mortgage payments on time. Since Freddie Mac was "backed by the full faith and credit" of the federal government even if it was primarily privately owned, investors were willing to pay top-dollar prices for these pooled mortgage securities offered by Freddie Mac and Fannie Mae.

The **Office of Federal Housing Enterprise Oversight (OFHEO)** was an agency that was a part of the **Department of Housing and Urban Development (HUD)** that was established under the **Federal Housing Enterprises Financial Safety and Soundness Act of 1992**. This agency was given the power to regulate the operations of both Freddie Mac and Fannie Mae partly due to concerns about how these two secondary-market investors possibly had too much control of the nation's mortgage and housing markets. For example, Fannie Mae and Freddie Mac held or guaranteed $5 trillion of the national-mortgage market by 2008.

Accounting scandals followed in the years after the formation of OFHEO for both Fannie Mae and Freddie Mac. Both groups were sued by private investors and the federal government for claims related to underreporting both gains and losses by as much as tens of billions of dollars each year.

Many of these class-action lawsuits filed alleged that top executives were not reporting the true income and expense numbers so that they could maximize their compensation packages that were tied to stock-share prices. Both Fannie Mae and Freddie Mac agreed to settle the civil complaints filed against them and pay massive fines in amounts in the tens to hundreds of millions of dollars. Many top executives were forced to resign as a result of the these multiple lawsuits and fines.

Following these highly publicized accounting scandals in 2004, OFHEO required that Fannie Mae and Freddie Mac raise their level of core capital by 30% over their previous levels. This was somewhat akin to raising their reserve ratio requirements (or saved cash on hand) just like the Federal Reserve decided to do with its member banks. By forcing the two largest secondary-market investors to set aside a much more significant amount of cash reserves, both groups did not have enough capital to purchase new lenders from primary banks.

Wall Street vs. Fannie and Freddie

More investors on Wall Street began to purchase mortgage-backed securities in the late 1980s and '90s. The annual yields and returns on a high percentage of these mortgage pools were more attractive and much better than many stocks and bonds being offered at the time. This was partly due to the fact that mortgage rates were much higher in the 1990s than now, and the collateral protection was much better for loans secured by individual homes rather than stocks backed by companies that could eventually go bankrupt.

Ironically, Salomon Brothers, one of the wealthiest firms on Wall Street, was alleged to be the first investment firm to offer "private label" mortgage-backed security investments that did not involve any Fannie Mae or Freddie Mac-type mortgages in the '70s. There was very little financial interest in these perceived "risky" investment offerings partly because there was no government backing of these mortgage pools.

Shortly after the initial private-label offering, the Salomon Brothers fund failed and shut down.

A few years later in the late 1970s, Lewis Ranieri of Salomon Brothers and Larry Fink of First Boston invested in the concept of "securitization" or mortgage debt. This is where mortgages are pooled or packaged together at first, and the pool is then sliced into tranches (or sections or layers of risk as determined by bond-rating agencies and other groups) in categories rated as Class A (lowest risk and rates), Class B, and Class C securities, and then are sold off to individual and/or institutional investors.

In 1981, Salomon Brothers would be the first Wall Street investment bank to convert their operations from a privately-held firm to a public corporation. The financial risk was shifted from the main partners in the investment bank to the new stock and bond shareholders. It also allowed Salomon Brothers to raise more capital to expand its business operations. One of the best ways to attract more investment capital is to offer the highest annual rates of return.

The firm began to offer more creative investment offerings that were tied to underlying mortgage pools to its shareholders and investor clients.

Investors on Wall Street became more willing to take financial risks with their funds, especially if the investments were tied to mortgage portfolios. The first **collateralized mortgage obligation (CMO)** was offered by First Boston that is made up of Freddie Mac mortgages that are sold off in smaller pieces. In 1986, the **Real Estate Mortgage Investment Conduit (REMIC)** law passed. This law prevents the double-taxation of mortgage securities for investors and investment bankers. It made mortgage investments even more appealing to investors and the "secondary market" for mortgages skyrocketed for Fannie Mae, Freddie Mac, and Wall Street.

Two of the most prominent early "subprime" mortgage lenders that opened its doors for business were not based in New York City on Wall Street. No, they were located near the beach in Southern California in the offices of **Guardian Savings and Loan** in Huntington Beach and in the neighboring city of Long Beach in the headquarters of **Long Beach Mortgage**. The city of Irvine, California later became home to some of the largest subprime lenders in the nation.

It has been said that Russell Jedinak, the founder of Guardian Savings, issued the first subprime-backed mortgage security. The early versions of these subprime mortgage loans were usually offered at 80% loan-to-value or below as compared with the much higher leveraged 96% LTV loans offered by FHA. The lower LTV terms and much higher rates that exceeded 10% for many of these loans appeared to be much better investment opportunities, regardless of whether or not borrowers qualified with no income and no asset verification on their original loan applications.

More and more subprime lenders entered the lending market in the late 1980s and '90s after Guardian Savings and Long Beach Mortgage started to pick up tremendous market share of the mortgage business. Some of the most aggressive and successful early subprime lenders that followed Guardian and Long Beach (later sold off to Washington Mutual) included:

- The Money Store
- New Century Mortgage (Irvine, CA)
- Southern Pacific Funding
- Option One
- FirstPlus Financial
- Plaza Savings & Loan (Santa Ana, CA)
- Encore Mortgage
- First Alliance Mortgage
- ResMae Mortgage
- Ameriquest Mortgage Corp.

Ironically, Angelo Mozilo, the former head of Countrywide, called subprime lenders "crooks" who charged too much. After seeing firsthand how much money these early subprime mortgage lenders were making in profit returns, Countrywide later entered the market before becoming America's top "EZ Doc" and subprime credit lender up until they ran out of cash and were bailed out by Bank of America, as discussed earlier in this course.

Wall Street started getting more creative and reckless with its investment offerings by issuing products like **credit default swaps (CDS)** (also referred to as a "derivative" in that the financial asset derives value from underlying assets that it is tied to in the contract) that were tied to billions of dollars of these subprime mortgages. It was the investment firm, JP Morgan, that was given formal credit for the invention of the credit-default swap concept.

A credit default swap is like a hybrid of a financial and insurance contract in which the seller of the CDS will compensate the buyer (also known as the creditor of the underlying loan) in the event of a loan default by the original borrower/debtor or some other credit event such as a bond rating downgrade from Moody's, Standard & Poor's, and Fitch due to too many defaults. Unfortunately, these same credit-rating agencies had given their highest AAA rating on many subprime mortgage pools that were rated as "safe" as a U.S. Treasury offering.

The seller of the CDS insures the buyer against the potential risk of a loan default partly out of proceeds from the CDS "fee" or "spread" payments that the buyer pays to the seller. In some ways, it was a complex version of an FHA-insured mortgage loan that was valued at more like $100 million instead of just $100,000, or a glorified "bet" that the original borrowers continue to make their monthly payments. These CDS investments were very profitable for so many years that they grew in size to an estimated $1,500 to $3,000 trillion around the world.

Wall Street is so efficient at raising capital directly from the public with its stock offerings that were associated with subprime and Alt-A credit-mortgage loans that Fannie Mae and Freddie Mac started to lose tremendous market share for secondary market loans. Wall Street had decided to operate more like banks and government agencies to pick up new clients, so it became time for Fannie Mae, Freddie Mac, and various primary lending banks to start operating like Wall Street.

In order to accomplish this task to become more aggressive with their investment options for higher rates of return, the **Glass-Steagall Act** needed to be repealed before Fannie, Freddie, and banks could compete head on with the powerful and wealthy Wall Street firms. The Glass-Steagall Act (also known as The Banking Act of 1933) was enacted to effectively separate commercial banking from more speculative or risky investment banking and insurance investments, while also creating the **Federal Deposit Insurance Corporation** (FDIC) after being signed into law by FDR in June 1933. The act was named after its two primary Congressional sponsors named Senator Carter Glass of Virginia and Representative Henry B. Steagall of Alabama.

The **Gramm-Leach-Bliley Act (GLBA)**, which was also known as the **Financial Services Modernization Act of 1999**, was enacted on November 12, 1999 to repeal portions of the Glass-Steagall Act which included the removal of barriers that had prohibited banks from acting as securities companies and insurance companies as well. With the passing of the GLBA, banks were allowed to offer similar risky financial products just like their competitors on Wall Street. These investments included credit default swaps, mortgage-backed securities backed by prime and subprime credit borrowers, and insurance products. Banks then took their depositors' funds that were insured by FDIC (ironically, created from Glass-Steagall) and invest them in more speculative derivatives investments that were tied to corporate bonds, mortgages, and even incredibly-risky credit card debt.

Citibank, the commercial bank holding company, had attempted to merge with the global insurance conglomerate, Travelers Group, in 1998 to form the new Citicorp entity just one year before the Glass-Steagall Act passed. Yet the Federal Reserve gave Citigroup a temporary waiver in September 1998 to complete the merger even though it would violate both the Glass-Steagall Act and the Bank Holding Company Act of 1956. One year later, the Glass-Steagall Act was passed which made this merger more permanent while other financial groups would try to merge and dominate the financial markets on as many sides of the business as possible.

Banks were given the green light to gamble with their depositors' funds after Glass-Steagall was repealed. Some of the investments that provided banks with the biggest returns included mortgage-backed securities. To compete with the banks and investment banks after Glass-Steagall was partially repealed, Fannie Mae and Freddie Mac began to invest in subprime and Alt-A credit mortgage pools and derivatives. Because subprime loans were not as highly regulated or supervised as conventional loans, banks began offering the easiest mortgage qualification options in the industry with loans that did not verify current employment status, income, or even assets in some cases.

After the telecommunications and dot-com busts that destroyed billions or trillions of value worldwide (especially for NASDAQ stocks), interest rates were lowered beginning in 2000. One year later, following the 9/11 attack in 2001, the Federal Reserve continued to lower interest rates much further until 2004 when conventional 30-year mortgage rates were near 30 year lows. The Fed kept its key short-term rates near 1% which also directly impacted the adjustable or short-term fixed subprime and Alt-A credit loans in a positive way.

Unlike older hard money (or subprime credit) loans offered in the 1980s that reached 20% or more in annual rates in addition to loan points at 20% of the funded loan amount (e.g., a $100,000 loan might cost $20,000 in loan fees for a net loan amount of just $80,000 to the borrower who still has to pay 20% annual interest (or $20,000 per year in interest payments) on a $100,000 loan amount), the newer subprime mortgage loans backed by banks, investment banks, Fannie Mae, and Freddie Mac were being offered for 7% or 8% at a cost of 1% or 2%. Lenders began to get even more creative by offering mortgage loans with longer 40-year terms and low adjustable starting payment rates for **negative amortization** loans that were as low as 1% for much lower monthly payment options or short-term 2 (2/28), 3 (3/27), and 5-year (5/25) fixed loan products that later would convert to adjustable loan terms. (Fixed for two years at a low rate, and then adjustable for the rest of the loan term, for example.)

Between 2000 and 2007, nonbank mortgage underwriting exploded or boomed right alongside the private label securitization market. Home prices, especially in California, doubled or tripled in value during these years due to much easier access to mortgage capital. More investors started to quit their primary jobs and focus most of their time on buying and flipping "fixer-uppers" primarily since the access to purchase loans was so relatively easy and the home prices continued to increase at a rapid annual pace.

Fannie Mae and Freddie Mac purchased fewer mortgage loans than the private investment firms during the 2000 to 2007 time frame. The majority of primary lenders who funded these subprime and Alt-A credit loans in the first seven years of the 21st century would sell the bulk of their loans to Wall Street instead of to Fannie Mae and Freddie Mac. The Wall Street firms were not under the jurisdiction of the FDIC or the Office of Thrift Supervision because they held no customer deposits like at commercial banks, so they were much freer to take more aggressive risks with their clients' investments.

The combined market share of the secondary market business for Fannie Mae and Freddie Mac fell from a high of 57% for all new mortgage originations in 2003 down to just 37% as the mortgage and housing bubbles grew much larger. A whopping 84% of the subprime mortgage funded in 2006 was issued by private lending institutions. Private securitizers of mortgage pools grew from 10% of the overall market in 2002 to nearly 40% in 2006. As a percentage of all mortgage-backed securities, the private secondary-market investors' interests grew from 23% in 2003 to 56% in 2006.

The Federal Reserve put the brakes on its years of lowering interest rates in 2004. Shortly thereafter, it raised short-term interest rates 17 separate times between just 2004 and 2006. Since most subprime and Alt-A credit mortgages were issued as adjustable loans, millions of homeowners saw their monthly mortgage payments double in a short period of time. The increase of rates so many times was perhaps the main catalyst for the popping mortgage bubble that become more readily apparent from 2006, to 2008.

The banks, investment banks, and secondary-market investors like Fannie Mae and Freddie Mac who now held trillions of dollars' worth of mortgage securities were not too keen on sharing their financial loss statements with their investors. Since most of those secondary-market investors and primary lending banks were now publicly traded on Wall Street and on other financial marketplaces worldwide, they did not want to release their increasing mortgage-default numbers to the general public. If they did, their stock prices might fall faster than the home prices would soon fall.

As more investors and governing agencies caught wind of the potential amount of non-performing mortgage pools held by investment banks, commercial banks, and by Fannie Mae and Freddie Mac, these groups were audited more and more to find out the true financial scope of the losses. The multi-million and billion dollar lawsuits were the next step in the unwinding of these mortgage assets.

Citigroup, ironically, was forced to pay $75 million to settle fraud claims made by the SEC (Securities and Exchange Commission) after the financial markets began worsening in 2008. The SEC alleged that

Citigroup failed to disclose more than $50 billion dollars' worth of potential losses from subprime mortgages held in their portfolio.

Fannie Mae was hit with multiple lawsuits from investors and agencies as well for underreporting its mortgage losses. One or more lawsuits made the claim that Fannie Mae had told investors in 2007 just before the subprime and housing market bubbles burst that it held only about $4.8 billion worth of subprime loans on its books (or just 0.2% of its overall financial portfolio). Yet the SEC claimed that Fannie held closer to $43 billion worth of subprime mortgage products on its books, which represented about 11% of all of their financial holdings. Other lawsuits made the claim that Freddie Mac held similar amounts of subprime mortgages.

Bailing Out Primary and Secondary-Market Investors

The rumors of the near financial insolvency of Fannie Mae and Freddie Mac in 2008 were a bit overwhelming for many investors and governmental agencies. At that time, Fannie Mae and Freddie Mac held close to $5 trillion dollars' worth of mortgage loans in their portfolios. The total amount of all outstanding residential and commercial mortgage loans **combined** back then was estimated at close to $10 trillion. If these publicly reported numbers were fairly accurate, then Fannie Mae and Freddie Mac held 50% of all open mortgages in their portfolios.

In 2008, Fannie Mae and Freddie Mac reported combined losses totaling $47 billion in their single-family mortgage investments. Almost half of these losses came from Alt-A credit loans that were considered much safer than subprime credit mortgages due to higher FICO-score requirements and other underwriting factors. Fannie Mae and Freddie Mac later reported losses much higher between January 2008 and March 2012, totaling about $265 billion. An estimated 60% of these losses were a result of riskier Alt-A loan products purchased in 2006 and 2007 near the peak of the housing bubble just before it burst.

Although the housing and mortgage-bubble crisis had officially begun in the summer of 2007, it became more apparent to a higher percentage of Americans by late summer in 2008 after the media began reporting on the severity of the financial losses and several once well-known financial institutions closed their doors. Wall Street investment firms, and other private and publicly-traded pension, hedge fund, and insurance funds tried unloading their subprime mortgage pools at steeply discounted prices. These firms also refused to purchase any newly-issued subprime mortgage loans from primary funding banks. As a result, these lenders closed for business after losing their primary access to capital.

Pension funds and investment firms from around the world held large shares of Fannie Mae and Freddie Mac stock in their portfolios. If Fannie Mae and Freddie Mac ran out of cash and imploded, it would potentially cause a financial shock around the world. The bank losses in America and other countries could have been equal to or worse than the Great

Depression if the federal government did not step up and bail out both Fannie Mae and Freddie Mac. Without Fannie and Freddie available to purchase future mortgage loans after most of the private secondary-market investors jumped the proverbial "sinking ship" of subprime and Alt-A mortgages, home values would have plummeted even further than they did.

As the subprime mortgage dominoes continued to fall and millions of homes were lost to foreclosure, the government reacted by passing the **Housing and Economic Recovery Act of 2008 (HERA)** that was signed by President George W. Bush on July 30, 2008. This act authorized the Federal Housing Administration (FHA) to guarantee $300 billion in new 30-year-fixed mortgages for borrowers in much more costly subprime mortgage loans at the time.

Lenders were first required to reduce their mortgage principal amount to 90% of the current appraised value for HERA to step up and cash out the existing subprime mortgages. Even if the original purchase loan was $150,000 several years earlier for a $165,000 purchase price and the new market value was $100,000, the new HERA fixed loan would be based upon 90% of the latest $100,000 property value (or a new $90,000 first loan). In this example, the original lender or mortgage-loan servicing company might lose $60,000 in principal amount. Yet it was a smaller loss for them than if the property went to foreclosure and there were no buyers willing to purchase the "upside down" property.

This HERA act also established the **Federal Housing Finance Agency (FHFA)** from the **Federal Housing Finance Board (FHFB)** and the **Office of Federal Housing Enterprise Oversight (OFHEO)**. The newly appointed FHFA director, James B. Lockhart III, announced that he was placing both Fannie Mae and Freddie Mac under the conversatorship of the FHFA. It was akin to handing over the ownership and control of these two secondary-market investors back to the federal government. FHFA was also granted the power to act as regulator for the 11 Federal Home Loan Banks across the nation and the Office of Finance. Under the guidance of FHFA, Fannie Mae and Freddie Mac received $187 billion in taxpayer support by way of financial instruments executed with the U.S. Department of Treasury.

The Federal Housing Finance Agency released its *FHFA's 2014 Strategic Plan* to the general public as a way to let others know about its primary goals. The three main FHFA goals were:

> 1) *MAINTAIN, in a safe and sound manner, foreclosure prevention activities and credit availability for new and refinanced mortgages to foster liquid, efficient, competitive and resilient national housing finance markets;*
>
> 2) *REDUCE taxpayer risk through increasing the role of private capital in the mortgage market.*
>
> 3) *BUILD a new single-family securitization infrastructure for use by the Enterprises and adaptable for use by other participants in the secondary market in the future."*
>
> *The 2014 Strategic Plan for the Conservatorships of Fannie Mae and Freddie Mac* link:
> https://www.fhfa.gov/AboutUs/Reports/ReportDocuments/2014StrategicPlan 05132014Final.pdf

Even though subprime mortgage loans are usually blamed as the primary reason why the financial markets almost collapsed in 2008, as discussed earlier in this course, they actually represented less than 1% of all derivatives sold worldwide. Some of the most complex derivatives that amounted to somewhere within the $1,500 to $3,000 plus trillion dollar range were linked to credit cards, automobile loans, A-credit home mortgages, commercial mortgages, business loans, and student loans. Yet most people today still think of the subprime mortgage implosion as the main cause of the official start of the Credit Crisis back in the summer of 2007.

Whether true or not, mortgage brokers and real estate agents were faced with the biggest changes to their professions with new licensing and disclosure requirements that will be detailed in other sections of this course.

Other subsidiary acts that were included in HERA, or in modified amendments issued in future years, that were designed with the intent to help homeowners, lenders, and secondary-market investors included these:

Housing Assistance Tax Act of 2008: This section provided a first-time home buyer refundable tax credit for home purchases made on or after April 9, 2008, and before July 1, 2009, that were equal to 10% of the purchase price for a primary residence up to $7,500. This section of the Act provided emergency assistance for the renovation or redevelopment of abandoned or foreclosed homes.

"Housing Assistance Tax Act of 2008 - Title I: Housing Tax Incentives - Subtitle A: Multi-Family Housing - Part 1: Low-Income Housing Tax Credit - Amends Internal Revenue Code provisions relating to the low-income housing tax credit and tax-exempt bond rules for financing low-income housing projects.

(Sec. 101) Increases in 2008 and 2009 the per capita amount of the low-income housing tax credit allocable by each state.

(Sec. 102) Modifies rules for the low-income housing tax credit to: (1) eliminate the distinction between new and existing buildings for purposes of such credit; (2) establish a minimum credit rate for non-federally subsidized buildings; (3) set forth criteria for designating a building as federally subsidized and for considering federal assistance in calculating such credit; and (4) revise basic rules for certain state buildings and community service facilities.

(Sec. 104) Repeals: (1) the prohibition against providing low-income housing tax credits to properties receiving moderate rehabilitation assistance under the Housing Act of 1937; and (2) bond posting

requirements relating to the disposition of buildings for which a low-income housing tax credit was claimed.

Requires states to consider the energy efficiency of a low-income housing project and its historical nature in allocating credit amounts among such projects.

Extends eligibility for the low-income housing tax credit to students who receive foster care assistance under title IV (Grants to States for Aid and Services to Needy Families with Children and for Child-Welfare Services) of the Social Security Act.

Part 2: Modifications to Tax-Exempt Housing Bond Rules - (Sec. 111) Modifies rules pertaining to tax-exempt housing bonds to: (1) permit treatment of certain residential rental project bonds as refunding bonds regardless of any change in the obligors of such bonds; and (2) allow continued eligibility for low-income housing tax benefits with respect to new tenants, students, and single-room occupancies.

Part 3: Reforms Related to the Low-Income Housing Credit and Tax-Exempt Housing Bonds - (Sec. 121) Requires that median gross income levels established for calendar years after 2008 for determining eligibility for low-income housing tax benefits remain at the same level as preceding calendar years.

(Sec. 122) Waives annual income recertification requirements for residents of low-income rental projects whose incomes do not exceed applicable limits.

Subtitle B: Single Family Housing - (Sec. 131) Allows first-time homebuyers a tax credit for 10% of the purchase price of a principal residence. Limits the dollar amount of such credit to $7,500."

H.R. 5720 - Housing Assistance Tax Act of 2009 link:
https://www.congress.gov/bill/110th-congress/house-bill/5720

FHA Modernization Act of 2008: The Federal Housing Administration had been insuring mortgage loans for primarily buyers of owner-occupied property with relatively small down payments dating back to its formation in 1934. Between 1934 and the end of 2007, the FHA stated that it had insured close to 34.6 million home loans in amounts near $2 trillion. This new "Modernization Act" for FHA allowed the FHA to increase its loan limit from 95% to 110% of the area median home price up to as high as 150% of the typical GSE (government-sponsored enterprise) as of January 1, 2009. The new maximum FHA loan limits were increased from the $400,000 plus range to $625,000 in some of the pricier home regions in some parts of California.

After 2009, FHA became the primary residential loan option for the vast majority of all funded mortgages nationwide partly due to the combination of the higher LTV and loan amount options and the relatively small 3.5% down payment requirements. Often, most of the down payments and closing costs can be gifted or credited from family or sellers. As a result, the true down-payment requirements might be closer to 0% to 1% for buyers.

Hope for Homeowners Act of 2008: This section was designed to help homeowners who were at risk of losing their properties to foreclosure. Many homeowners were months or even years behind on their mortgage payments and on the verge of being homeless after their adjustable-rate loan monthly payments had doubled in size after so many rate hikes between 2004 and 2006. To qualify for this HOPE program, the borrower must meet the following requirements:

- The mortgage was funded on or before January 1, 2008.

- The homeowner did not intentionally default on the mortgage.

- The homeowner did not hold multiple home loans.

- All information provided in the original loan application was true, including income, assets, and employment details.

- The homeowner had not been convicted of fraud.

The HOPE Act had access to $300 billion in 30-year fixed bailout loans, but few borrowers would agree to roll their higher-priced subprime mortgage loan into a new 30-year fixed rate because it was not a simple refinance loan option. Rather, it was a refinance and **equity share** program with the federal government for assisting homeowners with the bailout of their adjustable loan.

The equity share program had a sliding scale used for a profit split with the federal government in the HOPE program that was based upon the amount of time that the property owner stayed in the home after completing the home refinance.

The sliding scale terms and equity splits were as follows:

- Year 1: The owner had to give the government's FHA 100% of the profits from the sale of the home if sold in the first year that the HOPE loan funded.

- Year 2: The homeowner keeps 10% of the equity while the FHA retains 90% of the profits.

- Year 3: The homeowner keeps 20% of the gains while the FHA gets 80%.

- Year 4: The homeowner keeps 30% and the FHA retains 70% of the profits.

- Year 5: Homeowner keeps 40% while the FHA gets 60%.

- Year 6 and beyond: The homeowner and FHA split the gains equally 50/50.

In some cases, the funded HOPE loans were fixed for a much longer 40-year amortization term so that the monthly mortgage payments were more affordable. The HOPE for Homeowners program only ran until September 20, 2011 prior to being discontinued partly due to the lack of interest from property owners who were interested in sharing ownership of their home with the federal government.

American Recovery and Reinvestment Act of 2009 (ARRA): This act was an economic stimulus package that was enacted and signed into law by President Barack Obama on February 17, 2009. Congress approved this $787 billion dollar ARRA stimulus package to better stabilize the mortgage and housing markets as well as the overall national economy. One of the main goals for ARRA was to save between 900,000 to 2.3 million jobs.

The ARRA had three core spending goals from the bailout funds that included:

- The reduction of taxes by $288 billion.

- The spending of $224 billion in extended unemployment benefits, education, and health care.

- The creation of new jobs through the allocation of $275 billion in federal contracts, loans, and grants.

Congress designed the Act so that $720 billion, or 91.5% of the total original $787 billion, would be spent within the first three fiscal years as suggested with these amounts and years below:

- $185 billion was allocated to be spent in 2009.
- $400 billion was planned to be spent in 2010.
- $135 billion was to be spent in 2011.

In the 2012 fiscal budget, it was noted that Congress allocated additional funding that raised the total amount to $840 billion (or $120 billion higher than the proposed spending plan for the first three years). By December 31, 2013, the Obama administration had spent $816.3 billion. Of that amount, $290.7 billion was applied to tax relief, $264.4 billion was set aside for benefits, and $261.2 billion was provided for contracts, loans, and grants. (Source: Recovery.gov)

Chapter Seven Summary

- The **Federal National Mortgage Association (FNMA)** is most commonly called Fannie Mae, a reference to the FNMA acronym. It is America's largest secondary market investor for residential mortgage loans.

- Fannie Mae is a **government-sponsored enterprise (GSE)** that was originally founded as part of President Franklin D. Roosevelt's **New Deal** plan.

- The **Federal Housing Administration (FHA)** program was formed under the National Housing Act as a way to offer more credit options to lenders and borrowers for home repairs, construction, purchase, and refinance loans for low and moderate-income families.

- Fannie Mae was later acquired by the **Housing and Home Finance Agency**'s Federal Loan Agency in 1950. Subsequent amendments to the Fannie Mae charter allowed them to have both public and private ownership options by way of stock holdings.

- The **Government National Mortgage Association (GNMA)** commonly referred to as Ginnie Mae, was established in 1968 to promote homeownership by way of government-backed or insured loans. Ginnie Mae focused on purchasing FHA, VA, and rural USDA mortgage loans.

- In 1970, **Freddie Mac (FHLMC - Federal Home Loan Mortgage Corporation)** was created as another secondary mortgage investor to compete with Fannie Mae after being created by Congress. This initial government entity later went completely public with stock offerings in 1989.

- The **National Affordable Housing Act** was enacted in 1990 to protect borrowers from abuse by loan servicers in the secondary market.

- Both government and private investors from Wall Street and elsewhere began purchasing government, subprime, and Alt-A mortgage loans from places like Fannie Mae, Freddie Mac, New Century Mortgage, Encore Mortgage, and Option One in amounts ranging from millions to billions. This new flood of investment capital in mortgage loans made it more attractive for lenders to offer "EZ Doc" loans because they knew that secondary-market investors would buy it shortly after the funding.

- The **Gramm-Leach-Bliley Act** (also known as the **Financial Services Modernization Act of 1999**) was enacted on November 12, 1999 to repeal portions of the Glass-Steagall Act, which included the removal of barriers that had prohibited banks from acting as securities companies and insurance companies. From here on out, lenders started to recklessly invest in stocks, junk bonds, and complex derivatives like interest-rate options and credit-default swaps for higher returns.

- In 2008, Fannie Mae and Freddie Mac reported combined losses in the amount of $47 billion in their single-family mortgage investments. Over the next several years, the losses grew to at least $265 billion.

- **Housing and Economic Recovery Act of 2008 (HERA)** was signed by President George W. Bush on July 30, 2008. This act authorized the FHA to guarantee $300 billion of new 30-year fixed mortgages to replace more costly subprime loans.

- HERA established the **Federal Housing Finance Agency (FHFA)** out of the **Federal Housing Finance Board (FHFB)** and the **Office of Federal Housing Enterprise Oversight (OFHEO)**. Both Fannie Mae and Freddie Mac were placed under the conservatorship of the Federal Housing Finance Board so that they would not run out of capital.

- The **American Recovery and Reinvestment Act of 2009 (ARRA)** was an economic stimulus package that was signed into law by President Barack Obama on February 17, 2009. Congress approved this $787 billion dollar ARRA stimulus package to stabilize the mortgage and housing markets.

Chapter 7 Quiz

1. What is an example of a government-sponsored enterprise (GSE)?
   A. Commercial bank
   B. Fannie Mae
   C. Freddie Mac
   D. Both B and C

2. Which government program or legislative act created Fannie Mae?
   A. National Housing Act
   B. Mortgage Purchase Act
   C. New Deal
   D. FDIC

3. Which act or agency created the Federal Housing Administration (FHA)?
   A. National Housing Act
   B. SEC
   C. Federal Reserve
   D. Glass-Steagall Act

4. Which agency was created to reduce Fannie Mae's control of the national secondary market?
   A. FSLIC
   B. Freddie Mac
   C. Dodd-Frank Act
   D. Consumer Financial Protection Bureau

5. Which federal act was passed and enacted in 1990 to protect consumers or borrowers from abuse by loan services in the secondary market?

   A. National Housing Act
   B. Affordable Home Protection Act
   C. National Affordable Housing Act
   D. FIRREA

6. Which secondary market investor primarily purchases FHA, VA, and residential USDA loans?

   A. Fannie Mae
   B. Freddie Mac
   C. Sallie Mae
   D. Ginnie Mae

7. Which secondary market agency went from a government agency to a completely privately-held entity after raising money through the sale of stocks that were offered to private investors in 1989?

   A. Fannie Mae
   B. Sallie Mae
   C. Freddie Mac
   D. Ginnie Mae

8. Which legislative act would partially repeal the Glass-Steagall Act so that it would be legal for commercial banks to invest in complex, risky, and potentially profitable stock, insurance, and derivatives investments?

   A. Dodd-Frank Act
   B. Gramm-Leach-Bliley Act
   C. Financial Services Modernization Act of 1999
   D. Both B and C

9. Which legislative act was passed in 2008 to guarantee $300 billion in new 30-year fixed-mortgage loans to refinance more costly adjustable subprime mortgage loans for borrowers in need of financial relief?

A. Housing and Economic Recovery Act

B. Dodd-Frank Act

C. Wall Street Reform Protection Act

D. FHA Bailout Funding Act

10. Which agency placed both Fannie Mae and Freddie Mac under conservatorship (or supervisory power) after these secondary-market investors began to show significant multi-billion dollar losses?

A. FDIC

B. SEC

C. Federal Housing Finance Agency

D. Office of Thrift and Supervision

11. Which 21st century federal bailout program offered homeowners relief from current or impending foreclosure actions in exchange for the homeowner sharing equity or ownership interests in the property with the federal government?

A. Hope for Homeowners

B. The American Dream Plan

C. Home Owners' Loan Corporation

D. Equity Share Bailouts

12. Under the American Recovery and Reinvestment Act of 2009, what was the original approved dollar amount that was provided to stabilize the mortgage and housing markets?

A. $57 billion

B. $325 billion

C. $787 billion

D. $2.5 trillion

Answer Key:

1. D	6. D	11. A
2. C	7. C	12. C
3. A	8. D	
4. B	9. A	
5. C	10. C	

CHAPTER 8

REAL ESTATE CYCLES & ECONOMIC THEORIES

Overview

Over the past century or so, there have been many positive, flat, and negative housing-and-mortgage-rate cycles. Readers of this chapter will learn about the various reasons why housing markets may boom or bust. The available supply of homes is directly impacted by personal and external factors as well as the latest buyer demands. Economic theories that also help describe and define housing trends will be covered as well.

Demand, Supply, and Value

The value of a specific and unique property is determined primarily by what a willing and able buyer offers to pay and the price that is most acceptable to a seller who is hopefully not under any type of duress to sell the property. True value does exist in the "eye of the beholder" as the old saying goes. To a seller, his or her property may be worth much more than the actual latest sales comparables nearby because of years or decades of positive memories and emotional attachment to the property. A buyer usually wants the best property at the lowest price.

Three of the main elements of value are demand, scarcity, and transferability (or the ease of selling the asset or consumer good).

The **market price** for a home or for any other item for sale is the price at which a market clears (or the product sells) between a willing buyer and a willing seller, where they made their decisions under their own free will without any negative outside influences. The market price is the **equilibrium point** where the available supply is just meeting the demand at the time of sale.

Real Estate: Both Elastic and Inelastic

First and foremost, demand for housing is **elastic** like a rubber band. Housing cycles can snap back and forth from boom to bust (or vice versa). It can change value directions slowly or quickly depending upon a wide variety of factors. The demand for housing or any other type of asset, product, or service is likely to rise as the prices fall. On the other hand, the demand for anything for sale will probably fall as the prices for the same product continue to rise.

Markets for an asset or product can move rather swiftly up or down. A savvy business owner will make production adjustments to keep up with the latest positive or negative demand. An automobile assembly plant that has 100 workers on staff to quickly handle the increased demand for the latest car model can rather easily increase the production of cars to meet consumers' needs. This same is true for a video game manufacturer who can change production schedules to rapidly increase production to meet the latest demand for their product.

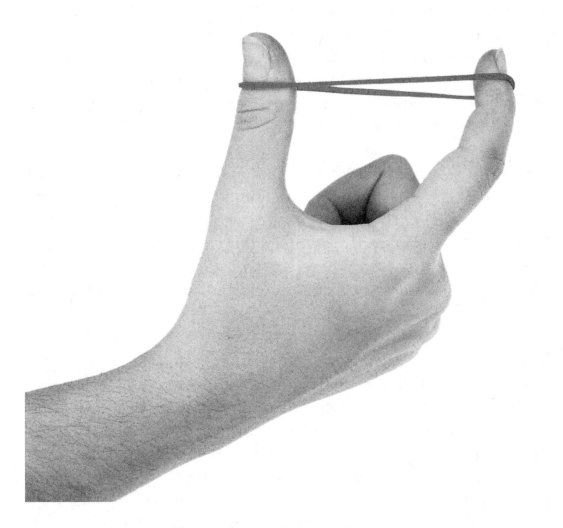

The real estate field is one that is more about people than properties. Without people, there would not be a need for the purchase of residential or commercial properties. The values associated with properties in a certain town or city are directly influenced by the latest population trends. When there are more tenant prospects than available apartment units or single-family homes to lease, then the rent prices will probably start to increase. And when a town's unemployment rate is high because of something like the shutdown of a local chemical plant that had once employed 5,000 people, that will likely have a negative impact in the near-term rent prices as vacancy rates increase and tenant demand decreases.

The local household size trends also play an important role in the movement of purchase and rental prices. When housing is relatively cheap at a specific time in the economic cycle, the number of households will expand as more people seek out their own places to live whether nearby or far away from their family and friends who they once lived with as roommates or housemates. If so, there will be fewer people per household.

During times when housing is costly such as currently in many coastal regions of California, the number of households may shrink in size. Young adults who have recently graduated from college may be forced to move back home with their parents because they can't afford the latest high-rent payments near the area where they work. Young families may put two, three, or four people in each bedroom instead of opting to move to larger places due to the unaffordable rent or home prices.

The supply of housing and land, however, is highly **inelastic** in that it takes a very long time to build a new home or an entire housing tract. The home builder must first acquire the available land from a motivated seller. Land is **finite** in that there is only so much of it to go around in any given region. The land must also be approved by the local planning and zoning department for the correct type of property that the owner wishes to build. If the owner wants to build five residential homes on a one-acre lot that is zoned for agriculture or farming, then he or she will probably be wasting his or her time and money should the builder move forward with the land purchase.

Regardless of the zoning type, it can take months or years to go through the planning and building process. The owner will usually have to pay fees for building permits, environmental inspections, zoning costs, and fees for access to roads and utilities. The owner will need to find an experienced contractor with a team of qualified subcontractors (e.g., plumbers, electricians, roofers, etc.) to assist him. Once the newly-constructed home is built, it is **immovable** and permanently fixed to the ground.

The primary housing characteristic that typically drives the direction of the property's value is **location**. A property seller with a 10,000-square-foot lot for sale on the sands of Newport Beach is much more likely to receive a higher offer price from a buyer than a seller with a similarly-sized land site 100 miles inland in the middle of the desert somewhere. Yet there will be more buyers who can afford the 10,000-square-foot land site in the middle of the desert that is priced at $30,000 than there will be buyers who can afford the beach lot that is probably priced well over $1 million dollars just for the land.

What is the most important factor affecting a home's value?

In addition to location, other factors that can directly impact the value for a property (home or raw land) include:

Lendability: The vast majority of property purchases in California and around the nation involve some type of third-party financing option needed to complete the acquisition. Raw land is generally considered the riskiest type of property on which to lend from a banker's point of view. This is especially true if the land site is located in the middle of nowhere with very little access to utility hookups, streets, schools, neighbors, or businesses nearby.

At best, some lenders may only offer loans at 50% loan-to-value (LTV) for the purchase of these land parcels. Other lenders may refuse to offer any type of construction loan based upon the future completed value of the finished property partly since there really are not any similar homes or structures within a 30-mile radius. A property will probably be much more valuable to a seller and buyer if there is some sort of decent access to third-party funds to get into and out of the property. This is partly why single-family homes that are surrounded by other similar sized and priced homes in the same neighborhood usually have access to the highest number of lenders interested in assisting them with mortgage loans and they sell faster than raw-land sites.

Leverage: Real estate agents need to truly understand that the residential mortgage programs that have been used the most by buyers over the past several years are the government-backed forms of financing. In many ways, the financial markets (both the primary and secondary markets, directly or indirectly) have been "socialized" or taken control of by the federal government and the Federal Reserve since the financial markets began showing significant signs of weakness in 2008.

Some financial analysts have made the claim that FHA, VA, and rural loans from the USDA (United States Department of Agriculture) comprise over 90% of all residential loans funded in certain regions of the state and nation. To borrowers, the most attractive feature of these government-assisted mortgage loans is the low down payment requirements (0% down for VA and 3.5% down for FHA). A relatively small percentage of home buyers these days have sufficient liquid cash funds available to put down 10% or 20% or more down payment, regardless of whether the home being purchased is $100,000, $300,000, or $500,000.

Many real estate agents who work in the pricey housing areas of California do not think that their clients will qualify for an FHA mortgage loan that is large enough to purchase a median-priced home in their area. But, over the past several decades, FHA loan limits have steadily risen from a few hundred thousand dollars to as much as $679,650 in the expensive areas of the state and the country.

In November 2017, an economist from the California Association of Realtors reported that the median price for existing single family homes in the state reached $546,820. Home prices in the state have increased on a consistent and fairly steady pace since early 2012 in California. Yet the median home price in late 2017 was still below the last peak price in May 2007 when the median existing home price hit $594,530. A high percentage of the homes purchased in the state since 2012 were acquired with FHA mortgage loans as the mortgage underwriting guidelines eased up to accommodate more buyer applicants who could not qualify for conventional loans. Conventional loans required and still require a higher down payment and FICO credit score requirement as well as much tougher debt-to-income ratio options for non-FHA loans. In the history of the state, the median price for existing homes has yet to exceed the latest high-cost-region FHA loan limits of $679,650, so these government-insured loans will continue to be used in the majority of housing transactions statewide.

Liquidity: How quickly can the property owner convert his or her ownership interests to cash? Some owners may have $200,000 or

$700,000 equity (current market value - mortgage debt) that they cannot spend at the local grocery store to buy food. Products or assets that are priced at $100 will probably have many more willing buyers able to hand over a $100 bill to the seller in the event that the seller needs to liquidate the product and turn it into spendable money. Yet it usually takes much longer to either refinance or sell a home in order to generate some cash for the owner. There are more lenders willing to offer a single-family homeowner a conventional, government-backed, or private money loan than there are lenders available for raw land or large commercial properties such as office buildings or industrial parks.

These four components above (location, lendability, leverage, and liquidity) are all key factors with respect to accessing financing for the purchase of property. Financing is the most important element that determines the value and saleability of a property. Money (100% cash offers or 96.5% LTV FHA loans) gets a buyer into a deal and a seller out of the same deal in almost every single transaction that a real estate agent will work on in their career (excluding some family gift transfers or other similar scenarios).

Let's review below some basic core economic theories that drive the housing and financial markets as we start with supply and demand:

Land

Land comprises all naturally-occurring resources that may consist of underground or above ground water access (lakes, rivers, streams, oceans), the dirt, sand, and rocks on the ground, and the air rights up to reasonable heights above the land site. Per various economic theories, land is inherently fixed, immovable, unique, and in finite supply. Even though few regions of the world have as much undeveloped and developed land as California, every single parcel is unique even if the size is identical to the adjacent parcels (e.g., a 7,000-square-foot lot with a 70-foot frontage that is adjacent to the street and a 100-foot depth that reaches the back fence). The main factor that makes each land site unique is the location that is defined by differing legal and/or street addresses.

To city or town planners, land is an intangible asset on which development activities will take place in the near future. Property owners and contractors will add buildings on the land which will contribute to its value and use. For farmers and ranchers, the main productivity of the land is the soil that is hopefully rich with nutrients for the production of new food crops. Economists may view land as a factor of production that is in addition to capital and labor.

Real estate is the term that includes the land, the air above it, the ground below it to the center of the earth in theory, any buildings or structures attached to the land, and any natural resources on it like gold, silver, or copper.

Ricardo's Theory of Rent

The prices paid to own, occupy, or cultivate land are based upon several factors. Since land is the absolute basis for real estate, real estate licensees should learn about how and why certain land parcels are more valuable than other land parcels that look almost identical.

One of the more interesting economic theories that describes how land value prices can widely fluctuate is the *Theory of Rent.* This economic theory was first proposed by the English Classical Economist David Ricardo (1773 --1823) in his book entitled *Principles of Political Economy and Taxation.*

David Ricardo was regarded as an eminent economist back in the 19th century. Before Ricardo, the well-known economist named Adam Smith viewed rent as the result of the bounty of nature. Both Smith and Ricardo believed land was the most valuable commodity of all to farmers and ranchers who needed land to raise crops and livestock. The most efficient and effective use of the land in addition to the quality of the labor employed to cultivate the land would reward the property owner by yielding produce (or food crops) many times more than the labor involved. This excess production was called **net production** or **rent** (or profit) for the property owner.

One of Ricardo's most famous quotes about his rent theory was as follows: *"Rent is that portion of the produce of earth which is paid to the landlord for the use of the original and indestructible powers of the soil."*

Ricardo believed that "rent" was a payment for the use of land only. It differed from contractual rent which included the returns on capital investment or upgrades made by the property owner who added drains, wells, buildings, and other fixed attachments to the land. Ricardo claimed that the deduction of the return on the capital investment made to the property from the contractual rent would leave the property owner with the pure land rent.

The Ricardian Theory of Rent was based upon certain assumptions such as:

1) The land had no alternative use as it could only be used for farming purposes.

2) The fertility of land differs from site to site due to issues such as access to water, weather patterns, and nutrients found in the soil.

3) The Law of Diminishing Returns economic theory that states that output will not increase at the same annual rate at which capital and labor increases.

4) The increase in population near the land site will likely be a positive influence for the production of more crops to feed the new residents.

5) This theory assumes that the supply of the available superior grade of high-quality land that can produce rich crops is somewhat limited in the immediate region.

6) Ricardo's theory is based upon the belief that land possesses some type of original and indestructible powers and will not be reduced in size or quality in the future.

7) Ricardo made the fundamental assumption that there was the existence of **perfect competition** in the market which the core product price is given, and the economic rent is he surplus which grows and compounds over and above the cost of production.

8) The theory assumes that the most fertile land in the best locations would be cultivated first before less desirable land is worked on at a later date.

Real Estate Principles or Theories

There are a number of core economic and real estate principles or theories that are used to describe the movement of property values, demand, and supply of available product at any given time. Each of these theories also can determine whether or not a property is financeable. They can be used by economists, investors, real estate agents, and appraisers. Some of the better-known theories follow:

Economies of Scale: As the production of a product or asset increases in number, the average cost to create the same product decreases. The price reductions are obtained by spreading out the fixed costs over a larger number of units during the production phase while providing much lower prices to consumers. Falling prices, in turn, will likely inspire more buyers to be interested in purchasing the product.

Law of Diminishing Returns: This theory is the opposite of the Economies of Scale theory above. With the Law of Diminishing Returns, the increase in production efforts and expenses will lead to **declining** returns or profits as the per unit cost increases partly due to inefficient production activities.

Economics of Assemblage: This theory applies more to land than any other type of real estate property. The assemblage of multiple adjacent lots into one large lot will probably increase the overall value of the owner's investment much higher than acquiring the smaller lot pieces separately. In many urban areas, there is a shortage of buildable land. For investors and their agents who can find multiple lots to purchase simultaneously, the returns may be much better and the costs to build much lower when attempting to assemble multiple lots into one larger parcel.

Economics of Subdividing: This economic theory is almost the exact opposite of the assemblage theory above. While real estate developers may prefer to build on larger land parcels at one time because of reduced construction costs, there are more individual buyers who can afford to purchase smaller lots with or without homes on them. An owner can subdivide or break their larger 5-acre parcel into 30 separate home sites that are all shaped equally with sizes near 7,000 square feet. One acre consists of 43,560 square feet. Six lots may be subdivided within each acre to create six lots per acre (6 lots x 5 acres = 30 homes) plus leave some extra room for common-area features, like parks and walking trails.

Principle of First Choice: Some buyers are more motivated than others to purchase a land parcel, home, or commercial property site for their business location and are willing to pay much more than any other buyer due to their own personal needs and preferences. A property that offers the **highest and best use** options for one particular seller may generate the highest offer price. A prime example is a golf course business owner who needs a minimum of 200 acres to build his new course in a specific town. If there is only one land site available to purchase with more than 200 acres and with the best zoning allowances, this property will be the first and only choice for the golf course owner if he plans to open his new course in this town.

Principle of Competition: When the profit margins are exceedingly high for the production of a good, service, or asset, it is quite reasonable to assume that more buyers and sellers will try to enter the same marketplace and compete for these near record profits. The increased competition to sell products may cause prices to fall because buyers will have more choices at the time of purchase. For two or more products that are almost equal, the buyer will likely purchase the most affordable one. As such, the increased competition may lead to price wars between the new sellers competing for business. If so, the buyers will benefit more than the sellers due to much lower prices.

Marginal Propensity to Save: "Truth" is just one's perspective in life. If one person believes that the economy is about to crash in the near future, he or she is likely to try to save additional money as some sort of a safety cushion in the event that he or she may lose their job or their stock, bond, or real estate, and their pension portfolio might fall in value. When more and more people across the state and the nation also have negative outlooks on the economic and financial future, they too will spend less money on consumer goods and services while trying to set aside more money as a safety net. Consumer spending represents 70% of our nation's overall economy. The reduction of demand for goods and services is **deflationary** as it may drive prices downward.

Marginal Propensity to Consume: Time periods that are more robust or positive can inspire consumers to spend more and save less. Sometimes, these boom economic periods can seem like they will last for years or decades, so consumers spend and borrow at much faster paces. The increase in demand for goods, services, and assets like real estate could become **inflationary** up until the prices get too high for many consumers. At that point, the economic curve may begin to fall to a point where there are more sellers than buyers for a product or asset which, in turn, can also cause prices to fall.

Principle of Substitution: This is both an economic and appraisal principle used to determine the demand and price for a product or asset like a home for sale. The maximum value of a property is determined by the available supply of similar properties nearby. If two homes are almost identical, the more affordably priced home is more likely to sell first. This principle runs somewhat parallel to the basic laws of supply and demand. There are very few buyers who willingly pay more to purchase the higher priced property if they are almost the same.

The appraiser, lender, investor, and agents may all use some type of income approach (especially for rental properties) to determine the current value of the subject property by trying to estimate the present worth of future benefits of the property. Other times, people will analyze the potential highest and best future use for the property that may make the future value much higher than the present value. An example might include a 20,000-square-foot land site that is zoned for agricultural or farming uses only that is in the process of growth for a nearby town and is about to be rezoned as residential or commercial. If so, the zoning and usage benefits are expected to improve right along with the future price.

Principle of Contribution: This refers to the value added (or not added) to a property after adding a new amenity or feature such as a new swimming pool or a remodeled kitchen. Sometimes, a property owner will add $10,000 in new upgrades to a home that will increase the overall price five times that amount to $50,000. Other times, the $20,000 spent for a new swimming pool placed in the backyard may add no value whatsoever because many buyers do not want a pool on their property either for safety reasons because they have young children or pets, or because of the expenses involved with maintaining a pool.

Principle of Balance: The maximum value of a property or other asset is maintained through an equal balance between supply and demand. Location is one of the key elements that can affect this desire for a balanced market with a steady supply of properties for sale and creditworthy and motivated buyers. The factors of production -- labor, capital, coordination, and land -- must all be in proper balance so that properties maintain maximum value.

Principle of Change: This theory states that real estate prices are always in a state of flux or change as they do not remain relatively constant. Even though the property's location and amenities may not change over the years, the economic market, buyer and seller trends, and the available supply of homes for sale will change every single month. The increased demand for homes in the same neighborhood will likely increase home prices while the decreased demand may lead to stagnate or falling prices. The only thing certain in both life and real estate is change.

Principle of Real Estate Cycles: The simplest way to explain this economic principle is that newer homes will probably have the highest value at a specific time in the real estate cycle than much older homes that are falling into disrepair or faced with **functional obsolescence** (or have outdated features that are no longer desired in modern times, such as homes with just one bathroom).

The are three main phases in a standard real estate cycle for properties that include:

1) **Development State/Integration:** The newly-built property adds value to the once raw land and the surrounding homes nearby.

2) **Maturity/Equilibrium State:** At some point in the future, the benefits of the new construction will begin to wear off and the values will reach a peak price.

3) **Decline/Disintegration:** The subject property and the homes nearby start to deteriorate as they age over several years or decades. The older homes may become less appealing to young buyers who aspire to find properties with the latest advanced kitchen appliances, internet and wireless access features, and flooring styles. If few buyers are interested in the property, a new buyer may decide to purchase the older home, demolish it, develop a new modern-style home, and start the real estate cycle stage all over again.

Economic Obsolescence: Negative external influences such as neighboring properties that are rapidly declining in appearance due to poor maintenance or age, increasing crime rates and unemployment rates, and even noisy neighbors can adversely impact the value of one's property even if the homeowner maintains his property in pristine condition.

Principle of Anticipation: This principle is used quite often by appraisers when attempting to value the current and future market value of a subject property. The value of a certain property depends on the anticipated income or usage that will accrue to the owner in the future. Often, this value is used for income-producing properties such as rental homes or apartment buildings.

Principle of Highest and Best Use: The root definition of highest and best use that is described by the Appraisal Institute of Canada is "the reasonably probable and legal use of the property, that is physically possible, appropriately supported, and financially feasible, and that results in the highest value." When determining the current market value, the appraiser, buyer, lender, and real estate agents will consider if the current zoning and usage is as profitable as the potential access to better zoning and use options that may be available now or in the near term. The potential highest and best use of a subject property will later lead to the highest value estimates for the property.

Principle of Conformity: This is the belief that a new or older existing home will probably increase in value if its size, style, age, and condition are similar to other properties that surround it. This concept is easiest to visualize when thinking about new master-planned single-family home developments in suburban areas in the state, like in the city of Irvine. Irvine has just three, four, or five identical home designs that are built in communities that feature hundreds or thousands of homes and share homeowners associations that make sure the property owners continue to maintain their same home style by not changing exterior paint colors, tiles, or door designs. If one adjacent property owner was allowed to paint his home a bright pink color, it would likely harm the values of the properties on both sides of it because it violates the principle of conformity rules.

Principle of Progression: This economic theory and real estate principle is based upon the belief that the acquisition of the smallest and oldest home on a neighborhood block will generally be positively affected by larger, nicer, and newer homes on the same block or subdivision. The larger properties that are well maintained may increase the value of the older property much more than the older property will hurt the value of the larger property. For "fix and flip" investors and their affiliate agents, this type of example can be one of the best ways to make a rather large profit in a relatively short period of time. The "fixer upper" home can be painted, the landscape can be improved, the flooring and window coverings can be upgraded, and one or two new appliances can be installed for a total cost of just $10,000 or so. But these minimal upgrades can increase the overall sales price by $100,000 (ten times the amount of repair work) due to the fact that the adjacent homes are selling for $300,000 or more higher.

Principle of Regression: This real estate principle is the exact opposite of the principle of progression in that an owner has the largest home on a block that is surrounding by smaller, older, and inferior properties. A prime example can be when a contractor buys a small home, levels it, and builds a custom "McMansion" type home that has no comparables anywhere within a five or ten mile radius. The same beautiful new home may be better suited to be built on the sands of Malibu or Santa Barbara as opposed to 75 miles inland on a street adjacent to a busy highway or toxic industrial plant. The owner will not gain much new value for his new custom home primarily since the smaller and older homes will be the most likely sales comparables used by an appraiser or buyer.

Inflation Cycles and Causes

Inflation can be good or bad, depending upon whether one is a creditor or debtor. Overall, inflation can eventually severely damage the purchasing power of the dollar. If so, a dollar will buy fewer goods and services in the future. A prime example is a $3 to $5 cup of coffee sold today that once sold for 50 cents.

The number one stated fear of the Federal Reserve is inflation. When the board members at the Fed get too concerned about how high prices are getting for goods and services, they may start raising short-term interest rates in order to apply figurative "brakes" on the economy. As such, higher inflation rates tend to cause short and long-term rates for loan products related to credit cards, automobiles, student loans, and home mortgages to rise as well. The higher rates and payments for these loans may cause fewer buyers to demand these products or properties, and prices will begin to stabilize to a new level that economists and Fed members appreciate.

Landlords who own rental properties may really enjoy it when their annual rent payments and overall property values increase on a consistent basis due to increasing inflation. Tenants, however, would usually not like periods of time when inflation moves too high in a relatively short time period and their monthly rent payments increase by 10% or more. The actions of consumers and their demand for goods and services, the supply of available items or properties for sale, and the actions of the Federal Reserve and U.S. Treasury as it relates to increasing or decreasing the available supply of money, are some of the most common reasons for increasing or decreasing current inflation levels.

There are three main types of inflation as it relates to the interactions of consumers and sellers. They are:

1) **Demand Pull Inflation:** Increasing inflation rates as a result of higher consumer demand for goods coupled with low unemployment.

2) **Cost Push Inflation:** The sudden decrease in the available supply of retail goods, services, or assets that would cause prices to rise because there may be more buyers than sellers at this point. On the wholesale side of the retail business, the producers of products who are hit with higher prices due to a shortage of supplies will then pass on the higher wholesale prices to their retail buyers. These store owners will then increase their prices on the store shelves that will be paid by consumers shopping in their stores.

3) **Anticipated Inflation:** Perceptions can become reality if enough people believe that future prices for a certain product may rise. An example may include the expectation that there will be more buyers than sellers at an art or real estate auction, so many individual buyers will pay more money and drive the prices higher just because they expect the prices to rise.

Consumer Price Index (CPI)

The CPI is a measurement of inflation that is published on a monthly or annual basis by economists or federal agencies. The index measures the weighted average of prices of a basket of consumer goods and services that includes food, transportation, and medical care. It is calculated by comparing the current prices with past periods of time to determine whether prices are increasing, decreasing, or remaining relatively flat from year-to-year, while also figuring out the general overall annual inflation rate for the nation.

A "market basket" for the calculation of the Consumer Price Index is really a sample of core prices analyzed by agencies, such as the Bureau of Labor Statistics. The most common items that are reviewed in this figurative "market basket" include:

- Apparel (men's and women's clothing, jewelry)
- Housing (tenants' rent, owners' equivalent rent, furnishing costs)
- Food and Beverages (milk, coffee, juice, meats, wine, snacks)
- Transportation (gasoline, airline fares, new car prices)
- Medical Care (prescription drugs, eyeglasses, hospital services)
- Recreation (toys, sports equipment, ticket prices for events)
- Education (school textbooks, college admission fees)

Let's take a look at the reported annual Consumer Price Index rates over the period of 30 years as determined by the Bureau of Labor Statistics:

Year	CPI Rate
1987	4.43%
1988	4.42%
1989	4.65%
1990	6.11%
1991	3.06%
1992	2.90%
1993	2.75%

1994	2.67%
1995	2.54%
1996	3.32%
1997	1.70%
1998	1.61%
1999	2.68%
2000	3.39%
2001	1.55%
2002	2.38%
2003	1.88%
2004	3.26%
2005	3.42%
2006	2.54%
2007	4.08%
2008	0.09%*
2009	2.72%
2010	1.50%
2011	2.96%
2012	1.74%
2013	1.50%
2014	0.76%
2015	0.73%
2016	2.07%
2017	2.11%

* Please note that the year 2008 had the lowest reported annual CPI rates over the past 30 years when it reached a low of just 0.09%. This was the same year when the financial markets had their worst year since the Great Depression and the federal government and Federal Reserve stepped up to bail out various large banks, insurance companies, automobile firms, and both Fannie Mae and Freddie Mac.

Since inflation is the main concern of the Federal Reserve, they will increase or decrease short-term rates such as the Effective Funds Rate depending upon their comfort level with the latest annual inflation numbers. Let's compare the same time period (1987 -- 2017) for the Fed's Effective Funds Rate with the CPI numbers to better understand how the Fed either increases or decreases access to money by changing consumers' and banks' borrowing rates (source: Board of Governors of the Federal Reserve):

Month and Year	Effective Funds Rate
December 1987	6.77%
December 1988	8.76%
December 1989	8.45%
December 1990	7.31%
December 1991	4.43%
December 1992	2.92%
December 1993	2.96%
December 1994	5.45%
December 1995	5.60%
December 1996	5.29%
December 1997	5.50%
December 1998	4.68%
December 1999	5.30%
December 2000	6.40%
December 2001	1.82%*
December 2002	1.24%
December 2003	0.98%
December 2004	2.16%
December 2005	4.16%
December 2006	5.24%
December 2007	4.24%
December 2008	0.16%**
December 2009	0.12%
December 2010	0.18%
December 2011	0.07%
December 2012	0.16%
December 2013	0.09%

December 2014	0.12%
December 2015	0.24%
December 2016	0.54%
December 2017	1.30%

* The Fed Funds Rate dropped dramatically in just one year between December 2000 and December 2001 due to factors such as the telecommunications and dot com stock and bond market busts and the 9/11 event that rattled the financial markets and Americans in general. The Fed cut rates from a high of 6.40% in December 2000 to 1.82% just 12 months later in an attempt to stimulate the economy.

** The Effective Fed Funds Rate fell from a high of 4.24% in December 2007 to a record all-time low at the time of just 0.16% in December 2008 after the severity of the Credit Crisis became more obvious to bankers, economists, and most people around the nation. Once again, the Fed was trying to boost the economy by making home, business, automobile, and other types of consumer loans much more affordable as well as attempting to rally the stock and bond markets.

During this same 30 year time period, the first four years had both the highest reported Consumer Price Index inflation rates and the highest Effective Funds Rate as listed below:

Year	CPI Rate	Fed Funds Rate
1987	4.43%	6.77%
1988	4.42%	8.76%
1989	4.65%	8.45%
1990	6.11%	7.31%

The correlation between the highest reported inflation rates and the Fed Funds Rate all happening in the four highest years of the past 30 years proves that the Fed will take swift action to slow down increasing inflation rates by raising short-term interest rates that make consumer borrowing much more expensive. The highest rates and payments for consumer loans will then drive down demand and stabilize prices.

The one year that had both the lowest reported CPI index and the lowest Effective Fed Funds Rate was the exact same year of 2008. It is no surprise that the Fed would try to boost the economy by taking a "near zero rate policy" approach as a way to boost asset prices and encourage consumers to spend again. Listed below are the comparisons between the lowest CPI rate and the once all-time record low Effective Funds Rate that were both the lowest rates ever for 2008 and earlier in U.S. history:

Year	CPI Rate	Fed Funds Rate
2008	0.09%	0.16%

Inflation Stage Cycles

Prices for goods, services, and assets can rise and fall like the ocean tides. Historically, home values have appreciated by at least the same pace or higher than the stated CPI inflation rate over the past 50 plus years. Real estate has proven to be an exceptional hedge against inflation in that properties tend to rise right alongside the reported inflation rates. Many times during booming economic periods, property values in California have increased more than two or three times the reported annual inflation rates. In years when the CPI rate is listed at 4%, the median prices for homes in the state have increased 8% or 12%.

The best time period for the ownership of property has proven to be when inflation levels are fairly consistent and interest rates are near historically low levels. Conversely, zero to negative rates of inflation combined with higher interest rates would be one of the worst times to try to sell property. Property owners want prices to increase while buyers standing by with cash and affordable loans want home prices to remain steady or fall so that they are able to find the best deals possible.

Depending upon factors such as unemployment levels (i.e., an underemployed or fully employed economy), wage income trends, the available supply of products or properties, currency fluctuations for the dollar, import and export numbers, and the annual government budget deficit, inflation rates can move wildly from positive to near zero rates and even to negative annual rates as noted below in these inflation stage cycles:

Deflation: The decrease in the general price of goods and services as compared with prior years is called deflation. Economists believe that deflation officially occurs when the annual inflation rates falls below 0% and becomes a negative inflation rate. Deflation is actually a positive for the purchasing power of the dollar in that a consumer can buy more goods and services for their same dollar. **Depreciation** differs from deflation in that it refers to the loss of value of an asset such as real estate for any cause like age and environmental damages.

Disinflation: This is a slowdown in the annual rate of inflation that is tied to the general price level of goods and services in a market basket as part of the nation's gross domestic product (GDP) over a certain time period. If the previous year's levels were relatively high, then this can be a solid sign for the overall economy as long as the inflation rates do not go negative and enter the deflation territory.

Hyperinflation: This inflation stage happens when prices and inflation rates are moving too high in a relatively short period of time. Often, this happens when the Federal Reserve and U.S. Treasury print too many new dollars or add credits to the financial system. If they do, there will be too many new dollars chasing goods and services before pushing prices higher. As a result, the purchasing power of the dollar will fall rather dramatically and that $4 cup of coffee may now cost $7.

Stagflation: This word is a hybrid of two words - *stagnation* and *inflation.* It is an economic period when the annual inflation rate is high, the overall economic growth rate slows, and unemployment continues to be rather high. The early to mid-1970s in the U.S. experienced this fairly overall negative combination of high rates and unemployment combined with a sluggish economy partly due to the "Oil Shock" years when oil prices were too high. Since energy costs are historically at the root of core inflation rates, high oil costs can make transportation, housing, and consumer products increase as well. The Fed might be unwilling to increase short-term interest rates to slow down the annual rate of inflation because they are fearful that higher interest rates might worsen the already high unemployment figures.

Reflation: This inflationary stage is generally considered to be positive for the national economy. It tends to follow sluggish, recessionary, or depressionary financial or housing cycles after the Fed moves to lower interest rates and/or reserve-ratio requirements for banks so they can lend more money; and/or when the federal government decides to cut taxes and increase spending as a way to improve consumer spending trends and lower national unemployment numbers. A reflationary phase is viewed by many economists as the upward movement after previous dips or lows in the business cycle while showing signs that the economy is getting back on track towards long-term positive growth.

Chapter Eight Summary

- **Value** is usually derived from a combination of consumer demand and available supply. Three of the main elements of value are demand, scarcity, and transferability (or the ease of selling the asset or consumer good).

- The market price is the **equilibrium point** where the available supply just meets the demand at the time of sale. It is established by a willing buyer and seller under no duress to sell.

- The supply of housing is relatively **inelastic** (or slow to change) while the demand for properties can be highly **elastic** (or quick to change).

- The primary housing characteristic that drives the direction of the property's value is **location**. The property's access to capital or mortgage sources (lendability, leverage, and liquidity) are important factors in determining current and future price trends.

- **Ricardo's Theory of Rent:** *"Rent is that portion of the produce of earth which is paid to the landlord for the use of the original and indestructible powers of the soil."*

- **Economics of Assemblage:** The assemblage of multiple adjacent lots into one large lot will probably increase the overall value of the owner's investment much more than acquiring or selling the smaller lot pieces separately.

- **Principle of Substitution:** The maximum value of a property is determined by the available supply of similar properties nearby. A buyer will usually buy the more affordable choice if given two or more options.

- **Principle of Balance:** The maximum value of a property or other asset is maintained through some sort of an equal balance between supply and demand.

- **Principle of Progression:** The real estate principle is based upon the belief that the acquisition of the smallest and oldest home on a neighborhood block will generally be positively affected by nearby larger homes.

- **Principle of Regression:** A larger and newer home's value in a subdivision will be adversely impacted by smaller, inferior properties that surround it.

- The **CPI (Consumer Price Index)** is a measurement of inflation that is published on a monthly or annual basis by economists or federal agencies. It is generally tied to a basket of goods associated with clothing, transportation, and retail supplies. Home prices have historically increased at annual rates higher than the CPI inflation index.

- **Deflation:** The decrease in the general price of goods and services as compared with prior years. **Hyperinflation** is a period of time when annual inflation rates and consumer prices move too high as the dollar's purchasing power falls too much at the same time.

Chapter Eight Quiz

1. The dollar amount at which a market clears (or the product sells) between a willing buyer and a willing seller where they made their decisions under their own free will without any negative outside influences is called____.
   A. Value
   B. Market price
   C. Appraised value
   D. Implied value

2. The place where the available supply of homes meets the most current demand is known as the____.
   A. Value point
   B. Equilibrium point
   C. Ultimate price
   D. Market plateau

3. The demand for a product like homes for sale that can change on a day-to-day or monthly basis rather quickly up or down is said to be____.
   A. Inelastic
   B. Elastic
   C. Fixed
   D. Constant

4. The finite or limited supply of a product like new homes for sale that takes a rather long time to add to in terms of new supply is called____.
   A. Elastic
   B. Inelastic
   C. Fluid
   D. Stable

5. What is the most important factor affecting a home's value?
   A. Lendability
   B. Leverage
   C. Location
   D. Liquidity

6. The ability to quickly convert an asset like a home to cash is called____.
   A. Liquidity
   B. Leverage
   C. Lendability
   D. Marketability

7. "As the production of a product or asset increases in number, the average cost to create the same product decreases" under the theory of ____.
   A. Law of Diminishing Returns
   B. Economies of Scale
   C. Supply and Demand
   D. Law of Assemblage

8. "The increase in production efforts and expenses will lead to **declining** profits as the per-unit cost increases partly due to inefficient production activities" under the economic theory of____.
   A. Economics of Assemblage
   B. Supply and Demand
   C. Ricardo's Theory of Returns
   D. Law of Diminishing Returns

9. "A property that offers the **highest and best use** options for one particular seller may generate the highest offer price" under the theory of ____.
    A. Supply and Demand
    B. Principle of Progression
    C. Principle of First Choice
    D. Principle of Competition

10. "If two homes are almost identical, the more affordably priced home is more likely to sell first" under what theory?
    A. Principle of Regression
    B. Supply and Demand
    C. Assemblage
    D. Principle of Substitution

11. What is the first stage in a real estate cycle?
    A. Maturity
    B. Development
    C. Integration
    D. Both B and C

12. What measures a "basket" of goods and services on an annual basis?
    A. Consumer Price Index
    B. Production Producer Index
    C. Fed Funds Rate
    D. Annual Inflation Index

Answer Key:

1. B	6. A	11. D
2. B	7. B	12. A
3. B	8. D	
4. B	9. C	
5. C	10. D	

CHAPTER 9

THE MORTGAGE INDUSTRY

Overview

This chapter is about the mortgage brokerage and banking process that many licensed real estate agents may choose to work in for some of their career, either as opposed to or in addition to their roles as real estate agents. The access to multiple lending sources will increase the chances of an agent's purchase transactions closing sooner rather than later or not at all. The funding and approval process for mortgage loans has changed significantly in recent years thanks to the passage of Dodd-Frank, the SAFE Act, the creation of the Consumer Financial Protection Bureau, and the new TRID requirements that will be discussed below. We will address the various roles that mortgage brokers play as well as learn details about the licensing and regulation requirements that mortgage professionals must follow both here in California and by way of governing federal guidelines.

Regulatory Agencies and Laws for Mortgage Brokers

Any person interested in originating mortgage loans in California must obtain either a salesperson or broker license before working with clients. All California mortgage licenses are handled through the **National Mortgage Licensing System**. The **Secure and Fair Enforcement for Mortgage Licensing Act of 2008 (SAFE Act)** is a federal law that was enacted in 2008 as a way to reduce mortgage fraud and improve consumer disclosure forms that are related to mortgage loan applications. The SAFE Act regulations were added to California state law through **Senate Bill 36** in 2009.

The SAFE Act and Senate Bill 36 both enhance consumer protection by establishing minimum standards for the licensing and registration of state-licensed mortgage loan originators (MLOs). An MLO is a person who accepts mortgage loan applications, or offers or negotiates primarily owner-occupied residential (one-to-four unit) loans to consumers in expectation of financial gain or a commission fee. Independent loan processors and underwriters are required to also hold a real estate broker license with an MLO endorsement even if they did not find the client.

As of 2018, there is a requirement for license applicants to complete at least 20 or more hours of pre-licensing courses before their mortgage license endorsement is issued. Applicants can still take the SAFE MLO exam without completing all 20 course hours, but the license will not be provided to the applicant. The pre-licensing courses that are required are:

- three hours of federal law and regulations;
- three hours of ethics (including fraud), consumer protection, and lending issues;
- two hours of training related to lending standards for nontraditional mortgage-loan products such as private money or "EZ Doc" loans; and
- 12 additional hours of various elective courses associated with mortgage origination.

Every 12 months, the MLO license endorsement holder is required to renew his or her license by the end of December in the following year. Licensees must complete eight (8) additional hours of MLO continuing education through an NMLS-approved course provider.

How often must the MLO license be renewed?

There are two regulatory agencies for mortgage brokers who work in the state of California. These agencies are the **California Division of Corporations** (formerly known as the Department of Corporations) that is a division of the **California Department of Business Oversight,** and the **California Department of Real Estate** (this license gives agents the best access to state and federal lenders).

A broker or agent licensed under the Department of Real Estate may have the right to work with most banks, savings banks, thrifts, credit unions, and other large state and national lenders. Agents licensed under the Division of Corporations can negotiate loans only with lenders licensed by the **California Finance Lenders Law**.

Applicants for a mortgage broker's endorsement license must submit their fingerprints for background checks when submitting their original license applications. In addition, applicants must confirm that they have not been convicted of any serious past frauds, especially related to past financial matters. A credit check will be reviewed for each applicant to find out how he or she handles his or her own personal credit. Please note that an MLO applicant does not need perfect credit to submit an application for an MLO license. In fact, California is one of the more flexible states that allow MLO license applicants with average to poor past credit histories to still qualify to take the exam on a case-by-case basis.

The MLO license endorsement is usually issued to currently licensed individuals who already hold a real estate salesperson or broker's license in California or to an employing corporation that has the correct licenses in place. Each real estate licensee is required to submit his or her original application through the Nationwide Mortgage Licensing System (NMLS) at http://mortgage.nationwidelicensingsystem.org/Pages/default.aspx.

The employing broker or corporation must create a business relationship with the mortgage license applicant as well as establish a formal sponsorship of the licensee.

The individual and company MLO license applications include the following forms for California applicants:

- Company (MU1) License Endorsement–Corporation
- Company (MU1) License Endorsement--Sole Proprietor Broker
- Branch (MU3) License Endorsement--Corporation and Sole Proprietor
- Individual MU4 Form-Broker and Salesperson

The MLO applicant's previous real estate salesperson or broker's license number issued by CalDRE does not change once he or she has been approved for the issuance of a new MLO endorsement. Real estate licensees will still be required to renew their licenses every four years while also renewing their MLO licenses every year. The education requirements for each license are separate, and do not crossover and apply towards both license renewals. Licensees must still pay the required fees each time when they renew one or both licenses.

The contact information (name, address, phone number, email, etc.) must be identical for each person holding both a real estate license and an MLO license endorsement that is issued by the NMLS. Any changes made about the licensee's contact information or employing firm name must be sent to both the CalDRE and the Nationwide Multistate Licensing System and Registry (NMLS) for amendments. Any employment or address changes must be sent to the NMLS within five (5) days of the starting date of employment at the new employing firm. It is the responsibility of the designated broker/officer of a corporation to also maintain and update their list of current MLO licensees working under them and to provide their company's most up-to-date contact information.

Full-time residency in California is *not* a requirement to be issued an MLO license from the state as long as the applicant passes the background check, pays the fee, completes the course, and passes the national exam. However, California does *not* have a reciprocity agreement in place with any other state to allow a waiver of requirements to obtain either a real estate or MLO license endorsement.

The Dodd-Frank Act

Over the past 111 years, America has experienced some significant boom and bust cycles that either created lots of newfound wealth for investors or a family's entire generation of wealth was lost forever after the financial markets crumbled in a relatively short time period. "Out of chaos comes opportunity" as the old saying goes, which also can be linked to the growth of new governing agencies and laws that were passed after the most recent financial scandal or crisis. Between 1907 and 2018, the four most significant financial crisis events that severely impacted a high number of consumers and banks included these events:

- Bank Panic of 1907
- The Great Depression (1929 - 1939)
- The Savings and Loan Crisis (1980s and 1990s)
- The Credit Crisis (2008)

What all of the negative financial events share in common is that these financial busts usually followed boom or bullish eras when access to cheap money was relatively easy. Each time the stock or housing markets would fall 10%, 20%, or 30% or more in value during one of these recessionary or depressionary financial periods, the federal government would usually pass new laws and create new governing agencies to ensure that these new laws were followed so that the economy could get back on track.

As discussed earlier, the Bank Panic of 1907 later led to the passage of the Federal Reserve Act of 1913. The Great Depression prompted the creation of a wide variety of laws, agencies, and job-works programs for citizens such as the enactment of the Glass-Steagall Act of 1933, which established the Federal Deposit Insurance Corporation (FDIC). The FHA program also came out of the ashes of some of the worst banking years in the 1930s in order to improve access to affordable home loans for borrowers. During the 1980s and 1990s, the bank industry was deregulated (eased banking laws) and regulated again and again with tightened banking guidelines several times after thousands of banks collapsed across the nation during some of the main "boom and bust" years.

The main new law that followed the Credit Crisis which caused the near implosion of the financial system in 2008 was the Dodd-Frank Act. It is essentially the 21st century version of the Glass-Steagall Act that was designed to inspire faith and confidence once again in the banking and overall financial system. Investors and real estate professionals must keep up to date with the latest changes to the financial and real estate markets that can affect them on a day-to-day basis. As such, it is critically important that real estate agents and mortgage brokers understand as much as possible about the Dodd-Frank Act that will be detailed below.

The full name of Dodd-Frank is the **Dodd-Frank Wall Street Reform and Consumer Protection Act**. It was signed into law in 2010 and changed the mortgage lending industry more than any other law ever passed in modern times. The stated primary intent was to prevent another collapse (or near collapse) of major financial firms like Washington Mutual (the number one bank collapse in U.S. history), Merrill Lynch (once the world's largest brokerage firm), AIG (one of the world's largest insurance companies), Countrywide Mortgage, IndyMac Mortgage, Downey Savings (one of California's largest mortgage lenders prior to 2007), World Savings, Lehman Brothers, and Bear Stearns.

The Dodd-Frank Act was named after the two main sponsoring politicians: Senator Christopher Dodd of Connecticut and Congressman Barney Frank of Massachusetts. Dodd-Frank was also designed to improve disclosure forms for consumers so that they truly understood what they were borrowing before signing their loan documents and funding their loans. There were at least 16 major areas of reform included in the Dodd-Frank Act that were covered in hundreds of pages.

The act created the **Financial Stability Oversight Council (FSOC)** to be in charge of the enforcement of the new regulations that came as a result of the passage of Dodd-Frank. The chairman of the FSOC who leads this agency is the Treasury Secretary. There are nine members including the Federal Reserve, the Securities and Exchange Commission, and the newly formed **Consumer Financial Protection Bureau**. The FSOC is also in charge of overseeing non-bank financial firms like equity or hedge funds.

Dodd-Frank has a section called the **Volcker Rule** which prohibits banks from owning (directly or indirectly) or managing private equity firms, hedge funds, or other types of sophisticated and risky financial firms in the U.S. or in other parts of the world. Dodd-Frank also required that complex derivatives like credit-default swaps and interest-rate option derivatives (these were the main catalyst for the bankruptcy filing of the County of Orange, California back in 1994) be regulated by the SEC or the **Commodity Futures Trading Commission (CFTC)**.

Insurance companies were to be managed by the new **Federal Insurance Office (FIO)** that was formed from Dodd-Frank to help audit and identify insurance companies that were financially unsound like AIG. In today's global financial world, the facets of the financial system (banks, equity firms, insurance companies, hedge funds, etc.) are interdependent, directly or indirectly, like a row of dominoes. Should one of these figurative "dominoes" fall down, then each financial entity that does business with it or holds billions of dollars' worth of its assets might implode as well.

As noted before, the U.S. and the world's financial systems had their worst days, months, and years starting in 2007 and 2008, primarily due to the "frozen" derivatives market that consisted of upwards of 1,500 to 3,000 trillion dollars worldwide. Delinquent subprime mortgage loans represented well under just 1% of all bad debt that froze up the markets in 2008. Yet Dodd-Frank focused much of the blame on subprime and Alt-A credit mortgage pools that were incorrectly rated as AAA (the highest and best credit rating possible) by the main credit-rating agencies such as Moody's, Fitch, and Standard & Poor's. Millions and billions of dollars' worth of these loan packages were sold off to investors around the world even though their credit quality was more like C, D, or F. So, Dodd-Frank also created an **Office of Credit Rating at the Securities and Exchange Commission (SEC)** to regulate and supervise credit-rating agencies so that they did their job properly.

The Consumer Financial Protection Bureau

The main governing agency that was formed as a result of the passage of the Dodd-Frank Act was the Consumer Financial Protection Bureau (CFPB). It officially opened for business back on July 21, 2011. The bureau was founded with the intent to consolidate employees and responsibilities from other regulatory agencies such as the Department of Housing and Urban Development (HUD), the Federal Trade Commission (FTC), the Federal Reserve (the Fed), the Federal Deposit Insurance Corporation (FDIC), and the National Credit Union Administration (NCUA). The bureau was formed as an independent entity that is located inside and funded by the Federal Reserve with partial affiliation and assistance by the U.S. Treasury Department.

The bureau's stated intent was to improve disclosure forms, education, and reduce fraud in the lending fields associated specifically with mortgages, student loans, and credit cards. The jurisdiction covered by the CFPB includes credit unions, commercial banks, securities firms, payday lenders, foreclosure relief or debt-consolidation companies, and other financial businesses operated anywhere in the U.S. The CFPB writes and enforces rules for the bulk of the financial sector and has the power to audit and examine both bank and non-bank financial institutions. It also keeps track of the latest financial market numbers and collects and investigates consumer complaints that have reached over 700,000 complaints in the six plus year of existence.

Truth-in-Lending Act (TILA)

The Truth-in-Lending Act was a federal law enacted in 1968 as a way to offer more protection and assistance to consumers in their dealings with their creditors and lenders. TILA was implemented by the Federal Reserve Board by way of a number of new regulations that lenders and creditors were forced to follow before providing funds to their customers. TILA came as a result of the enactment of **Regulation Z** (see 12 CFR Part

226 at https://www.gpo.gov/fdsys/granule/CFR-2012-title12-vol3/CFR-2012-title12-vol3-part226). It applies to most types of credit such as closed-end credit (mortgages), or installment loans, and open-ended revolving credit like credit cards or credit lines (or HELOCs - Home Equity Lines of Credit). New disclosure forms such as the Good Faith Estimate and HUD-1 closing statement originated from TILA.

The main financial contract items that lenders were required to fully and properly disclose to their clients included the following details:

- the annual percentage rate (APR);
- the term of the loan; and
- the total costs to the borrower.

These disclosure items were required to be easily found on the contract and understandable to the customers *before* they verbally agreed to the terms and signed the contract. The monthly billing statements must also contain the latest APR, loan terms, and costs in each and every statement sent out to customers.

TILA especially impacts how creditors or banks can advertise their loan products to the general public. The loans offered to consumers must clearly state whether the loans are for fixed or adjustable-rate mortgages, the length of the loan, whether or not there are any near-term balloon-payment requirements (or payments much larger than the usual monthly payments), and the total points and fees that the consumer will have to pay upon the receipt of open-ended or closed-ended funds.

One of the most important features of TILA involved the requirement that consumers be given a **right of rescission** to back out of the loan up to three days after signing the original contract. Many consumers were adversely influence by the lender, who used high-pressure salesmanship tactics to get the client to agree to the loan. The right of rescission gives each customer a few more days to change his or her mind after signing the contract.

RESPA

The Real Estate Settlement Procedures Act (RESPA) was a consumer protection law that was passed by Congress in 1974. This act is codified at Title 12, Chapter 27 of the United States Code, 12 U.S.C. §§ 2601 -- 2617. Between 1974 and 2011, HUD was in charge of the administration of this act. In July 2011, the enforcement duties for RESPA were transferred from HUD to the Consumer Financial Protection Bureau.

RESPA had two main purposes:

> 1) To offer consumers assistance so that they would become better consumers of loan services; and

> 2) To eliminate kickbacks and referral fees paid to licensed or unlicensed individuals that partly increased the borrower's total closing costs.

RESPA made it mandatory that lenders provide borrowers with disclosures at certain times during the mortgage-loan borrowing process that clearly outline the proposed and final terms of the loan. These terms must include all settlement service charges associated with the loan such as title, appraisal, credit reporting fees, escrow, mortgage-loan broker points, processing and underwriting fees, and other charges that were directly related to the borrower's transaction for both refinance and purchase loans. The primary form associated with RESPA in mortgage transactions was the **HUD-1** settlement form.

RESPA applies specifically to "federally related" mortgage loans that are secured by residential (one-to-four unit) properties. A lender is described as offering "federally related" mortgage loans when they hold deposits or accounts that are insured by any federal agency such as the FDIC, and / or a lender that sells their funded loans to a government-sponsored enterprise (GSE) in the secondary mortgage markets (e.g., Fannie Mae, Freddie Mac).

TRID

TRID - the Consumer Financial Protection Bureau's *Know-Before-You-Owe* rule was created as a hybrid between TILA (Truth-in-Lending) Act and RESPA (Real Estate Settlement Procedures Act). RESPA was developed with the intent to help consumers shop for the best rates and terms as well as to eliminate referral fees that increased the borrower's closing costs. Most types of closed-end mortgages secured by real estate must now follow the TRID rules of disclosure. The loans that are exempt or free from the TRID guidelines include reverse mortgages, open-ended lines of credit, and mobile or manufactured homes not attached to the land.

TRID was created to improve the disclosure forms to make them more understandable for consumers as well as to give people more time to agree or disagree and cancel the loan request either near the start or the end of the loan-application process. Prior to TRID, there were four main disclosure forms that were sent by lenders to the consumers, in accordance with the RESPA requirements. These four forms were:

- Good Faith Estimate
- Initial Truth-in-Lending Statement
- HUD-1
- Final Truth-in-Lending Statement

TRID merged the Good Faith Estimate and the Initial Truth-in-Lending Statement into one document called the **Loan Estimate** statement. The Loan Estimate (formerly known as the Good Faith Estimate) form must be sent out to the borrower within **three (3) days** of the submitted loan application. This new form was sent out to borrowers with proposed loan terms shortly after they submitted their original loan application to the lender. The old HUD-1 form and the Final Truth-in-Lending Statement were consolidated into a new **Closing Disclosure** statement under the TRID regulations.

Mortgage Operations

There are many different types of mortgage operations that exist around the state and nation. The best known types of mortgage lenders include:

- Commercial banks
- Savings banks
- Online mortgage lenders
- Credit Unions
- Mortgage companies

Commercial banks, savings banks or thrifts, and credit unions all may provide the majority of their mortgage loans from their customers' savings deposits. The online mortgage lenders and mortgage companies may have credit lines (or warehouse lines) that they draw or borrow from before funding the loan for their clients.

Or, these same lenders may reach out to 50, 100, or more affiliate lenders and use the affiliate's funds to close the loans primarily so that they may collect closing-cost fees like broker, processing, and underwriting fees. The funding mortgage company may fund the loan in its name that is listed as the primary lender on the loan documents and disclosure statements or it will be listed as a separate mortgage broker on behalf of another lender that provided 100% of the loan amount.

Most mortgage companies are not depository institutions. They do not offer savings or checking accounts in their physical or online office locations to their customers. Yet there are many mortgage companies that are directly owned by much larger depository institutions (commercial banks, savings banks, etc.) while acting as kind of a separate business entity that has some autonomy or independence. The earliest known truly independent mortgage-banking companies that were established in the U.S. dates back to the 1930s during the Great Depression.

Within the "mortgage broker/banker" designation, there are a large number of subcategories for the brokerage and lending functions that real estate agents should be familiar with while working in the real estate field. Over the past few decades, the job titles have changed somewhat right alongside the licensing and education requirements. Let's take a closer look at some of the core descriptions of jobs associated with the mortgage industry.

First off, a **lender** is the actual party who provides money or capital to the borrower at the closing table or close of escrow. In exchange for the funds provided to the borrower, the lender (or their appointed trustee or mortgage loan service company) will receive a promissory note (a glorified "IOU" for the debt that includes the loan terms such as the interest rate and due date) that is the primary evidence of the mortgage debt as well as a lien on the subject property by way of a trust deed (in the state of California).

A person described as a **loan officer** may represent a commercial or savings bank directly as a fully employed representative with a yearly salary with or without bonuses and additional benefits. Or, the loan officer may act as more of an independent contractor at a large mortgage brokerage firm that may have anywhere from two to a hundred licensed mortgage brokers/loan officers who specialize in offering residential or commercial mortgage loans (or both). Many of these independent mortgage brokers who work at a mortgage firm that is not a depository institution will be paid 100% commission only after they fund or close one or more mortgage loans. Some larger, well-capitalized mortgage firms may offer monthly draw options where they advance money to mortgage brokers until they close their next loan.

A true loan officer does not lend his or her own funds. He or she works as a middleman between the client(s) and the lender. These loan officers may work with many different **wholesale lenders** that provide slightly discounted rates and fees to mortgage brokers who send them enough monthly business volume. These wholesale lenders may represent some of the largest state, national, and international banks on the planet or financial firms that are backed by funds provided by insurance groups, hedge funds, or equity firms on or near Wall Street. The largest source of profit for a wholesale lender comes from the collection of their mortgage-loan servicing fees over several years on average.

The loan officer/mortgage broker is usually the main person who will interact with the client throughout the mortgage application and funding process. If the mortgage broker is not familiar with all of the loan terms being offered by his wholesale lender, then the broker may call the wholesale lenders' representatives or their associates for the best answers to their client's questions. The loan officer/mortgage broker will help the client fill out their 1003 loan application and gather up all of the requested financial and credit documents at the start of the application process.

The mortgage broker may speak on an almost daily basis with the clients, one or more real estate agents (buyer's agent and listing agent), the lender's appointed appraiser, a title insurance company representative, the escrow officer, and even one or more of the third-party inspectors (pest, natural hazard, home inspector, etc.) to ensure that the loan eventually funds and the deal closes escrow. Some lenders may have concerns with value, building defects, or environmental hazards that must be addressed before the lender approves the funding of the loan. Most often, the mortgage broker will not receive any money for all of his hard work unless the deal closes escrow. As such, the broker is quite motivated to pacify all parties involved in the transaction that most especially includes the borrowing client.

The commission collected by a mortgage broker on just one residential or commercial loan transaction can be incredibly high (1% or more of the funded loan amount that is paid at the close of escrow is the norm as a loan origination fee). For true loan officers acting as independent contractors, it is their primary job to find clients who are searching for loans. Once the clients have been found directly by the loan officer, or by way of referrals from online sources, real estate brokers, or other contacts, the loan officer will usually work as quickly as possible to ensure that the loan funds in a timely manner. The loan officer is motivated to meet the target loan contingency and closing guidelines set by the client and brokers for purchase transactions as well as to earn his or her commission income.

A loan officer working as an independent contractor will likely have brokerage commission splits with their main individual or corporate employing broker just like real estate agents at their office. Newer loan officers may start out at the lower 50/50 splits (50% of the gross commission goes to the loan officer and the other 50% goes to the employing broker). As they build their careers over time and close a fairly high dollar amount of loans, the loan officer may move up to higher 65/35, 70/30, and 80/20 splits with the largest percentages going to the loan officer (i.e., 65%, 70%, or 80% of the gross commission will be paid to the loan officer).

Let's review below some potential loan brokerage commission fees that are based upon the entire funded loan amount. Please note that most independent loan officers earn the vast majority of their income from the points charged on the loan. These loan fees may be paid from the borrower directly or some combination of the borrower and the funding lender from their side of the profit. Because property values are so much higher in California as compared to the rest of the nation, the loan and property dollar amounts will usually be consistently well above the lower national averages. The loan fees may vary from low to high depending upon factors such as low credit scores, higher loan-to-value loans, private money options (instead of conventional bank loans that are much cheaper), and the type of loan-documentation options selected such as "full doc" or "EZ doc" (or "stated income") type loans.

The loan options for both simple residential loans and much larger commercial loans for more expensive properties such as high-rise office buildings, hotels, or retail shopping malls are as follows:

Residential Loan (Single-Family Home)

Loan Amount	Points Charged	Gross Commission Fee
$100,000	1%	$1,000
$300,000	2%	$6,000
$500,000	3%	$15,000
$1,000,000	2%	$20,000
$2,000,000	2%	$40,000

Commercial Loan (Office, Retail, Industrial, Multifamily Apartments)

Loan Amount	Points Charged	Gross Commission Fee
$3,000,000	1.0%	$30,000
$5,000,000	2.0%	$100,000
$7,000,000	1.5%	$105,000
$10,000,000	2.0%	$200,000
$20,000,000	1.5%	$300,000

Some mortgage brokerage firms will promote to the public that they are both "brokers" with access to hundreds of lenders as well as a **direct lender**. If so, this means that the mortgage company has its own sources to fund loans using its own cash reserves or borrowed funds from warehouse lines (also referred to as "credit lines") or private investors. Often, a direct lender-type of a mortgage broker will refer to itself as a **mortgage banker** because it offers both types of services to customers.

Many private money lenders these days use a pool of hundreds of private investors to fund loans for residential, commercial, or construction loans. The private investors are secured by a deed of trust against one or more properties and generally receive rates of interest much higher than the best conventional banks. Billions of dollars have been raised by privately-held **crowdfunding platforms** for real estate since 2012 after the passage of the JOBS (Jumpstart Our Business Startups) Act (and subsequent amended acts like Title II and Title III) that eased securities regulations so that it was easier to raise capital directly from the public for real estate investments and business needs from crowdfunding sources.

Other mortgage professional designations that cater directly to the consumers themselves or through the mortgage broker contact include:

Wholesale Lenders: These wholesale representatives may send out daily rate sheets to their mortgage brokerage offices and to individual loan officers by email or text. It will be the wholesale lender that has the final absolute authority in determining whether or not the borrower applicant is creditworthy enough for the loan. It is the wholesale lender who is taking the bulk of the financial risk when approving each loan that comes across their desks.

A mortgage broker will have a signed agreement in place with their wholesale lender before they work together. The agreement may include such provisions as the broker will be required to buy back the funded loan at a later date should any fraud be proven to have been committed by either the client or the loan officer. The wholesale lender's primary client is their mortgage brokerage firms more so than the individual clients. Some brokerage firms may send hundreds or thousands of loans to some of the larger wholesale lenders who offer the best rates, terms, and service.

Retail Lenders: A lender who lends money directly to individual consumers rather than to mortgage brokerage firms or other types of financial or business institutions. The multi-billion dollar commercial banks or conglomerates like JPMorgan Chase, Wells Fargo, Bank of America, and Citigroup are some of the most powerful and successful retail lenders in the nation. Of these tens or hundreds of thousands of employees around the nation and the world, they can generate a very high volume of incoming calls or email requests partly due to the fact that they spend a great deal of money each year advertising their loan products. Other types of retail lenders include credit unions, savings banks, and some mortgage bankers with access to their own money pools.

Portfolio Lenders: This type of lender may both originate the loan using their own funds and also hold the funded loan in their portfolio while collecting the monthly mortgage payments from the borrower. The portfolio lender can make money from the funding fees (i.e., loan points, loan processing and underwriting fees, etc.) at the time of closing, and later collect a small percentage of fees each month from the spread (or difference) between the interest-earning assets (or the mortgage payment) and the interest paid on the deposits in their mortgage portfolio. The lender may also collect some loan service management fees for each monthly payment amount collected.

Warehouse Lenders: This type of lender pulls money from their business line of credit that is then given to a loan originator like a mortgage brokerage firm as a way to provide a new mortgage loan to a borrower for the purchase or refinance of a property. The life of this warehouse line or loan will typically last from the time of funding the original loan for the borrower up until the loan is sold to investors (private or government) in the secondary market. Other times, the lender may sell the individual loan to an individual investor, equity firm, hedge fund, or pension fund, especially for smaller loan amounts under $1 million.

Sometimes, the warehouse line will only be open for a week or so before the credit line is paid off in full once sold to a secondary market-type investor. Each time the warehouse line is paid off, the line of credit balance may go back to zero for the warehouse lender. If the lender cannot sell the loan to another investor, then they may quickly run out of funds to offer new mortgage loans to brokerage firms and their customers.

Correspondent Lenders: A correspondent lender is defined as one that originates and funds home loans in their own name. Shortly after the close of escrow, the lender will likely sell these loans to much larger mortgage lenders. These same lenders, in turn, may retain the loans in their portfolio just like a portfolio lender while collecting the fees for handling the servicing of the loan. Or, these larger lenders may choose to sell these loans to secondary-market investors like Fannie Mae, Freddie Mac, pension funds, or equity firms.

Correspondent lenders will usually employ their own in-house mortgage underwriters to closely analyze each individual loan request before the lender will approve and fund the loan. Often, the loans are underwritten and approved to the exact same mortgage underwriting guidelines that are required at larger banks. Because the correspondent lender knows that the approved loan meets all of the underwriting guidelines at the larger lender who might buy their loan a few days after funding, the odds are fairly good that the larger lender will buy the funded loan from the correspondent lender.

In some ways, the correspondent lender acts like a subsidiary of a larger bank if they send most of their loans to them after funding, regardless of whether or not the larger bank has any ownership interests in the correspondent lender. The mortgage borrower who uses a correspondent lender to close their loan will often see that their monthly mortgage statements will have new bank names and addresses for the payments.

Private Money Lenders: In the old days, private money (also called **hard money**) was often the loan choice of last resort for borrowers. Some of the more expensive mortgage rates offered in the 1980s and 1990s ranged from 10% to 20% plus in annual interest rates with loan points varying between five and 20 points. A $100,000 loan that costs 10 points to close would cost the borrower at least $10,000 in closing costs (plus additional processing, underwriting, and other valid or not so valid fees).

With interest rates at or near historical lows over the past several years for mortgages and other types of loans, private money loan rates have fallen to fairly low rates and fees. Given the choice between some private money loans and conventional bank loans, many non-owner occupied property investors who own multiple rental properties prefer the private money options better than conventional bank funds. This is especially true if the investor is planning to "fix and flip" the rental property and needs to close as soon as possible partly to beat out competing bid offers. In recent years, these private money sources have offered rates closer to 6% to 8% from funding sources that originate from individual investors, pension funds, or equity firms. Some private money firms specialize in offering capital for both residential and commercial properties across the state or in several states outside of California.

National Mortgage Lenders

A report issued by or compiled from data prepared by iEmergent and the Federal Financial Institutions Examination Council after their review of the latest Home Mortgage Disclosure Act details showed the list of the top 10 mortgage lenders nationwide in 2016. The details included in this data noted that the number of originated loans for all types of properties had increased by close to one million loans between 2015 and 2016 (or a 13% increase). The number of refinance originations increased by 16% between 2015 and 2016, and the home purchase lending applications increased by almost 11%.

Here is the list of the top 10 mortgage lenders nationwide for 2016:

1) Quicken Loans - 436,289 funded loans
   Share of total loans: 5.7%
   Total combined loan amounts: $90.6 billion

2) Wells Fargo Bank - 393,568 funded loans
   Share of total loans: 5.2%
   Total combined loan amounts: $126 billion

3) JPMorgan Chase Bank - 173,702 funded loans
   Share of total loans: 2.3%
   Total combined loan amounts: $74 billion

4) Bank of America - 152,811 funded loans
   Share of total loans: 2%
   Total combined loan amounts: $58.1 billion

5) Freedom Mortgage Corporation - 152,017 funded loans
   Share of total loans: 2%
   Total combined loan amounts: $31.8 billion

6) LoanDepot - 132,440 funded loans
   Share of total loans: 1.7%
   Total combined loan amounts: $35.7 billion

7) U.S. Bank - 108,171 funded loans
   Share of total loans: 1.4%
   Total combined loan amounts: $28.6 billion

8) Caliber Home Loans - 105,371 funded loans
   Share of total loans: 1.4%
   Total combined loan amounts: $27.6 billion

9) Flagstar Bank - 99,341 funded loans
   Share of total loans: 1.3%
   Total combined loan amounts: $26.5 billion

10) United Wholesale Mortgage - 82,231 funded loans
   Share of total loans: 1.1%
   Total combined loan amounts: $22.9 billion

Chapter Nine Summary

- All California mortgage licenses are handled through the **National Mortgage Licensing System** after the passage of the **Secure and Fair Enforcement for Mortgage Licensing Act of 2008 (SAFE Act)**. The SAFE Act regulations were added to California state law through **Senate Bill 36** in 2009.

- The SAFE Act and Senate Bill 36 established minimum qualification standards for the licensing and registration of state-licensed **mortgage loan originators (MLOs)**.

- There are two regulatory agencies for mortgage brokers who work in the state of California that include the **California Division of Corporations** (formerly known as the Department of Corporations) that is a division of the **California Department of Business Oversight** and the **California Department of Real Estate** (this license gives agents the best access to state and federal lenders).

- Agents licensed under the Division of Corporations can only negotiate loans with lenders licensed by the **California Finance**

Lenders Law. Agents with **CalDRE** approval can work with most types of state and federal lenders.

- As of 2018, there is a requirement for license applicants to complete at least **20 hours** of pre-licensing courses before the MLO license endorsement is issued. Each year by December, the MLO license must be renewed after completing eight (8) additional course hours and paying the fees.

- The **Dodd-Frank Wall Street Reform and Consumer Protection Act** was signed into law in 2010. The act was designed to reduce mortgage fraud, improve access to capital, and to make disclosure forms more understandable for consumers.

- The **Truth-in-Lending Act (TILA)** was a federal law enacted in 1968 as a way to offer more protection to consumers in their dealings with their creditors and lenders. New disclosure forms such as the Good Faith Estimate and HUD-1 closing statement originated from TILA.

- The primary agency that was formed as a result of the passage of the Dodd-Frank Act was the **Consumer Financial Protection Bureau (CFPB)**. The CFPB opened for business on July 21, 2011.

- The **Real Estate Settlement Procedures Act (RESPA)** was a consumer protection law that was passed by Congress in 1974. RESPA was implemented with the intent to give consumers better access to financial services so that they could shop for the lowest rates, and to eliminate kickback or referral fees that were increasing borrowers' loan costs.

- **TRID** merged RESPA and TILA rules and mortgage disclosure forms. The Good Faith Estimate and Initial Truth-in-Lending Statement combined to form a new **Loan Estimate** form. The HUD-1 and Final Truth-in-Lending were merged to become a new **Closing Disclosure** statement.

- **Retail Lenders:** A lender who lends money directly to individual consumers.

- **Wholesale Lenders:** A lender who provides discounted mortgage loan products to banks and mortgage companies that are then later offered to consumers.

Chapter Nine Quiz

1. The federal law that was passed in 2008 as a way to reduce mortgage fraud and improve consumer disclosure forms for mortgage loan applications was called ____.
    A. Dodd-Frank Act
    B. Consumer Financial Protection Bureau
    C. SAFE Act
    D. Graham-Bliley Act

2. How many hours of pre-licensing course work does a new applicant for a mortgage loan originator (MLO) license endorsement need in order to qualify to take the first national exam?
    A. 8
    B. 12
    C. 16
    D. 20

3. How often must the MLO license be renewed?
    A. Every year
    B. Every two years
    C. Every three years
    D. Every four years

4. How many course hours must be completed to renew the MLO license?
    A. 3
    B. 8
    C. 14
    D. 20

5. The main governing agency that was formed to protect consumers and improve mortgage disclosures as a result of the passage of the Dodd-Frank Act was the ____.
    A. Mortgage Compliance Agency
    B. Consumer Financial Protection Bureau
    C. TRID
    D. SAFE Agency

6. Which federal law was enacted in 1968 as a way to offer more protection and assistance to consumers in their dealings with their creditors and lenders?
    A. Truth-in-Lending Act
    B. RESPA
    C. TRID
    D. Fair Lending Act

7. Which laws, agencies, or programs require lenders to provide the true annual percentage rate, the term of the loan, and the total borrower costs?
    A. Consumer Financial Protection Act
    B. Truth-in-Lending Act
    C. TRID
    D. All of the above

8. A borrower's right to back out of a signed financial contract like a mortgage up to three days after signing the document is called a ____.
    A. Cancellation clause
    B. Right of rescission
    C. Revocation right
    D. None of the above

9. What is the name of the first mortgage disclosure statement that is mailed or handed over to a borrower at the start of a mortgage application process thanks to TRID guidelines?

  A. Good Faith Estimate

  B. HUD-1

  C. Loan Estimate

  D. Initial Truth-in-Lending Statement

10. Which commission amount below will generate the highest gross commission fee for a mortgage broker?

  A. 1% on $1,000,000

  B. 2% on $450,000

  C. 3% on $275,000

  D. 6% on $150,000

11. Which type of financial group may both originate the loan using their own funds and also hold the funded loan while collecting the monthly mortgage payments from the borrower?

  A. Retail lender

  B. Secondary market investor

  C. Portfolio lender

  D. Correspondent lender

12. What California agencies regulate mortgage loan originators?

  A. Division of Corporations

  B. Department of Business Oversight

  C. Department of Real Estate

  D. All of the above

Answer Key:

1. C	6. A	11. C
2. D	7. D	12. D
3. A	8. B	
4. B	9. C	
5. B	10. A	

CHAPTER 10

LOAN UNDERWRITING PROCESS

Overview

There is no magic involved with the mortgage underwriting process. Today, lenders may likely use a combination of human beings and computer software systems to analyze the credit and loan-risk potential for each of their mortgage applicants. This section of the course will cover the basic parts of the 1003 loan application, the usual items requested by the lender for the borrower applicant, and how loans are either approved or denied due to factors such as FICO credit scores, low or high cash reserves, current net worth levels (assets - liabilities), and property quality. Real estate agents should learn as much as they can about the mortgage process because third party loans will probably be involved in most of their transactions throughout the agent's career.

Loan Origination

Real estate agents will usually spend much of their time on each transaction worrying about whether or not the buyer has formally qualified for a loan. Most often, real estate purchasers will find their mortgage lender through a referral from their own buyer's agent or from the listing agent in the same transaction.

Because the vast majority of buyers in the state are likely to apply for some type of government-assisted mortgage loan product (FHA and VA, especially) when making a purchase offer, real estate professionals may have a few sleepless nights hoping that the buyer/borrower qualifies for the loan and the subject property appraises at the full purchase price offer. Some loan applications can take 21, 30, 45, or 60 or more days to get approved prior to the issuance of loan documents for signing and the subsequent closing, so the wait process can be excruciating in some lengthy deals.

Many borrowers will work with a mortgage broker who has access to many lenders as opposed to just one loan officer at a bank with only two or three home loan options. Often, the buyer's agent has an established long-time working relationship with a mortgage broker who visits his or her office on a weekly or monthly basis. A mortgage broker with a proven track record of funding the bulk of their loan requests in a timely manner -- well before the loan contingency time periods that are typically 17 to 21 days in each purchase offer -- is one who may continue to receive a consistent number of loan applications from brokers and clients. A mortgage broker is usually only as good as their last deal with each real estate agent, so the loss of just one mortgage deal that was expected to close last week on time may end the relationship between the agent and mortgage broker.

The mortgage broker (also referred to as the **loan originator**) is responsible for finding new loan prospects either on their own or by way of referrals. Those referrals typically come from real estate agents, but may also come from online sources, accountants, attorneys, wealth advisors, other business professionals, or through the mortgage broker's "sphere of influence" circle of friends, family, former co-workers, or fellow church, synagogue, temple, or club members.

The mortgage broker will sit down with the mortgage borrower applicant and help the client correctly fill out the 1003 loan application form (also referred to as the **Uniform Residential Loan Application**) that is approved by both Fannie Mae and Freddie Mac as well as the issuing lender.

The main sections in the 1003 loan application form are:

1) Instructions and Signatures: The borrower(s) are given brief instructions at the top of the loan application form that are acknowledged with a signature.

2) Section I - Type of Property and Term of Loan: The borrower must confirm which type of loan product they are seeking such as a conventional, VA, FHA, or USDA/Rural type loan. The loan applicant will also fill in the proposed loan amount, interest, amortization type (fixed or adjustable), and desired loan term that is desired for the property.

3) Section II - Property Information and Purpose of Loan: The applicant will write in details about the subject property being refinanced or purchased which include the legal and street or physical address, the purpose of the loan (purchase, refinance, construction), the age of the property, the source of the borrower's choice for title interests in the property such as "joint tenancy" or "sole and separate" vesting interests.

4) Section III - Borrower Information: This section is more about the specific details about the borrower applicant(s) such as their full legal name, social security number, educational background, marital status, and current and former addresses within the past two years.

5) Section IV - Employment Information: Because lenders want to be paid each month with timely mortgage payments and eventually paid in full, the employment section will show the lender how consistent the borrower's income is each month.

6) Section V - Monthly Income and Combined Housing Expense Information: The lender wants an itemized list of total overall monthly income (base income, bonuses, commissions,

dividends/interest, and net rental income) for the borrower to compare with the proposed new mortgage payment. Is the borrower's income high enough to cover the proposed new mortgage payments (principal, interest, taxes, and insurance) plus the borrower's other monthly debt obligations related to credit card, school, business, and/or automobile loans?

7) Section VI - Assets and Liabilities: The borrower will provide a detailed list of assets and liabilities partly so the lender can determine if the borrower has sufficient access to cash to close on a purchase loan or enough cash reserves to make mortgage payments on time for either a purchase or refinance loan. Lenders are generally most interested in how much liquid assets (or assets that can easily be converted into cash) they hold in their accounts or as cash on hand.

8) Section VII - Details of Transaction: This section is about the purchase price or refinance amount as well as the potential closing costs or total amounts that are targeted for payoff. With some refinance transactions, the borrower is looking to refinance the existing mortgage debt plus outstanding or unpaid credit card, student, or business loans and/or wish to pull additional cash out from the equity in their home for construction remodels or to improve their cash reserves.

9) Section VIII - Declarations: This section includes a series of questions with "Yes" or "No" answers that are associated with issues such as past or current judgments, lawsuits, delinquent or defaulted government debt, and whether or not the applicant is obligated to pay spousal support, child support, or other types of financial obligation.

10) Section IX - Acknowledgement and Agreement: After reading the statement about the rights of the lender and the borrower that include the fact that the borrower has been honest and forthright

with the completed loan application, the borrower applicant signs and dates this section.

11) Section X - Information for Government Monitoring Purposes: This is an optional section that is completed by both the borrower(s) and the loan originator that has boxes to be checked for topics related to gender, race, and ethnic backgrounds. The federal government likes to keep track of this information to ensure that lenders are providing equal credit and lending opportunities for all people.

12) Continuation Sheet/Residential Loan Application: This optional separate continuation sheet (page 5 of 5) gives more room to borrower applicants to explain positive or negative issues that can help or hurt their overall loan application process. Specifically, the borrower may explain why he or she was forced to filed for bankruptcy protection several years ago, or the reasons why his or her previously owned home went into foreclosure back in 2009 after temporarily losing his or her job.

1003 form link:
https://www.fanniemae.com/content/guide_form/1003rev.pdf

The mortgage broker/loan originator may also assist the client with gathering the required documentation that is submitted along with the completed 1003 application form such as follows:

- A check for the applicant's credit report
- Last 2 years tax returns (self-employed, investors, retirees, etc.)
- Last 2 years W2 forms (if employed)
- Last 2 months pay stubs
- Last 2 months bank statements (all pages)
- Last 2 months investment accounts
- Last 2 months pension accounts

- A signed gift letter if any of the down payment or closing cost funds are provided by anyone other than the buyer or seller
- A signed explanation letter from the borrower in regard to any past negative credit-history issues such as foreclosures, judgments, or bankruptcies.

The loan officer/mortgage broker/loan originator (all the same thing) will then bring in the completed mortgage application file to his or her office for a more thorough review or analysis. The loan officer will sit down with his or her personal assistant, loan processor, or in-house mortgage underwriter to go over the loan request with them. It is the main duty of this team of mortgage professionals and staff members to make sure that the borrower's mortgage-loan request is matched with the most appropriate lender that offers the same desired 30-year fixed mortgage loan program that the borrower had requested.

The Underwriting Process

It is up to the loan originator, the loan processor or assistant, and one or more mortgage underwriters to quickly gather as much information as possible in regard to the borrower(s) and the subject property. The signed 1003 form and the copies of the borrower's financials are just the first steps in the application process. Shortly thereafter, the underwriter will request an updated copy of the borrower's credit report as long as the client has provided a check or paid the fee online for the credit search (typically $25 or more).

Data Verification

There has been lots of fraud in the mortgage industry dating back as far as the 1930s when the industry started to really develop parallel to the commercial banks' significant growth. Well before so much information could be found out about a person's credit, income, and asset profile with sophisticated credit reporting and data analysis systems, there were many borrower applicants who would create phony W2 tax forms for jobs that they did not actually hold and/or would cut and paste existing or completely fraudulent bank statements that showed $10,000, $20,000, or $50,000 cash on hand when the borrower applicant actually had no money of their own.

With the more advanced online data confirmation and analysis programs, underwriters can quickly verify whether or not a borrower applicant's 1003 form is valid, accurate, and worthy of a solid approval, or find out that the borrower applicant committed a federal crime by lying on their loan application. Some of the most important components of a loan application that a mortgage underwriter must confirm include:

Deposits: The borrower applicant must first sign a Verification of Deposit (VOD) form that gives the mortgage company the legal authority to verify the latest and past banking, investment, and pension deposits. In some past fraudulent mortgage deals, the borrower will add thousands or tens of thousands of dollars in cash from family or friends in an attempt to show the lender enough cash reserves to buy a home for the mortgage applicant or for another buyer. If the mortgage prospect was acting as some kind of a "straw buyer" just because the person had a much higher credit score than the actual buyer or due to other issues such as the hidden buyer was trying to hide assets from an ex-spouse during a messy divorce, it could be challenging for some lenders to verify whether the applicant was using his own funds to complete the purchase.

Which underwriter form is used to confirm a customer's bank account balance?

The underwriter at the mortgage company or bank will then send out a cover letter to the mortgage applicant's financial institution or investment firm along with the person's signed Verification of Deposit firm either via regular mail, a scanned email, or while using an older fax machine.

The depository institution or investment company will then write in the borrower applicant's most current balance amount as well as their account balance history in recent months. If the account balance was $5 last month and now is listed as $35,000 after some large cash and blank cashier's check deposits were added to the account from unknown sources, then the underwriter might think that there is enough potential fraud involved with this deal to deny the application. For any questionable recent large deposits, the underwriter may ask for some additional "proof of funds" to confirm that the funds are, in fact, the applicant's funds 100% and not hidden gift or loan money from other parties not listed on the mortgage application or purchase contract. The signed VOD form is one of the main documents that may inspire more borrowers to be truthful with their stated deposits that are listed on the original 1003 application.

Employment: Each mortgage applicant will be required to sign a VOE (Verification of Employment) form if he or she is employed as a part or full-time employee for one or more jobs. Many times, a mortgage applicant works one full-time job and one or two other part-time jobs to generate enough monthly income to qualify for a mortgage in the first place. If so, the underwriter will send out the VOE forms to all of the listed direct employers and will ask for additional information for any self-employed type of jobs, such as copies of a business or professional license, tax returns, 1099 tax forms, or other documentation.

The employer who receives the signed Verification of Employment form from the mortgage underwriter must then reveal very confidential income and job history details by filling out the form. The employer will include the monthly and annual income history over the past year or few years. The employer may also be asked to give his or her honest opinion about their employee's job skills and overall attitude as well as offer a favorable or not so favorable prognosis for the employee's continued employment and prospects for advancement or future promotions at higher wage levels.

Income: The **Equal Credit Opportunity Act** prohibits lenders from discriminating against loan applicants because some, most, or all of their income comes from sources other than part or full-time jobs. This is especially true for income received from a public assistance program such as welfare or food stamps. The public assistance income may, however, only be counted as stable monthly income if it meets the test of durability over a projected future long period of time. Should these public assistance agencies confirm with the mortgage underwriter that the public benefits are about to run out in the next few months, then the underwriter cannot count this income as an acceptable income source. Older mortgage applicants may not be discriminated against under the federal **Equal Credit Opportunity Act** either.

Often, an older American receives the bulk of their consistent monthly income from pension income (especially former teachers, postal workers, and other former government employees) that may equate to 60% to almost 100% of their peak monthly income highs received while they were working full-time. These retirees may receive the second or first largest share of their monthly income from social security or from rental income on investment properties that they've owned for many years or decades. A mortgage underwriter must consider all of these income sources that are not related to current part or full-time work income.

An exception to this rule is when the applicant is in their 90s and they request a new 30-year mortgage. Some lenders may offer shorter term mortgage-loan options to the older retiree because the loan will likely outlive the mortgage applicant. Or, the loan originator and underwriter may suggest that the older American bring in a young person such as a child or grandchild to co-sign with him or her on the loan.

The income received from a former spouse as part of a divorce settlement may also be counted towards a mortgage applicant's loan request. With a 50% plus national divorce rate and an almost 60% divorce rate in the state of California, it is very likely that a high percentage of mortgage applications will include some type of **alimony (or spousal support)** and **child support** income.

The underwriter will review the payment history of the spousal and/or child support as well as review a copy of the **divorce decree** that shows how much money is to be paid out by the non-custodial parent and received by the custodial parent each month. The divorce decree will also show the underwriter how long the spousal and/or child support is supposed to last without any future support modification requests made by either side that could increase, decrease, or completely eliminate these monthly payment amounts.

Some mortgage applicants are part or full-time stock and/or real estate investors with a rather large investment portfolio that amount to millions of dollars. With the Dow Jones Industrial Average index recently surpassing 26,000 (or almost 19,500 higher than previous lows in March 2009), there are many investors who can show relatively high monthly income from their **dividends** or **interest** on investments. The underwriter may likely consider the average monthly return over the past two years. Since stocks have been on an upward ascent for the past nine years, the odds are fairly good that these stock gains will probably be on an increasing slope. A really fortunate borrower will find a lender who qualified them at their potential highest annual income received over the past year as many stocks reached record highs.

It is not uncommon for a mortgage applicant to have more than one open mortgage at the time that they submit their package. Many investors own their primary residence in addition to one or more rental properties. Some investors might hold several properties in their rental property portfolio. The mortgage underwriter might request copies of lease agreements, front and back-cancelled checks of the monthly rent payments received for each home, apartment unit, or commercial building tenant(s).

There are so many potential expenses related to the ownership of rental properties such as repair costs, management fees, advertising costs to find new tenants, unknown utility and common-area landscaping expenses, and vacancy rates that can fluctuate in a short time period. As a result, many lenders will count only 75% of the gross monthly income for the mortgage applicant's rental properties when attempting to determine the stability of the borrower's income levels. If so, $10,000 in monthly rental income will be counted as $7,500 (75%) on the borrower's loan application.

Tax Forms: In years past, there were so many phony social security numbers provided on 1003 loan applications as well as phony tax forms like the W-2, 1099-MISC, or other forms on which lenders had to tighten down their verification strategies to ensure that the borrower really was who he said he was and not someone using a stolen identity to gain access to a new property or to cash. The mortgage applicant will sign a **Borrower's Authorization** form along with their original 1003 loan application that gives the mortgage company the right to order the client's credit report and verify any information provided on the application. This information includes the right to confirm if the provided social security number, tax forms, and tax returns are in fact valid along with the stated deposits and employment documentation.

A signed **Form 4506-T (Request for Transcript of Tax Return)** by the borrower applicant gives authority to the lender to verify the validity of the applicant's submitted tax documents. The submission of phony federal tax documents related to the Internal Revenue Service or the Franchise Tax Board for California is a federal crime, so few borrower applicants are dumb enough to submit fraudulent tax records to lenders that can later send them to prison and be subject to serious fines. (Form 4506-T link: https://www.irs.gov/pub/irs-pdf/f4506t.pdf)

Property Details: Believe it or not, there have been many loan transactions throughout the state that involved properties that did not exist. The mortgage applicants might have stolen identities and created phony property descriptions and addresses (or even placed the mortgage on someone else's home while pulling all of the cash out and skipping town) to qualify for a loan. There have been examples where older retirees were shocked to learn that they had two or more mortgages on their property when they thought they owned the home "free and clear" with no mortgage debt due to various financial scams committed by others who they did not know.

Sadly, some family members like children or grandchildren also have filled out loan applications for cash-out refinance loans in order to steal tens or hundreds of thousands of dollars out of their parents' or grandparents' homes unbeknownst to the relatives who actually owned the home. There have been many sad and tragic stories where the true owners of the home lost the home to foreclosure without even being aware that there were one or two new mortgages on the home that hadn't been paid for several months or longer. Often, the same relative who might live with the property owner will run to the mailbox (or forward their mail to a new P.O. Box address nearby) and hide the monthly mortgage statements, late notices, and eventually the lender's foreclosure notices (Notice of Default, Notice of Trustee's Sale, and Final Trustee's Auction Notice).

As a result of so many financial and real estate frauds (especially in states like California), lenders will order preliminary title reports to verify that the legal and physical street addresses are valid. Additionally, the title reports will show the name(s) of the current and past owners of the property, all recorded liens (mortgage, judgment, tax, etc.), and the current lien balances against the property for refinance type of transactions. For purchase deals, the confirmation that the seller really does own the property and the total amount of the liens to be paid off are important as well for buyers and all real estate agents involved.

The designated escrow companies will also work to confirm that the properties are held in title by the individuals or entities (corporations, LLCs, partnerships, etc.) that are listed on the MLS or listing agreement. The escrow companies will also send out a **Demand for Payoff** statement to the individuals, lenders, or businesses listed as holding lien rights, loans, or judgments on the subject property. Escrow will also verify the current status of the property tax and insurance balances that they will later prorate to the exact day of payoff. The escrow officer, in turn, will apply the proper payoff credits and debits to the buyer on their respective closing statements.

Credit

A borrower's past credit payment history is a good indicator of what their future payment trends may be that also include whether or not the borrower applicant will make timely monthly mortgage payments to the lender if and when this deal funds and closes escrow. Today's modern credit scoring systems are based more on a FICO (Fair, Isaac and Company) scoring number system that can vary from a low of 300 (a negative score) to a high of 850 (the highest and best score possible). The FICO data will include personal information, credit history, and public-record information on the consumer. No tax return details will be added to the FICO file.

Most lenders will request a "tri-merge" credit pull that includes the three main credit reporting agencies in the U.S.: Experian, Equifax, and TransUnion. Their FICO scoring numbers may vary as much as 100 points or more depending upon what data each credit reporting system has available online. Generally, most lenders will take the middle of the three scores when deciding whether or not to approve a borrower applicant for one or more of their loan products.

The individual FICO scores are said to be calculated or weighted using the factors below as a percentage of overall importance in the final scores:

Payment history (35%): Over one third of a person's FICO credit score is determined by their past payment history. A credit applicant with no 30, 60, or 90-day lates on their payment history for loans associated with current and past automobile, credit card, student loan, child support, and mortgage loans, especially, will be viewed as a solid loan prospect by most lenders.

Amount owed (30%): Thirty percent of a person's credit score is based upon the amount of current unpaid or outstanding debt as well as past high-credit amounts that were paid off in full. In addition, a credit applicant who uses only a relatively small percentage of their available credit (i.e., they maintain zero balances on credit cards that allow $10,000 credit limits or unused credit lines for business or real estate that have zero to low balances on lines that can go as high as a few hundred thousand) is seen as a good credit risk.

Length of credit history (15%): An applicant with a credit history that dates back several years or decades is rated as a stronger borrower. Other credit applicants with histories that go back only a few months or years aren't seen as great credit risks unless their payment histories are primarily paid on time and as agreed.

New credit (10%): The credit scoring agencies will analyze the mix of existing credit types that each consumer uses at present as well as in the past. A positive use of credit cards, car loans, and mortgages that are borrowed and paid off on a consistent basis can improve a consumer's FICO score. However, the use of multiple credit cards that are all maxed out after reaching the highest ceiling amount allowed while the borrower pays the minimum monthly payment either on time or late can reduce credit scores. In situations where the consumer seems to be living off of their credit card loans more than receiving consistent employment or investment income, most lenders will deny the new mortgage-loan request due to the high-perceived risk of default on the current credit-card debt as well as a high probability of mortgage default shortly after the requested loan closes.

Mortgage applicants and their real estate agents need to know that not everyone has perfect credit these days. In fact, many California residents have past foreclosures and bankruptcies on their credit-report history profiles. Lenders and credit reporting companies like to see consumers who were able to bounce back from their troubles. Shortly after a recent foreclosure or bankruptcy discharge, consumers should apply for new credit as soon as possible in order to rebuild their credit scores. If credit card companies will not approve the consumer's application after a recent huge negative credit event like a foreclosure or bankruptcy, then there are hundreds of **secured credit card** companies that may consider issuing a new card after the customer sends in a small deposit for the credit issuer to hold and apply towards future charges ($50 to $200).

It is imperative that the customer find out if the secured credit card sends reports to the three major credit-reporting bureaus before submitting their application and paying their fees. If not, the consumer will not be positively improving their FICO scores even if they pay their monthly payments on time to the secured credit-card companies. Two or three years after new credit is reestablished after a bankruptcy discharge, a consumer may have FICO credit scores that exceed 720 or 750 (a solid "A" credit rating, per many lenders). FHA mortgage-loan underwriters may consider FICO scores in the high 500s and low 600s, so agents should keep working hard.

Other factors:

The mortgage underwriter may focus on these key items in a mortgage applicant's credit report history to get a better sense of whether the person is creditworthy:

- the mortgage applicant's length of credit history;
- the positive and timely payment record;
- derogatory credit incidents (30 and 60-day lates, etc.); and
- the three main FICO scores.

Everyone in the United States has a right to receive one free copy of their credit report as of September 2005 from each of the three major credit-reporting agencies: Equifax, TransUnion, and Experian. Real estate agents should consider suggesting that the clients or prospects request a copy of their credit report sooner rather than later before they start shopping for mortgage loans or looking at properties. Should there be any mistakes on the credit report, it may take a few weeks or months to rectify or repair the negative items that are keeping the scores much lower than they should be based upon the consumer's actual more positive payment history.

Automated Underwriting

The minimum standards used in the mortgage underwriting process can be fairly consistent for certain types of loan categories such as conventional, conforming, jumbo, FHA, VA, or even for non-owner occupied, no-income verification private money loans that require much larger down payments due to the higher risk factor. Loans that meet the lender's in-house underwriting standards (or the standards of the lenders or investors in the secondary markets) are likely to be considered as acceptable risks that can be approved. Loans that do not meet the minimal established underwriting, on the other hand, will probably be denied.

Who determines these "acceptable" minimum underwriting standards like FICO scores, cash assets on hand, monthly income, and the ratio of income to expenses that must be reached before the loan is approved? If the lender is using its own funds and plans to retain the loans in their personal portfolio, then this same lender can create its own mortgage underwriting guidelines for both the borrowers who will be considered as well as for the types of properties. Unless this portfolio-like lender eventually runs out of cash or is faced with too many future foreclosures due to fairly easy-approval guidelines, then the lender can continue onward while funding almost any loan that looks decent.

Most lenders do not have limitless money at their disposal, so they will normally apply similar qualifying standards for residential (one-to-four unit) properties that are set by Fannie Mae, Freddie Mac, FHA, or VA. Any funded conventional loan that is sold off to Fannie Mae or Freddie Mac in the secondary market must meet the minimal standards that are considered acceptable to them. Otherwise, the lender may be forced to hold its funded loan in its own portfolio, or discount the loan and sell it off to a private investor who is seeking a much higher yield or annual rate of return than just 4% or 5%.

Some mortgage underwriters have years or just months of experience when analyzing the possibly hundreds or thousands of loans that may cross their desks in a year or over the course of their entire career. Sometimes, a mortgage underwriter may get too personally attached to a deal and sign off as approved because they personally liked the clients who submitted the loan application after the loan originator introduced them to one another, regardless of whether the borrowers have sufficient levels of income to actually qualify.

By removing the human element somewhat, more and more lenders rely upon powerful and sophisticated **automated underwriting (AU)** software programs that will sort through the applicant's numbers before determining which loan product or products might be right for them if they meet the computer program's minimal guidelines. These automated underwriting systems came about in the 1990s. They were not meant to completely eliminate the living and breathing underwriters. Rather, the software systems were designed to complement and assist the mortgage underwriter by making their jobs even more efficient at a much faster pace of analysis.

Some of the larger lenders and mortgage companies might hire their own computer designers to create a mortgage underwriting system that they use to analyze their own files. Yet many lenders are likely to use one of the underwriting software systems below that were developed by Fannie Mae or Freddie Mac several years ago:

- Desktop Underwriter
- Desktop Originator
- Loan Prospector

The first step in the automated underwriting process is for the loan originator or underwriter to manually submit the information submitted on the 1003 loan application into the software's database system either as newly typed in using a computer keyboard or some type of scanning system that copies the loan application, tax forms, and financial information. Parallel to this loan submission, the borrower's credit report will be merged into the automated underwriting system for an efficient analysis of potential credit risks with this particular borrower.

After the AU system does a thorough analysis of the borrower's credit, appraisal and some third-party inspection reports, and mortgage application and profile, the system then provides a report for the underwriter and loan officer to review.

There may be three or more main categories that are included in the AU report:

- a risk classification for the borrower;

- a recommended level of income documentation (full or EZ doc); and
- any recommendations about possible acceptable appraisal (full or drive-by appraisal) or inspection reports.

If ultimately Fannie Mae or Freddie Mac may likely purchase the bulk of funded owner-occupied residential loans across the nation, then most primary lenders (commercial banks, savings banks, credit unions, etc.) are wise to follow the underwriting regulations established by the two largest secondary market investors in the nation. Even for loans that are not sold off to Fannie Mae or Freddie Mac, a lender might be smart to still use their automated underwriting systems because they can later find buyers for these loans by noting that the loans meet acceptable Fannie and Freddie underwriting guidelines.

Debt-to-Income Ratio

Shortly after the underwriter has done a thorough analysis of an applicant's potential income and expenses, the next step in the underwriting process is to measure the adequacy of the income levels. Does the borrower have sufficient levels of income that will more than cover their proposed new monthly payments (principal, interest, taxes, and insurance)? Equally as important, does the borrower also have enough income to cover his or her monthly debt obligations with other creditors or lenders such as their credit card, automobile, business, and student loans? If not, the underwriter may decide to deny the loan as soon as it crosses her desk.

The **Front End Ratios** for underwriting calculation purposes are found by dividing the proposed monthly mortgage payment (principal, interest, taxes, and insurance) by the borrower's gross monthly income.

Let's take a look below at a front-end ratio example:

```
* Proposed mortgage payment (principal and interest) = $1,750
* Proposed property taxes (1/12 of annual payments) =    $150
* Proposed monthly home insurance payment =              $100
                                                      ---------
Proposed total monthly mortgage payment (PITI) =       $2,000
```

If the borrower applicant consistently earns $6,000 per month in income at their full-time job (W-2 form shows $72,000/year), then the front-end debt ratio is calculated this way:

$$\$2,000 \ / \ \$6,000 = 33\%$$

Now, let's calculate the **Back End Debt Ratios** by adding up the proposed monthly mortgage payment plus other monthly debt obligations to arrive at the backend number below:

```
* Car payments =                              $300 / month
* Minimum credit card payments =              $250 / month
* Student loan payments =                     $200 / month
* Other monthly payments =                    $100 / month
                                           ----------------
Total payments (excluding mortgage) =         $850 / month
                                           ----------------
Total payments (including mortgage) =       $2,850 / month
```

The back end debt ratio is then calculated in the following way"

$$\$2,850 \ / \ \$6,000 = 47.5\%$$

The front and back-end debt ratios (33% / 47.5%) may be too high for some types of conventional loans funded by primary banks that are later sold off to Fannie Mae and Freddie Mac. Yet there may be private money loans or loans insured by FHA or partially guaranteed by VA that will be offered to the same borrower.

The acceptable debt-to-income ratios that lenders and various loan programs will allow may change every year or few years, depending upon the needs and interests of the funding banks or investors purchasing the loans in the secondary markets. Other times, the government may encourage banks and secondary-market investors to ease up their guidelines so that more loans are funded by offering some type of partial guarantee or financial assistance. This has been especially true in recent decades when the real estate market has boomed and busted a few times. If and when there are times when there are more sellers than buyers for properties and home prices are beginning to plateau or even fall, banks, with or without government influence, might decide to change their underwriting guidelines so that more loans are funded.

Over the past few decades, the allowable back-end debt ratios have risen from 36% or 38% for some conventional loan programs (about 60% of all funded residential loans nationwide) to as high as 50%. Also, FHA has approved many loans with back-end debt ratios as high as 60% on a case-by-case basis.

Stacking Order

The loan originator/loan officer is usually the first party from a bank or mortgage company who will interact with the borrower applicant. Once the completed 1003 form is received along with copies of financial documents related to income, expenses, and property details, the loan officer will work with his or her assistant and/or loan processor to make sure that the file is in the right stacking order before the loan package is submitted to the in-house underwriter or out of the office to the funding lender's main underwriters for formal approval.

Each funding lender may have similar or fairly different stacking orders. But a bank or mortgage office that plans on quickly selling off the loan to a larger bank or to a secondary-market lender should probably create a similar stacking order that is acceptable to the end-loan buyer. The more organized that a loan package is in a style that the underwriter is used to for most of his or her files, the quicker the approval process. Conventional, private money, FHA, and VA loans may all have different stacking order requirements that loan originators, processors, and underwriters should be aware of before they submit their files to the lender for formal approval.

Let's review below several different stacking styles for a Letter of Intent or prequalification mortgage letter, private money, FHA, VA, conventional, and commercial mortgage loans:

The first step in the underwriting and loan file package status may likely be a borrower and/or real estate broker request for a pre-approval letter, especially for purchase transactions. Borrower applicants and their affiliated buyer's agents want to be fairly certain that the loan prospect can qualify for his or her loan as well as afford the required down payment, closing costs, and monthly payments. Sellers, especially in a solid housing market cycle, want to know that the buyers really do have access to enough third-party funds to buy the seller's property at the mutually agreed-upon sales price. As such, a Letter of Intent or pre-approval letter from a lender interested in funding the deal is usually the first step in the loan packaging process.

In order for a lender to issue a pre-approval letter that is subject to the review of future items yet to be received like appraisal and various inspection reports, the lender may need at least the following items stacked in a file folder before the bank or mortgage company can issue some type of a Letter of Interest. Please note that the requested stacking order list will normally be much longer than a private money loan request and may have several code designations or numbers. These items for private or conventional loans may include:

Letter of Intent/Pre-Qualification Letter

1) Submission Form/Loan Summary (loan details, debt servicing, and borrower's "exit strategy" or how they plan to eventually pay back the loan)
2) Completed 1003 form and/or Personal Financial Statement
3) Property Photos or Recent Appraisal
4) Recent Credit Report

Non-Owner Occupied Residential Loans - Private Money

1) Submission Form (list desired loan terms and programs)
2) Completed 1003
3) Credit Report (90 days or sooner)
4) One or Two Years Personal & Corporation Taxes (if applicable)
5) Loan Summary/Letter of Explanation with exit strategy
6) Investment Properties - Rent Roll or Lease Copies
7) Copy of Signed Purchase Contract
8) Appraisal (or photographs and MLS sales comps)

* Please note that underwriters may analyze **gross income** from a residential or commercial investment property by taking the total rental income minus the vacancy or rental expenses.

Multifamily (5-plus Units) and Other Commercial Loans - Private Money

1) Submission Form
2) Completed 1003
3) Credit Report (90 days or sooner)
4) One or Two Year Personal & Corporate Taxes (if applicable)
5) Loan Summary/Letter of Explanation with exit strategy
6) Rent Roll or Lease Copies
7) Copy of Signed Purchase Contract
8) Appraisal (or photographs and MLS sales comps)
9) Year-to-date Balance Sheet (net worth) & Profit and Loss Statement

New Construction or Remodel Loans - Private and Bank

1) The first nine items listed above (if applicable)
Plus:
2) Construction Costs Breakdown Sheet
3) Construction Draw Schedule (amounts and dates for the funds needed)
4) Contractor's Resume

Conventional, FHA, & VA Loans

1) FHA Case Number Assignment (if applicable)
2) FHA Streamline Worksheet or VA IRRRL (if applicable)
3) Original FHA / VA 92900
4) Original VA Certificate of Eligibility
5) 1008, Mortgage Credit Analysis Worksheet (MCAW), or VA Loan Analysis
6) Completed 1003 form
7) Credit LOE (letter of explanation)
8) Credit Report
9) Bankruptcy Papers (if applicable)
10) Divorce Decree (if applicable)
11) Verification of Employment (VOE)
12) Pay Stubs (30 days or sooner)
13) 2 Years W2's and/or Tax Returns
14) Lease Agreements (if applicable)
15) Additional Misc. Income Sources
16) Last 2 months' Bank Statements (all pages)
17) Last 2 months' Investment Statements (all pages)
18) Last 2 months' Pension Statements (all pages)
19) Gift letter for purchases
20) Copy of HUD-1 or Closing Disclosure statement from past home sale
21) Other source of funds information

22) Verification of deposits (VOD)

23) Purchase contract

24) Signed payoff demand letters for all mortgages to be refinanced

25) Preliminary Title Report

26) Hazard Insurance (lenders want to see proof of a one-year policy)

27) Closing Doc Order Form

28) Initial Loan Estimate

29) Any additional signed disclosure forms

30) Signed 4506-T form for tax return verification

31) Borrower's Authorization

California Foreclosure Trends

By sheer numbers, California has had literally millions of foreclosures since the official start of the Credit Crisis back in the summer of 2007 to 2008. A person is most likely to walk away from their home if it is "upside down," where the mortgage debt exceeds the current market value. Fortunately, home values have rebounded and skyrocketed in several regions of the state. As a result of the improve equity gains, more distressed property owners were able to refinance their more expensive mortgages with lower rates or sell the property and walk away with an actual positive cash gain.

Millions of properties have been foreclosed in California over the past 10 or 20 years. With a population base approaching 40 million residents as of 2018, California has more properties and mortgage loans than any other state in the union. Even during positive economic time periods, there may be tens of thousands of properties foreclosed in the state each year.

During the depths of the worst foreclosure years in the state as well as in some of the other "bubble" states (where the prices rose too quickly in prior years before the values burst) like Nevada, Arizona, and Florida, there were many lenders who refused to issue foreclosure notices because they already had thousands or tens of thousands of nonperforming or delinquent mortgages on their financial books. Many of the largest commercial banks are publicly traded on Wall Street.

Some banking officials were worried that their stock-share prices might drop too much if their investors and banking customers really understood the severity of the bank's declining mortgage portfolio, so they kept postponing the filing of foreclosure notices for months or even years.

Between 2009 and 2013, it was a common strategy for banks to offer cash to delinquent mortgage borrowers in exchange for the keys to the home and the signing of a quitclaim deed from the property owner back over to the lending bank. These "cash for keys" programs might have generated upwards of $5,000 to $25,000 for the property owner who hadn't made a mortgage payment in months or several years in exchange for the owner to vacate the property without damaging the home and stealing valuable kitchen appliances or lighting systems.

In California during normal market times, the main steps in the foreclosure process are as follows:

First, the lender sends out warning letters to their borrower after they have missed one or two mortgage payments.

Second, the lender files a **Notice of Default (NOD)** filing that is served upon the borrower at their home. This notice officially notifies the borrower that the foreclosure process has formally begun.

Third, the lender files a **Notice of Trustee's Sale (NTS)** ninety (90) days after the NOD was filed if the loan hasn't been cured or reinstated by the borrower. The Notice of Trustee's Sale gives a proposed date and time for the scheduled foreclosure auction sale. The lender will publicly post and advertise this foreclosure auction at least once in a local legal newspaper for three consecutive weeks (or 21 days).

Fourth, the auction sale will be held on the court steps of a government building, at a title company, or somewhere else. The lender will set a minimum bid that includes the most recent mortgage principal balance plus unpaid back interest, missed mortgage payments, late fees, trustee and legal fees, and any other fees. The auctioneer will start the bidding at this minimum dollar amount established by the lender. If no investor shows up with a cashier's check (or some other type of solid proof of funds), then the property will revert back to the lender as they become the official owner of the property.

Fifth, the lender will work with the local court and Sheriff's office to initiate an eviction process that involves the previous homeowner. An official from the local Sheriff's department will literally knock on the former owner's door and politely ask them to vacate the property that day or shortly thereafter. If the former owner refuses, the Sheriff has the legal right to physically remove the occupant from the property.

The foreclosure rates have slowed down considerably in recent years in California. As of November 2017, there is now one foreclosure filing for every 2,249 open mortgages, per *RealtyTrac* (www.realtytrac.com). The top five counties in the state with the highest percentage of foreclosure filings were as follows:

San Joaquin - 1 in every 850
Madera - 1 in every 949
Riverside - 1 in every 1,043
Shasta - 1 in every 1,076
Sierra - 1 in every 1,128

Chapter Ten Summary

- The **mortgage broker** (also referred to as the **loan originator**) is responsible for finding new loan prospects either on their own or by way of referrals from real estate agents, online sources, accountants, attorneys, wealth advisors, and other business professionals.

- The main document used in the residential loan application process is the **Form 1003 (Uniform Residential Loan Application)**.

- The borrower will likely sign a **Verification of Deposit (VOD)** form that gives the mortgage company the legal authority to verify the latest and past banking, investment, and pension deposits.

- Employment is verified by the signing of the **Verification of Employment (VOE)** form.

- The **Equal Credit Opportunity Act** prohibits lenders from discrimination against loan applicants because some, most, or all of their income comes from sources other than part or full-time jobs. These sources may include government assistance programs such as welfare, food stamps, and social security.

- The borrower's signed **4506-T (Request for Transcript of Tax Return)** form grants authority to the lender to verify the validity of the applicant's submitted tax documents.

- A borrower's credit report is usually based upon a low-to-high **FICO** score range between 300 and 850. The three main credit reporting agencies are Experian, TransUnion, and Equifax.

- Both primary and secondary-market investors will probably use some type of **automated underwriting (AU)** system along with a human underwriter before approving or denying a loan request.

- A **debt-to-income (DTI) ratio** measures a borrower's monthly debt obligations that include the proposed new mortgage loan payments against the applicant's monthly gross income. The lower the DTI numbers, the more likely the lender will approve the loan request.

- The three stages in the California foreclosure process include: 1) the Notice of Default; 2) the Notice of Trustee's Sale; and 3) the Trustee's Sale (final

- auction). It generally takes at least 111 days from start to finish in the foreclosure process.

Chapter Ten Quiz

1. What is another name for the Uniform Residential Loan Application?
   A. Truth-in-Lending Statement
   B. TRID
   C. 1003
   D. Automated Underwriting

2. What group(s) approved the Uniform Residential Loan Application for wide distribution across the nation?
   A. Dodd-Frank
   B. Fannie Mae
   C. Freddie Mac
   D. Both B and C

3. Which section of the loan application includes a series of questions with "Yes" or "No" answers that are associated with issues such as past or current judgments, lawsuits, or delinquent or defaulted government debt?
   A. Acknowledgement and Agreement
   B. Declarations
   C. Borrower Information
   D. Instructions

4. What underwriter form is used to confirm a customer's bank account balance?

    A. Verification of Balance

    B. Verification of Deposits

    C. Financial Asset Review form

    D. Verification of Funds

5. What federal law prohibits lenders from discriminating against loan applicants because some, most, or all of their income comes from sources other than part or full-time jobs such as public assistance programs (welfare, food stamps, and social security income)?

    A. Fair Housing Act

    B. Fair Lending Act

    C. Equal Credit Opportunity Act

    D. Glass-Steagall Act

6. To confirm spousal or child support income for a divorced applicant, a mortgage underwriter or loan officer may request a copy of what document?

    A. Former spouse's tax returns

    B. Divorce decree

    C. Form 3701

    D. Borrower's tax returns dating back five (5) years

7. Which mortgage form will an applicant sign that gives the legal right to the mortgage company to order a credit report and verify bank assets and employment?

    A. 1099-MISC

    B. Verification of Funding

    C. Borrower's Authorization

    D. 1003 form

8. Which signed mortgage application form allows the lender to verify how authentic or valid the borrower's tax returns are for the years submitted?

    A. Form 1003

    B. Form 1008

    C. Form 2406-A

    D. Form 4506-T

9. What form does an escrow company send out when attempting to close out an older mortgage account on a property that is being sold?

    A. Demand for Payoff

    B. Verification of Balance

    C. Request for Closing

    D. Closing Statement

10. What is the lowest and worst FICO credit score possible?

    A. 600

    B. 500

    C. 400

    D. 300

11. What is the absolute highest FICO credit score possible?

    A. 850

    B. 800

    C. 750

    D. 700

12. What is the main credit factor that impacts a consumer's overall FICO score?

    A. Payment history

    B. Income

    C. Amount owed

    D. Credit mix

Answer Key:

1. C	6. B	11. A
2. D	7. C	12. A
3. B	8. D	
4. B	9. A	
5. C	10. D	

CHAPTER 11

LOAN TYPES AND MORTGAGE INSTRUMENTS

Overview

This chapter revolves around the many different types of mortgage-loan products available to consumers. Some of these loans are originated or backed by private institutions while others are directly or indirectly funded or held by government agencies. Over the past several years, conventional or conforming mortgage loans that used to traditionally differ quite a lot from more flexible FHA-insured mortgages are now competing for many of the same borrower prospects with much easier underwriting guidelines. Readers will also learn about the main types of mortgage instruments used in loan and real estate transactions such as promissory notes, mortgages, and deeds of trust.

Mortgage Loan Types

There are several different types of mortgage loan descriptions that are available for mortgage applicants and home buyers across the state and the nation. Between 2007 and 2017, the guidelines have shifted dramatically for obtaining many of these loan products from fairly strict to much easier in order to accommodate the higher monthly debt ratios that more Americans are faced with these days. Few states are more expensive to live in than California, so the loan limits are higher there than in most parts of the state. And they are certainly higher than most other areas of the nation. Thus, higher debt-to-income ratios may be allowed for borrowers.

Under RESPA (Real Estate Settlement Procedures Act), borrowers are to be provided with a special information booklet -- a Good Faith Estimate or Loan Estimate (new name) -- and a mortgage-loan servicing disclosure statement for every type of loan applied for at the start of the lending process.

Listed below are some of the most common mortgage categories used by lenders in California:

Conventional Loans

A conventional loan falls into two types of subcategories: **conforming and nonconforming loans**. Conforming loans follow the main underwriting guidelines established by Fannie Mae and Freddie Mac. These are the two largest government-controlled secondary-market investors in the nation with ownership or beneficial interests in at least 60% of all outstanding residential mortgage loans across the nation.

In the 1980s, '90s, and earlier years of the 21st century, most types of conforming loans required 10% or 20% down payments when the median home prices were quite a bit lower than they are today. The loans that were funded at 80% loan-to-value (LTV) or below did not have any type of PMI (private mortgage insurance) or MIP (mortgage insurance premium) that borrowers had to pay each month in addition to the principal and interest for the mortgage loan.

Most people would have considered a true conforming loan as one that required a 20% down payment, had no monthly mortgage insurance premiums, and was structured as an 80% LTV first mortgage loan. Once the primary lender funded and closed the loan, the loan was quickly sold off to either Fannie Mae or Freddie Mac. These types of loans that were typically created as 30-year fixed-rate mortgage, were usually priced at the best available 30-year fixed rates at the time because they were considered to not be very risky.

How times have changed in recent years. After the financial markets began to crumble in 2008, the U.S. government was forced to make tremendous changes to their underwriting allowances to handle more new purchase-and-refinance loans that helped millions of Americans get out of higher-priced subprime and Alt-A type credit mortgage loans. The new changes to conforming loan programs rapidly increased the size of the maximum loan amount and loan-to-value limits that have now reached as high as $729,750 in certain high-priced regions such as various coastal counties in the state. And LTV ranges have crept up to 97% of the purchase price or property value.

*What is the all-time high loan limit for a **high-cost** conventional loan at up to 97% LTV that was still purchased by Fannie Mae?*

Let's take a closer look at how much the maximum loan limits for conventional loans have changed as far back as 1980 for one, two, three, and four unit properties across the nation as determined by Fannie Mae:

Fannie Mae - Historical Conventional Loan Limits
(Excludes Alaska, Hawaii, the U.S. Virgin Islands and Guam)

Year	1 Unit	2 Units	3 Units	4 Units
1980	$93,750	$120,000	$145,000	$180,000
1981	$98,500	$126,000	$152,000	$189,000
1982	$107,000	$136,800	$165,100	$205,300
1983	$108,300	$138,500	$167,200	$207,900
1984	$114,000	$145,800	$176,100	$218,900
1985	$115,300	$147,500	$178,200	$221,500
1986	$133,250	$170,450	$205,950	$256,000
1987	$153,100	$195,850	$236,650	$294,150
1988	$168,700	$215,800	$260,800	$324,150
1989	$187,600	$239,950	$290,000	$360,450
1990	$187,450	$239,750	$289,750	$360,150
1991	$191,250	$244,650	$295,650	$367,500
1992	$202,300	$258,800	$312,800	$388,800
1993	$203,150	$259,850	$314,100	$390,400
1994	$203,150	$259,850	$314,100	$390,400
1995	$203,150	$259,850	$314,100	$390,400
1996	$207,000	$264,750	$320,050	$397,800
1997	$214,600	$274,550	$331,300	$412,450
1998	$227,150	$290,650	$351,300	$436,600
1999	$240,000	$307,100	$371,200	$461,350
2000	$252,700	$323,400	$390,900	$485,800
2001	$275,000	$351,950	$425,400	$528,700
2002	$300,700	$384,900	$465,200	$578,150
2003	$322,700	$413,100	$499,300	$620,500
2004	$333,700	$427,150	$516,300	$641,650
2005	$359,650	$460,400	$556,500	$691,600
2006	$417,000	$533,850	$645,300	$801,950

2007	$417,000	$533,850	$645,300	$801,950
2008*G	$417,000	$533,850	$645,300	$801,950
2008*HC	$729,750	$934,200	$1,129,250	$1,403,400
2009*G	$417,000	$533,850	$645,300	$801,950
2009*HC	$729,750	$934,200	$1,129,250	$1,403,400
2010*G	$417,000	$533,850	$645,300	$801,950
2010*HC	$729,750	$934,200	$1,129,250	$1,403,400
2011*G	$417,000	$533,850	$645,300	$801,950
2011*HC	$625,500	$800,775	$967,950	$1,202,925
2012*G	$417,000	$533,850	$645,300	$801,950
2018*G	$453,100	$580,150	$701,250	$871,450
2018*HC	$679,650	$870,225	$1,051,875	$1,307,175

* G = "General" conforming loan limits
**HC = "High Cost" conforming loan limits

The Economic Stimulus Act of 2008 temporarily increased the loan limits in certain high-cost areas like California. A short time later, the Housing and Economic Recovery Act (HERA) permanently changed Fannie Mae's charter designation to expand the definition of a "conforming loan" to include various "high cost" areas on loans that were originated on or after January 1, 2009.

The American Recovery and Reinvestment Act of 2009, beginning on January 1, 2009 through January 31, 2009, gave the power to Fannie Mae to purchase loans up to $729,750 for a one-unit dwelling (single-family home, condominium, townhome, etc.) in certain designated high-cost areas. A high-cost region was classified as one with much higher median-home prices than other portions of the state or the nation. In October 2009, Congress extended the $729,750 loan limit through the end of 2010.

The peak high loan limit amount of $729,750 was put into place for just a short time during some of the worst recessionary years as a way to stabilize the higher-priced housing market that had lost access to so many jumbo-type loan amounts that were over $500,000, especially for states like California. Once the housing market began showing signs of improvement and prices began increasing rather than decreasing, the $729,750 loan ceiling amount was adjusted downward as other lenders started making larger loans again.

The following year, in September 2010, Congress extended the high-cost loan limit to September 30, 2011. The "permanent" loan limits for HCAs (High Cost Areas) that were set by HERA went into effect on October 1, 2011 for loans that were purchased in 2011 and had mortgage-note dates that started on or after October 1, 2011.

A California "conforming" residential mortgage is one that falls within the maximum loan limits that are used by both Fannie Mae and Freddie Mac. These maximum limits were established by the Federal Housing Finance Agency (FHFA). Any loan funded in the state that falls below these upper loan limits can be sold off to Fannie Mae and Freddie Mac in the secondary market. Any loan that is larger than these conforming loan limits is considered a **jumbo** mortgage that cannot be sold off to the government-backed secondary market.

The maximum new high-cost loan limits for California in 2018 were announced on November 28, 2017. As of January 2018, here are the California counties that are deemed "high cost" counties for much higher loan limits for one-to-four-unit properties:

Maximum High Cost Conforming Amounts in California as of 2018:

1-Unit	2-Unit	3-Unit	4-Unit
$679,650	$870,225	$1,051,875	$1,307,175

These are the California counties below which qualify for the largest high-cost conforming loan limits as of January 2018 (subject to change):

- Alameda
- Contra Costa
- Los Angeles
- Marin
- Napa
- Orange
- San Benito
- San Francisco
- San Mateo
- Santa Clara
- Santa Cruz

Conventional loans

The easiest way to explain the difference between a "conventional" and a "conforming" loan is whether or not it is insured or backed by the federal government in some way. A **conventional loan** is a kind of mortgage loan product that is *not* insured by the federal government. The conforming loan limits have increased by several hundred thousands of dollars over the past 17-plus years. For example, the conforming loan limit was closer to $255,200 or less back on January 1, 2000.

Loan products that are insured or partly guaranteed in some form by the federal government include **FHA** and **VA** loans. A true conventional loan that is originated in California is from the private sector side of the mortgage industry that has absolutely no direct government backing.

Fannie Mae and Freddie Mac will even purchase second home and non-owner occupied residential loans from funding primary banks at slightly lower loan-to-value ranges that seem to continually change over the years (85% - 90% loan-to-value or combined loan-to-value). In the old days, Fannie and Freddie both preferred owner-occupied properties that were the primary residence of the borrower at loan-to-value ratios at or below 80%. After the government became the primary money source for residential loans after 2008, the underwriting approval process became much more flexible as the government strove to increase the availability of mortgage capital for many consumers.

Listed below are some of the highlights from the **Eligibility Matrix** issued by Fannie Mae for its affiliated banks that shows the types of loan products that are now acceptable enough for Fannie Mae to purchase in the secondary market.

The main acronyms and abbreviations used in this loan matrix are:

ARM: Adjustable-rate mortgage, fully amortizing
DTI: Debt-to-income ratio
DU: Desktop Underwriter
FRM: Fixed-rate mortgage, fully amortizing
LTV: Loan-to-value ratio
CLTV: Combined loan-to-value ratio
HCLTV: Home equity combined loan-to-value ratio

Transaction Type	# of Units	Maximum LTV, CLTV, HCLTV
Primary Home		
Purchase/		FRM: 97%
Limited Cash-Out Refi	1	ARM: 95%
	2	FRM/ARM: 85%
	3-4	FRM/ARM: 75%
Cash-Out Refinance	1	FRM/ARM: 80%
	2-4	FRM/ARM: 75%
Second Home		
Purchase/		
Limited Cash-Out Refi	1	FRM/ARM: 90%
Cash-Out Refi	1	FRM/ARM: 75%
Investment Property		
Purchase	1	FRM/ARM: 85%
	2-4	FRM/ARM: 75%
Limited Cash-Out Refi	1-4	FRM/ARM: 75%
Cash-Out Refinance	2-4	FRM/ARM: 70%

Over the past few decades, the acceptable debt-to-income ratios that Fannie and Freddie would consider for their conforming loan programs increased from low levels near 36% and 38% for back-end debt ratios to as high as 45% to 50% DTI levels (with recent rule changes made in 2017 and 2018). Several conforming loan products now have loan-to-value ranges as high as 95% to 97% of the purchase price with much higher allowable loan amounts. In recent years, conforming loans and FHA loans have begun to look more like one another since they both offer higher loan amounts in general and "high-cost" loan amounts in regions like the several expensive counties in California (discussed above). And now conforming loans and FHA loans offer down payment options at or near just 3% down payments.

Lenders and secondary-market investors like Fannie Mae and Freddie Mac take a great deal of financial risk by approving, funding, and later purchasing and holding mortgage loans in their portfolios at loan-to-value levels that exceed 80% at the time of funding. There have been some years in California when the median price levels for some state regions have fallen 5%, 10%, 15% or even 20% in just a year or two during turbulent economic times. The factoring in of closing costs to sell a listed home during a boom or bust economic time period (i.e., 6% commission fees to the buyer's agent and listing agent, title, escrow, inspection fees, and the payment of the documentary transfer tax fee) can really lower a property owner's true equity gains even more.

Just like with FHA loans which include monthly mortgage insurance premium (MIP) fees, the higher-conforming loan amounts that exceed 80% LTV levels were required to have private mortgage insurance (PMI) to help insure and reduce financial risks for the lenders and secondary-market investors.

The LTV amounts for Fannie Mae conforming loans that must have PMI are determined in the following ways:

- Purchase money loans: The value is the lower of the sales price or appraised value of the subject property being funded with a new mortgage.

- Refinance loans: The value that is established is derived from the appraised value, AVM (Automated Valuation Model), or other types of acceptable valuation methods.

The cost of PMI (private mortgage insurance) can vary on a year-to-year basis. In 2017, the typical private mortgage insurance premium cost somewhere between 0.5% to 1% of the **entire loan amount** on an annual basis. Mortgage insurance can be described as co-insurance, full coverage, and self-insurance. "No fault liability" coverage does **not** exist.

This PMI fee option would be much cheaper for borrowers if the PMI fee was based on the loan amount over and above the 80% LTV dollar amount up to as high as 95% to 97% of the purchase price or appraised value. If so, the borrower would be paying fees only on 15% to 17% of the loan amount (95% - 80% = 15%; 97% - 80% = 17%). However, lenders charge premium insurance fees on the entire loan amount that might reach up to the high $600,000 range in those high-cost counties in California that we have discussed.

For a $100,000 first mortgage loan in California or elsewhere, the 0.5% to 1% private mortgage insurance premium fees might equal up to $1,000 per year.

For loan amounts that are higher and more common in California, let's review how expensive these mortgage insurance premium fees can be for conforming loan amounts higher than 80%:

$200,000 loan = $2,000/year PMI
$300,000 loan = $3,000/year PMI
$400,000 loan = $4,000/year PMI
$500,000 loan = $5,000/year PMI
$600,000 loan = $6,000/year PMI
$679,650 loan = $6,796/year PMI

Some California homeowners may be able to write off the payment of the private mortgage insurance as a deduction on their tax returns if they meet the latest single or dual-income wage limits that are subject to change every so often. Unlike other types of insurance such as life or property insurance, there is no potential monetary gain for the property owners or their heirs. The lending institution is the sole beneficiary of the PMI policy. The proceeds are paid directly to the lender, mortgage loan servicing company, or the current secondary-market investor.

The PMI fees can be later waived or removed from the loan well after the loan has funded if the homeowner and/or an appraiser can provide the lender or mortgage loan service company enough solid new sales comparables that show the lender that the subject property has increased in value much higher than the original purchase price. If so, the loan-to-value range for the loan may have dropped from 95% on a $100,000 condominium purchase down to 80% LTV if the property appraises a year or two later for at least $118,750 (80% of this amount is equal to the original $95,000 loan amount).

An **80/10/10 piggyback loan** option is one way that borrowers get around the payment of monthly private mortgage insurance fees on their conforming loan amounts. The borrower will usually request an 80% first mortgage without PMI for a 30-year fixed rate mortgage. They will then seek out a concurrent second mortgage that represents 10% of the purchase price while coming in with 10% in the form of a cash down payment. The loan term for the second mortgage may be a much shorter duration over 10 or 15 years and at a higher rate due to the lender's risk taken by agreeing to fund behind the new first mortgage. Because the first mortgage is at 80% LTV or less, there is no PMI.

Here is an example of a $1 million dollar purchase loan for a coastal property in California:

Loan Amount	Loan Position	Rate	Monthly Payments
$900,000	First	4.75%	$4,694.83
$100,000	Second	6.00%	$843.86
Total Monthly Payments:			$5,538.69

Amortization Schedules: The loan terms or amortization schedules for the repayment of loans can vary greatly from five, seven, or 10 year-fixed to 15, 20, 30, 40, or even 50-year fixed. Or, the loan could be an adjustable-rate mortgage (ARM). The longer the loan term, the lower the monthly payment. However, a borrower will generally pay much higher amounts of interest over the life of a loan with a much longer term. Loans can be fixed for a portion of the loan terms prior to automatically converting to adjustable rate products (also known as **hybrid loans**). These loan terms may vary as well:

5/1 = Fixed for five years before later rolling into an adjustable-rate term
7/1 = Fixed for seven years before converting to an adjustable loan
10/1 = Fixed for 10 years prior to rolling into an adjustable loan

How do fixed and adjustable-rate lenders set their prices?

A 30-year fixed-rate mortgage will always remain priced at the exact same rate during the life of the loan. The 30-year fixed rate is usually set at the latest 10-year Treasury yields that act as the core rate for most 30-year fixed-rate mortgage products. Each time that the U.S. Treasury needs to raise funds, they borrow funds from individuals, institutions, and foreign governments through their Treasury securities offerings. The most popular types of Treasury securities that are offered to the general public include:

Treasury Bills: Loan terms of less than 1 year.

Treasury Notes: Loan terms of two, three, five, and 10 years. The 10-year note (also called a Treasury bond) is the most popular government investment offering. As the demand for 10-year Treasuries increases and the prices rise, the yields on these investments will fall. The **Treasury yield** is the return on investment, expressed as a percentage, on the U.S. government's debt obligations, or the interest rate that the federal government pays to borrow money for different lengths of time. The 30-

year mortgage rate will fluctuate daily up or down tied to the directions of the day's latest Treasury yield price trends.

Treasury Bonds: A true bond is issued for a term of 30 years. The investment offerings with the longest terms generally pay investors the highest rates for the risk that they are willing to take at the time of purchase.

On June 1, 2012, the yield on the 10-year Treasury note dropped briefly to an intra-day trading price. At the time, it was the lowest yield in 200 years. By day's end, the rate closed up just slightly higher at 1.47%. In recent years, it has not been uncommon to see some 30-year fixed mortgage rates offered in the high 3% or low 4%-rate range. Historically, fixed rates have ranged more from 6% to 8% over the past few decades, so the current rates are almost half of the more normal rates offered to borrowers.

The underwriter or the loan originator will typically confirm the day's best 30 year fixed rates with the client before locking in the loan term for 10 or 15 days. The client then must sign the loan documents that arrive at either the mortgage escrow, title or real estate company. The loan must fund on time within the rate-lock time period or the rate lock guarantee will expire, and the lender will have to draw up or create new loan documents after locking in the new rate that might be higher or lower than the previous rate.

It is the **Fed Funds Rate** that sets the pace for most types of adjustable-rate indexes. Shortly after the Federal Reserve will either increase or decrease this key short-term interest rate that affects both banks and consumers, other indexes around the country will move up or down as well. Adjustable-rate loan payments are likely to go higher than lower over the years, regardless of the index that is tied to the loan.

Some of the most common index rates selected for adjustable rate mortgages in California may be tied to one of the following underlying indexes:

- 1-year T-Bill
- 2-year T-Note
- 5-year T-Note
- Prime Rate
- 1-year Treasury Constant Maturity (TCM)
- 12-month MAT (Moving Average Treasury)
- 12-month MTA (Monthly Treasury Average)
- Cost of Funds Index (COFI) - National
- Cost of Funds Index (COFI) - 11th District (near California)
- LIBOR (London Interbank Offered Rate)

The two main rate numbers that borrowers and real estate agents should keep a close eye on when pricing the best adjustable-rate products are the **margin** and **index** rate. The margin is a constant throughout the life of the loan term and is equivalent to the bulk of the lender's profit margin. The index rate, in turn, is variable and changes based upon the type of underlying index that it is tied to for durations that may vary from as short as one, three, six, or twelve months.

Margin + Index Rate = Note Rate (or the true mortgage rate)

The adjustable-rate loan may be priced with starting and lifetime payment or rate caps that are based upon the lender's fixed margin rate plus the current floating index rate.

The lifetime cap, or the maximum ceiling rate that an adjustable loan can reach might be 5% or 6% higher than the starting true note rate (original margin + index rate). Borrowers with the best credit will usually qualify for loans that have lower margin and starting index rates than people with worse credit.

Here are examples of three different types of adjustable-rate loans:

Index Rate	Margin	Note Rate	Lifetime Cap
0.85%	3.0%	3.85%	9.85%
1.25%	3.25%	4.50%	10.50%
1.62%	3.35%	4.97%	10.97%

Qualified Mortgages (QM)

The Consumer Financial Protection Bureau (CFPB) issued guidelines on January 10, 2013 about both the **Ability-to-Repay** rule and the new **Qualified Mortgage (QM)** loan product that later took effect on January

10, 2014. To simplify these rules, they require mortgage lenders to consider their potential borrowers' ability to pay back the home loans before extending credit to them. If the lender does not underwrite these loans with the best interests of their borrowers in mind, the funding lender may be forced to buy back the defaulted loans at a later date from the secondary-market investor that purchased the loan or from other capital sources, *and* the borrower in default may have the legal right to file a lawsuit against the lender for offering them a loan that the borrower really should not have qualified for in the first place.

The QM loan products are priced as the best (or one of the best) 30-year-fixed mortgage products anywhere in the nation. Yet these stringent guidelines seem to go against the much more flexible guidelines offered by so many lenders for conforming and FHA loan products.

"Certain risky loan features are not permitted, such as:

- *An "interest-only" period, when you pay only the interest without paying down the principal, which is the amount of money you borrowed.*
- *"Negative amortization," which can allow your loan principal to increase over time, even though you're making payments.*
- *"Balloon payments," which are larger-than-usual payments at the end of a loan term. The loan term is the length of time over which your loan should be paid back. Note that balloon payments are allowed under certain conditions for loans made by small lenders.*
- *Loan terms that are longer than 30 years."*

Fannie Mae's general criteria/information that must be provided and that lenders must adhere to when offering a mortgage loan deemed a Qualified Mortgage and information that must be provided are as follows:

1. *The borrower's current or expected income or assets.*

2. *The borrower's income and employment status if the borrower is claiming to have employment income.*

3. *Monthly payments on the loan, including any possible changes if the interest rate is adjustable.*

4. *Monthly payments on other loans being made at the same time secured by the property that the lender is aware of.*

5. *Monthly costs of other mortgage-related obligations the borrower has, such as homeowners' association dues or property taxes.*

6. *Other loans and debts the consumer has, such as alimony, child support, or credit card debt.*

7. *The borrower's debt-to-income ratio.*

8. *Credit history.*

Fannie Mae criteria link:

http://www.fanniemae.com/portal/media/business/qualified-mortgages-121013.html

The maximum allowable back-end debt ratios for a Qualified Mortgage are **43% DTI (Debt-to-Income ratio)**. Per the Consumer Finance Protection Bureau, the amount of total overall closing costs are capped to represent 3% or less of the funded loan as noted below in the CFPB rules:

"For a loan of $100,000 or more: 3% of the total loan amount or less.
- *For a loan of $60,000 to $100,000: $3,000 or less.*

- *For a loan of $20,000 to $60,000: 5% of the total loan amount or less.*
- *For a loan of $12,500 to $20,000: $1,000 or less.*
- *For a loan of $12,500 or less: 8% of the total loan amount or less."*

FHA Loans

The most popular loan type selected for a purchase loan over the past ten years or so has been the FHA-insured loan. FHA allows lower FICO credit scores down to 580 to 620 (with multiple exception options) and higher debt-to-income ratio allowances that may exceed 50% DTI numbers. For borrowers with $5,000 in monthly gross household income, they may qualify for a new mortgage (plus all of their monthly debt obligations for car, school, and credit card loans) even if their back-end debt ratios reach $2,500 per month (50% DTI).

FHA loans are best known as loans that require only about 3.5% down payments. Most to all of the down payment funds can even be gifted by family or through some government grant programs. The seller, in turn, can provide credits towards most of the buyer's closing costs. A creatively structured FHA purchase deal might include cash down payments that originate from the buyer's own personal funds that are truly closer to 0% to 1% of the purchase price. In some ways, it can almost be like a VA mortgage loan that does allow zero down options up to 100% LTV of the purchase price. But unlike a VA loan, there is no requirement to work in the military or with the federal government to qualify for a new FHA loan.

Before all of the significant changes to conforming loans after 2008, there was a big difference between the much-more-flexible FHA loans as compared with the previously fairly conservative conforming loans. In many ways, conforming loan programs began to copy FHA loan products because these FHA-insured lenders were picking up most of the loans from new customers. Now it is almost hard to tell the difference between a conforming (not government insured) and an FHA loan.

There are 58 counties in California. The loan amounts will vary for FHA loan ceilings based on the median-priced homes for each region. Some counties will fall into the most affordable areas that have the lowest maximum loan amounts, while other pricey regions like Los Angeles County will be in the most expensive "high cost" regions. The other counties in the state that are not the lowest or highest-priced counties will have loan amount ceilings that fall somewhere in between.

Listed below are the **maximum** FHA loan limits for the most affordable counties in California and the most expensive "high cost" counties as of 2017:

Most Affordable California County Limits for FHA

The most affordable counties in California include these below:

- Butte
- Trinity
- Lassen
- Siskiyou
- Kern
- Modoc
- Shasta
- Glenn
- Kings
- Lake
- Merced
- Tehama
- Colusa
- Madera

The FHA loan limits for the most affordable counties in the state are as follows:

1-Unit	2-Unit	3-Unit	4-Unit
$294,515	$377,075	$455,800	$566,425

Most Expensive California County Limits for FHA

As discussed earlier, the counties in the state that are designated as the most expensive "high cost" county regions that allow the largest loan size limits include:

- Los Angeles
- San Francisco
- Contra Costa
- San Mateo
- Santa Cruz
- Orange
- Santa Clara
- Alameda
- Marin
- San Benito
- Napa

The FHA loan limits for the most expensive "high cost" counties in the state are as follows:

1-Unit	2-Unit	3-Unit	4-Unit
$679,650	$870,225	$1,051,875	$1,307,175

The Federal Housing Administration (FHA) loan is backed or insured by the federal government. The program came about near the depths of the Great Depression as a way to restore faith in the American banking system as well as a way to help more families get into their dream home. FHA usually charges two types of mortgage insurance premium fees that include (subject to change):

Upfront Mortgage Insurance Premium (UFMIP): It may be an amount equal to up to 1.75% of the base loan amount at the time of closing. For a loan amount of $100,000, this is equivalent to $1,750. For larger loans up to $600,000, this UFMIP fee would be $10,500.

Monthly Mortgage Insurance Premium: The borrower will pay a monthly fee to the lender or mortgage loan service fee **in addition** to the UFMIP fee that was collected at the time of funding and closing the loan (paid by borrower, seller, gifts, added to the original loan amount, or some combination of all four). If some or all of the UFMIP fee is rolled into the original loan balance, then the borrower will pay even more monthly MIP fees on the much higher loan balance.

The monthly mortgage insurance premium rates have changed a few times in recent years for FHA. This is partly due to the fact that the federal government has asked the FHA and VA to provide more loans to borrowers as a way to stimulate or boost the housing market. It is also because the FHA and conforming loans with private mortgage insurance (over 80% LTV is when these fee mortgage insurance fees are applied) keep battling for new customers with their similar maximum 96.5% LTV (FHA) and 97% LTV (conforming) programs by trying to make their loan products more affordable for new customers.

Borrowers should *not* have a delayed or delinquent mortgage payment for 30 days over the past year or for more than 60 days within the past two years of their private mortgage cancellation when asking to remove the PMI. This is true even if the current loan-to-value ratio is under 80%.

Listed below are some of the MIP rates for FHA loans that are amortized for 15 years up to a 30-year loan term as of 2017 pricing (subject to change), and then FHA loans amortized under 15 years:

Loan Terms Over 15 Years

Base Loan Amount	Loan-to-Value	Annual MIP
Less than $625,000	Less than 95%	80 bps[6] (0.80%)
Less than $625,000	Greater than 95%	85 bps (0.85%)
Greater than $625,500	Less than 95%	100 bps (1.00%)
Greater than $625,500	Greater than 95%	105 bps (1.05%)

---

[6]   bps = "basis points" or fractions of loan-amount fees in amounts written as one hundredth of one percent

A new FHA mortgage loan that was below $625,500 in size and had an original loan-to-value ratio of under 95% would be priced this way for monthly insurance premium (MIP) fees:

$625,000 loan x 80 basis points (.008%) = $5,000 per year

$5,000/12 months = $416.67 per month (MIP fees)

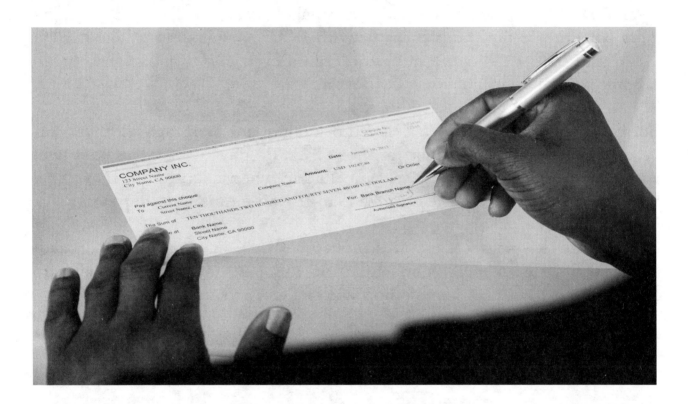

Loan Terms Under 15 Years

Base Loan Amount	Loan-to-Value	Annual MIP
Less than $625,500	Less than 90%	45 bps (0.45%)
Less than $625,500	Greater than 90%	70 bps (0.70%)
Greater than $625,500	Less than 78%	45 bps (0.45%)
Greater than $625,500	78.01% to 90%	70 bps (0.70%)
Greater than $625,500	Greater than 90%	95 bps (0.95%)

VA Loans

As of 2017, VA loan limits for single-family owner-occupied properties in the priciest counties in California reached up to $679,650 (subject to change). VA offers 100% LTV loans (or no money down) to active and former military and to surviving spouses. An applicant must provide a **Certificate of Eligibility** form that confirms that they are eligible to apply for a VA loan. An appraiser may hold one of the following licenses when appraising many types of properties: a **Trainee License** or a **Certified General License** that can be renewable.

VA loan products available do not require any upfront or monthly mortgage insurance like with FHA or conforming loan amounts that exceed 80%. This is surprising because the typical VA loan is at 100% LTV for purchase transactions. Fifteen and 30-year fixed rate mortgage loans are available. Many VA loan products prefer debt-to-income ratios somewhere in the low 40% range instead of the higher allowable 50% DTI levels for some FHA loans, and FICO credit scores currently are acceptable as low as 600 (subject to change).

The VA guarantees a portion of the borrower's loan amount for the lender which actually funds the loan. In the event of a future mortgage default and foreclosure, the VA will pay the lender a portion of their overall financial losses. The fixed-rate pricing is very competitive with other conforming loan amounts at much lower loan-to-value ratios in spite of the lender's higher risk associated with offering the loans at no money down. A VA-approved appraiser will provide a **Certificate of Reasonable Value (CRV)** for each property that will be funded with a VA mortgage.

Mortgage Instruments

The funding lender's main evidence of the loan debt is the **promissory note**. As discussed earlier, the promissory note is effectively a fancy version of an "IOU" for the original loan. The note includes the interest rate, borrower's full name and vesting, and the loan term. The promissory note is not normally recorded on public record as the deed of trust is at the time of closing. As such, it can be challenging for people besides the borrower and the lender to know the full details of the loan terms.

The one who makes the promise to pay the loan is called the **debtor**. The debtor/borrower is the **maker** of the note. The debtor promises to pay back the **creditor/lender** at some point in the future on or before the scheduled due date of the loan. The creditor/lender is also referred to as the **payee** while the borrower/debtor is the **payor** for the loan debt. The owner will use the property as security or the main collateral to guarantee the repayment of the loan, which is referred to as the **hypothecation** process.

Upon the closing of the purchase of a property, the owner can notify the public via **constructive notice** (the public should have known of the ownership change since it was of public record)[7] and by occupying the same property. The most **absolute** form of ownership interests for property owners is an **estate in fee** (**fee estate** or **estate in fee simple absolute**). The same owner has freedom to lease, sell, gift, or transfer interests to heirs (**estates of inheritance**) upon the owner's passing without any limitations. A **less-than-freehold estate** is generally defined as a lease held by a tenant.

A note can be a fairly brief and simple document, especially for some fixed-rate loans. Or, it can be several pages and fairly complex for many adjustable-rate mortgages because the explanation of how the underlying floating index (e.g., 11th District Cost of Funds or LIBOR) can change

---

[7]   The doctrine of constructive notice is generally regarding legal notices published, either by posting them at a designated place in a courthouse, or publishing them in a newspaper designated for legal notices. Because both methods of publication are available to the general public (courthouses being open to all members of the general public, and newspapers readily available in public places such as libraries), the person to whom the notice is being issued (even if issued in a generic form, such as "To All Heirs of John Smith, a Resident of Smith County") is considered to have received notice even if they were not actually aware of it.

over time might take up several paragraphs alone.

The promissory note will likely include the following key provisions:

- The names of the borrowers involved
- The total amount of the original principal or debt
- The interest rate (fixed or adjustable)
- The loan term or due date
- How and where the borrower shall make the payments and final payoff

Other details in the promissory note will likely include the lender's right to take action to foreclose on the mortgage debt if the borrower does not make timely monthly payments. Additional remedies or actions that the lender might take include the right to charge late-fee penalties or accelerate the loan as "all due and payable" (also referred to as an "acceleration" or "alienation" clause) should the borrower try to transfer title to another party who is not on the original loan or title.

A promissory note is generally deemed a **negotiable instrument**. The Uniform Commercial Code (UCC), which is included in various laws in all 50 states, sets forth some of the main rules or legal guidelines for negotiable instruments. The UCC defines a negotiable instrument as a written, unconditional promise to pay a certain sum of money either on demand or by a certain date. This type of negotiable instrument must be payable "to the order of" a specified person, business entity, or bearer just like a regular check that is written from a person's bank account.

A negotiable instrument is freely transferable. This means that the payee/creditor has the legal right to sell off a portion or the entire amount of the debt to another investor at any time it desires. Upon the sale and assignment of the promissory note to a new third-party investor, all rights transfer to the new owner of the negotiable instrument.

The new third party who acquired the promissory note or some other type of negotiable instrument in good faith with no notice to the borrower is referred to as the **holder in due course**. The original debtor/borrower/payor is now responsible to pay off the holder of the promissory note at some point in the future on or before the loan term ends.

A **homestead exemption** that is used by an owner-occupant for their primary residence may provide upwards of $75,000 to $175,000 equity protection from some debts, like certain creditor judgments, against which a home can be used to satisfy that judgment. The homestead exemption may still offer protection to the property owner even if requested after a judgment has been recorded as well as for newer mechanic's liens. (For this exemption to apply, the owner must be over the age of 65 and must earn less than $15,000 per year.)

An **easement** is the right to use another person's property or a portion of that property. An example might be driving across part of the land to reach another property. It can be held by a neighbor through mutual agreement. The easement does not usually run with the land (or stay with the property) upon the sale to a new buyer unless agreed to by the neighbors either ahead of time or at a later date.

A **standard coverage title insurance policy** will generally protect new buyers against risks associated with publicly disclosed items like easements, tax liens, and judgments. An **extended coverage title policy** (also known as a **lender's policy**) will provide the title protection as a standard policy plus offer some off-record risk protection regarding certain unrecorded mortgages, liens, and easements.

An **express easement** (or **easement by reservation**) is created by a written will or deed. A landlocked property can be accessed via an **easement by necessity** or some other kind of written or **express grant**.

An **encroachment** is where a property owner violates the property rights of his or her neighbor by building on or extending a structure onto the neighbor's land or property, such as a fence.

Mortgages

A mortgage is a two-party security instrument in which the **borrower/mortgagor** agrees to place his or her property up as collateral for a new loan. The lender who offers the loan to the borrower is called the **mortgagee**. The mortgage document must include the names of all parties involved with the transaction, the full legal description of the subject property and/or physical street address, and make a reference to the promissory note that the mortgage secures.

There are **covenants** (or agreement clauses) in a mortgage document in which the mortgagor/borrower fully agrees and promises to pay the property taxes, keep the property insured against fire or other hazards, and to always maintain the property in good condition. These covenants in the mortgage are meant to insure that the owner will take good care of the lender's source of collateral for the loan.

If the property burns down during a time when the property owner let their home insurance lapse, then the lender's collateral asset is greatly reduced from a home structure to just a land parcel. In situations like this, the $500,000 home that burned to the ground with a $400,000 first mortgage is now worth $50,000 (the land value). The lender might lose $350,000 if it is forced to foreclose and sell the land site after the home burns down.

Deed of Trust

The deed of trust (or trust deed) is used for the same purpose as a mortgage. The different ways to hold title to a mortgaged property is called **title theory** or **lien theory**. In California, most residential mortgage transactions are likely to involve a deed of trust. Three of the main elements contained in a trust deed include a date of execution, a reference to a promissory note, and a power-of-sale clause.

There are three main parties in a deed of trust transaction:

- The borrower is referred to as the **grantor** or **trustor.**
- The lender is called the **beneficiary.**
- The independent third party who holds the main mortgage documents on behalf of both the borrower and lender is the **trustee.**

DEED OF TRUST

:tions of this document are defined below and ot
and 21. Certain rules regarding the usage of wo

means this document, which is dated , toge

It is up to the trustee to help with the release of the lien at the time of the payoff by the borrower. The trustee will execute and issue a **deed of reconveyance** to the borrower once the entire loan has been paid off. The deed of reconveyance is the formal document that is proof that the property is now free and clear of any mortgage liens. Or, the trustee will assist with the filing of the foreclosure process if the borrower does not make his or her payments on time.

The trust deed includes a **power-of-sale clause** for the foreclosure filing process and an **assignment of rents clause** (a section that gives the lender the right to collect the rents during times when the mortgage payments are not paid). Personal property (also known as **chattel**) that is part of the real property sale may be sold using a **bill-of-sale** instrument. Food crops sold from a farmer's land are called **emblements** and are considered personal property once removed from the ground. A **package loan** may include a combination of real and personal property.

Land interests that are offered as loan collateral are defined as the land itself plus airspace, mineral rights, and water rights. Anything that is attached to the land is acquired by the buyer at the close of escrow. When lenders, investors, and tax agencies look at land, they will generally completely exclude land from future depreciation (or "wear and tear over time") calculations because dirt will still be just about the same dirt 10, 20, or 30-plus years from now as long as it is not flooded or severely damaged by earthquakes. Land can be shaped as 1,000 acre land parcels or by smaller lot parcels such as a cul-de-sac, key lot, flag lot, or corner lot.

Residential Investment Properties

Residential investment properties have a 27 ½-year depreciable life for tax, underwriting, and investment purposes. For a $100,000 home, for example, the land may be valued at $25,000 which makes the home value itself $75,000. The $75,000 home value is then divided by 27.5 years ($75,000 / 27.5 = $2,727 per year). This $2,727 is the number that represents that the building structure will either lose approximately $2,727 per year or need new maintenance close to that number for underwriting or tax purposes. The **operational expense** for a residential or commercial investment property includes the **capital improvements** made to a property as a way to modernize it or keep it in good shape with updated appliances, for example, or installation of air conditioning.

Junior Liens and Subordination Clause

The first loan that funds and is secured by a specific property shall remain in first lien position until paid off in full either with a future refinance or sales transaction. Any loans funded behind the first mortgage will be placed in second, third, or fourth position and are referred to as **junior liens** or **junior loans**. At a foreclosure sale, the trustee will pay off each lender in their priority of recordation.

Creditors who hold judgments on properties such as contractors or subcontractors who file **mechanics' liens** (or formal notices of unpaid fees due to them for their construction efforts) can adversely "cloud" (or negatively impact) a property owner's title on a home or commercial building. Typically, a creditor, like a contractor or judgment holder, will send out a **lis pendens** action notice that is public record to other potential buyers that there may be additional debt on the property besides the existing mortgage liens. If that occurs, it can severely impact the seller's ability to sell the property without first clearing up this negative title issue.

Often, a property will be "upside down" at the time of a foreclosure sale in which the mortgage debt, late fees, trustee's fees, and legal fees are much greater than the foreclosed or selling price of the property. Because of the risk factor associated with junior liens and the chance that they can be completely wiped out behind a first mortgage at a foreclosure sale, lenders generally charge more points and higher rates for second-mortgage loans. Additionally, loan terms for second loans are usually much shorter than a senior loan partly because the junior lienholder does not want the senior lien to "balloon" at the due date and foreclose.

Across the nation and especially in California, there are many investors or owner-occupants who purchase raw-land parcels or older homes that they plan on remodeling with new construction upgrades. In cases like these, there may be existing first mortgages on the property that will agree to subordinate to future construction loans if they are at low enough loan-to-value ratios.

Loans that confirm that the lender is willing to move from first to second lien position include a **subordination clause**. The brand new home or newly remodeled home that is built on the property will greatly increase the value of the property. Both loans on the property may later be at much lower loan-to-value ratios in some cases where the home value doubled after the completion of the home construction.

A **blanket mortgage** is a loan secured by two or more parcels is used in many real estate development transactions, such as a large loan secured by a development of 20 individual lots. A **partial release clause** that is included in some of these blanket mortgages will allow a partial release of the loan's collateral each time a significant or certain amount of funds are paid back by the borrower.

An **"or more"** clause in a mortgage allows a borrower to pay off a loan in full early or make larger principal payments. A borrower usually has a **grace period** in which they can make monthly payments a few days or longer beyond the due date without incurring any late fees.

A **reverse mortgage** is a type of insurance and mortgage hybrid product that older Americans use to pull money out of their home on a fairly consistent monthly basis. It is generally used by retirees or older Americans who still work part or full-time because they have low monthly incomes that need to be supplemented by the reverse mortgage income. The loan will be paid off when the borrower sells the home or passes away.

Land and other types of real properties can be described by a few different measurement methods such as **metes and bounds** (land and oddly-shaped properties, especially), **rectangular** or **government survey**, and **lot and block** with a recorded tract map (legal description). All types of properties are individual and unique as confirmed by their different legal descriptions or measurements. In a government survey method in California, the starting points to measure distances might include:

- The Humboldt Baseline and Meridian
- The Mt. Diablo Baseline and Meridian
- The San Bernardino Baseline and Meridian

For example, a **speculative developer** (or a "spec builder" who develops homes before they have a commitment from a buyer) has a $100,000 loan secured by 10 individual lots that are each valued at $20,000 and the individual loan amounts are estimated at $10,000 per lot (50% LTV). Each time that the builder finishes construction of one home, sells it to a new buyer, and the buyer's loan pays off the developer's loan (lot number one in this case), the partial release clause will remove lot number from the loan and reduce the $100,000 amount down to $90,000.

California Lending Programs

CalHFA: The California Housing Finance Agency (CalHFA) provides fixed-rate mortgage loans with very low down payment requirements for conventional mortgage products that include state-sponsored mortgage insurance premiums. CalHFA also offers some second mortgages that may eliminate the need for a California resident to even come up with a 3% down payment (or akin to 100% conventional financing with no money down). There are affiliate programs that may be available for some types of FHA and VA loan products.

Cal-Vet: This type of loan for military veterans or active duty service members is California's version of a VA loan with even better fixed rates and closing cost credits than federal VA loans. The main difference with the Cal-Vet loan is that the state of California will hold legal title to the property until the loan is paid off in full. The buyer, in turn, holds "equitable title" by way of a land contract (or contract for deed). Once the loan is paid off in full upon a future sale or refinance, the deed will be transferred to the owner who will then hold both legal and equitable ownership interests in the property.

Chapter Eleven Summary

- A conventional loan falls into two types of subcategories: **conforming and nonconforming loans**. Conforming loans will follow the main underwriting guidelines established by Fannie Mae and Freddie Mac. Fannie and Freddie own about 60% of the national residential market.

- Conforming loans used to be fairly low as compared with much higher California prices in amounts of a few hundred to the low $400,000 range. Over the past several years, the new **high-cost loans** in certain pricey counties in California and elsewhere reached up to $729,750 for 97% LTV loans.

- **The American Recovery and Reinvestment Act of 2009** gave the power to Fannie Mae to purchase loans up to $729,750 for a one-unit dwelling in certain designated high-cost areas starting in January 2009.

- Any loan that is larger than these conforming loan limits is considered a **jumbo** or **non-conforming** mortgage loan that cannot be sold off to the government-backed secondary market. Yet there are many private, insurance, and pension investors willing to purchase these larger loans.

- Loans that are insured or partly guaranteed in some form by the federal government include **FHA** and **VA** loans. FHA loan features include up to 96.5% LTV ratios while VA offers 100% financing for owner-occupied one-to-four-unit residential properties.

- FHA loans have **mortgage insurance premium (MIP)** fees that are paid by borrowers to insure the lender's risk related to providing loans over 80% LTV. Conforming or conventional loans that are not backed by or insured by any government agency may have their own **private mortgage insurance (PMI)** fees that borrowers pay for loans over 80% LTV.

- 30-year fixed-mortgage rates are tied to the direction of 10-year Treasury yields. Adjustable-rate mortgages are usually directly impacted by an underlying index tied to the Fed Funds Rate.

- The margin is the lender's fixed profit percentage rate + index rate = True Note Rate for an adjustable-rate mortgage.

- The CFPB's **Ability-to-Repay** rule requires mortgage lenders to consider their potential borrowers' ability to pay back the home loans before extending credit to them. If they do not, the borrower could later sue the lender, even if the borrower defaulted on the mortgage.

- The lender's main evidence of the loan debt is the **promissory note**. The promissory note is effectively an "IOU" for the original loan. The note includes the interest rate, borrower's full name and vesting, and the loan term.

- The one who makes the promise to pay the loan is called the **debtor**. The debtor/borrower is the **maker** of the note.

- A mortgage is a two-party security instrument in which the **borrower/mortgagor** offers the property as collateral for a new loan. The lender who offers the loan to the borrower is called the **mortgagee**.

- The three main parties to a trust deed include the **trustor** (borrower), **trustee**, and the **beneficiary** (lender). This is the most commonly used security instrument in California.

- Real properties may be described by a few different measurement methods like **metes and bounds**, **rectangular** or **government survey**, and/or **lot and block** with a recorded tract map (legal description).

Chapter Eleven Quiz

1. What is another name for a conforming or nonconforming loan?
   A. Federally-insured loan
   B. Loan guarantee
   C. Conventional loan
   D. Subprime mortgage

2. What is the all-time high loan limit for a **high-cost** conventional loan at up to 97% LTV that was still purchased by Fannie Mae?
   A. $417,000
   B. $525,000
   C. $679,000
   D. $729,750

3. Which agency sets the maximum conforming loan limits that will be purchased by Fannie Mae and Freddie Mac?
   A. HUD
   B. U.S. Treasury
   C. Federal Reserve
   D. Federal Housing Finance Agency

4. What kind of residential loans will Fannie Mae and Freddie Mac purchase in the secondary market?
   A. Owner-occupied home loans
   B. Second home loans
   C. Non-owner occupied home loans
   D. All of the above

5. Which mortgage product offers the smallest down payment option?
   A. Conforming
   B. FHA
   C. VA
   D. Jumbo

6. Which loan-to-value ratio is considered the riskiest for a lender?
    A. 96%
    B. 88%
    C. 75%
    D. 65%

7. Which debt-to-income ratio is considered the least risky for lenders?
    A. 28%
    B. 34%
    C. 43%
    D. 50%

8. What affects the directions of a 30-year mortgage rate the most?
    A. Fed Funds Rate
    B. 10-year Treasury Yields
    C. 1-year Treasury Bill
    D. LIBOR

9. Margin + Index Rate =
    A. Minimum payment
    B. True note rate
    C. Lifetime cap
    D. Principal amount

10. What is the maximum allowable debt-to-income ratio for a Qualified Mortgage?
    A. 28%
    B. 33%
    C. 43%
    D. 50%

11. What is the maximum FHA ceiling amount for a high-cost region in California as of 2018?
   A. $525,000
   B. $575,000
   C. $679,650
   D. $729,750

12. What is the maximum homestead-exemption amount that an older Californian with limited annual income can claim in order to protect equity in their primary home from certain creditors?
   A. $50,000
   B. $75,000
   C. $125,000
   D. $175,000

Answer Key:

1. C	6. A	11. C
2. D	7. A	12. D
3. D	8. B	
4. D	9. B	
5. C	10. C	

CHAPTER 12

SELLER FINANCING & CONSUMER PROTECTION LAWS

Overview

Commercial banks, savings banks, and private money lenders are not the only sources of capital available for the structuring of purchases or sales transactions involving real property. The seller financing of a property can be an exceptional option in a high percentage of real estate sales transactions if the seller has a fair amount of equity (difference between the sales price and existing mortgage debt) in the property and he or she has an open mind to creative financing strategies. These types of seller financing mortgage instruments include purchase money mortgage loans, land contracts, and the AITD (all-inclusive trust deed). Readers will also learn how older and new state and federal laws can make this type of sales strategy risky for both the seller and real estate agents involved if they do not follow the rules.

Seller Financing

The **capital gains** (or taxes paid on the home profits) can be payable over several years instead of in one lump sum by using an installment sale. Another tax deferral option for investment property sales transactions that can defer gains is the **1031-tax deferred exchange.** This is simplified as the deferral of capital gains if the property owner increases their debt, equity, and overall value when purchasing a new property within six months of the previous closing date for the old investment property. The investor must identify one or more potential investment properties within 45 days of the closing of the last property sale.

Upwards of 33% of all residential properties in the U.S. now are owned free and clear with no existing mortgage debt whatsoever. Of the other 66% of properties that have mortgages, a high number of these properties might have anywhere from 20% to 80% equity in the property after years of timely mortgage payments and the magic of compound growth associated with annual inflation rates.

The access to many different types of capital options might be the key to increasing the odds of a closed sales transaction. Not every buyer these days has sufficient cash reserves to even meet a relatively small 3% to 3.5% down payment plus closing costs, moving fees, and upfront prorated expenses for the first month's mortgage payment, homeowner's insurance, and property taxes. Many buyers also may not have debt-to-income ratios below 45% to 50% to qualify for any type of institutional mortgage, and some have FICO credit scores slightly below the acceptable limit for most lenders.

A seller-financed sales transaction effectively cuts out the middleman known as a bank or other kind of financial institution. Just like how the real estate crowdfunding platform industry has swept the nation by raising millions or billions of dollars' worth of capital directly from private investors online within a matter of just a few hours or days for new purchase and construction loans, seller financing is just a smaller version of this party-to-party funding solution. Both investors in crowdfunding platforms and sellers willing to carry a new first or second mortgage or structure some type of wraparound mortgage over existing loan debt may likely receive high rates of return that are better than most investment options these days.

Both banks and sellers can use a promissory note that is accompanied by a mortgage or deed of trust to finance the buyer's purchase. The buyer will take some type of title (equitable, legal, or both) and hold ownership interests in the property during the time that the buyer makes monthly payments to the seller as the borrower or **mortgagor**. The seller is the beneficiary or lender who is also referred to as the **mortgagee**.

These types of seller-financed deals in which the mortgage or deed of trust is handed by the buyer to the seller instead of to a third-party financial institution is often called a **purchase money loan**. It is the seller who is extending credit to the buyer as opposed to providing actual hard cash. The seller will usually finance the bulk of the purchase credit offered in installments over time instead of requiring that the buyer come up with all of the cash at the closing. Often, the seller will require that the buyer come up with some hard cash for a down payment at the time of closing as a way to make the buyer committed to the deal and less willing to walk away at a later date.

Seller-financing options become much more attractive to both buyers and sellers during times of tight credit or lending markets when lenders aren't as flexible with their underwriting decisions and/or mortgage rates are on the higher cycle. The faster way to close a sale is by using a form of seller financing rather than a bank loan. There are literally investors and sellers out there who have opened and closed sales transactions within the same day or over the period of just a few days by using creative types of seller financing methods. For some owners about to receive a foreclosure notice or in desperate need of some cash, they might be more willing to sell to a willing buyer who can close escrow within a week using seller-financing strategies rather than a buyer who needs up to 45 to 60 days for an FHA loan to close.

Sellers are more likely to receive prices well above market value at the time if they agree to finance a portion of the transaction for a buyer. No appraisals are required for a seller-financed deal unlike a bank loan. Buyers, sellers, and their respective real estate agents can work together to find the best sales comparables that are near the subject property before finalizing the price. A detailed **CMA (Comparative Market Analysis)** provided by one or both agents involved in the transaction can be helpful to both principals in the transaction when determining a mutually acceptable price. Yet it still might be wise for both agents to suggest to the buyer and seller that they chip in money together to appoint a neutral third-party appraiser for their expert value opinions.

After the exact purchase price has been determined, the buyer and seller must both agree to the amount of the down payment that the buyer must hand over to the seller. In some cases, the seller may agree to the receipt of personal property like a car or boat in lieu of cash. However, it is recommended as a safer strategy that the buyer actually gives the seller a decent amount of cash at the time of closing. It is also wise for the seller to order a copy of the buyer's credit report and even ask him to complete a 1003 loan application form that provides details about the buyer's employment status, income history, current assets, and whether or not he is a fairly good credit risk.

The buyer, in turn, should request an updated copy of a detailed title preliminary report prior to closing the transaction as a way to search for any unknown liens, judgments, or other types of encumbrances or easements that can adversely affect the property value. The buyer and seller should select an experienced escrow or title officer who can assist with the closing of the transaction as well as retain copies of the documents and grant deed that will eventually be formally signed over to the buyer upon completion of the seller-financed contract.

Most types of seller-financed deals are of a shorter duration or term. Many times, they have some type of **balloon payment** (a lump sum that is much greater than the monthly payments in the contract) that must be paid off in full at the end of the mutually-agreed contract. Several years ago, it was fairly common for sellers to offer seller-financed terms for as short as six months to two years. The seller financing was offered as just a short-term funding option that was beneficial for both the buyer and seller at the time.

The danger involved for the buyer who agreed to a one or two-year seller-financed purchase deal is that sometimes the buyer cannot find a lender who is willing to refinance the buyer out of the seller-financed deal. The lack of a formal credit history for a private mortgage or a deal that did not include a recorded deed transfer from the seller to the buyer made it appear as more of a **lease-option** (a rental contract with an option to purchase at a certain price in the future) deal. After the balloon date is reached, the seller has the legal right to file foreclosure and evict the buyer from the property.

Seller-Financing Options

Properties that are free and clear with no mortgages are usually the easiest properties to structure for new seller-financing methods. The buyer and seller will mutually agree to a down payment amount, the loan amount to be financed, and the length of the term for the new first mortgage. The promissory note will include the parties' names, the interest rate, the loan term, and any potential remedies for default such as the charging of late fees and foreclosure-filing notices. Both parties should seek legal assistance before agreeing to the signing of the note and deed for the property.

Occasionally, the buyer will qualify for a new 80% first mortgage from an outside lender, but he or she still needs the seller to carry some equity as a second mortgage (or **junior lienholder**) behind the new bank loan that will be placed in first lien position on the property (also called a **seller carryback**). Most lenders want any proposed second mortgages to have loan terms of at least 5 years so that the buyer is not at or near term risk for being foreclosed by the second lender. The first lender must review the proposed terms of the second loan while analyzing the rate, terms, and payments to see if the buyer's debt-to-income ratios do not move too high with the new debt. Some lenders may allow a CLTV (combined loan-to-value) up to 90% or 95% behind the 80% first mortgage. If so, the buyer will come in with just 5% or 10% cash down payment to close the deal.

An example of a concurrent 80% LTV/95% CLTV loan request is as follows for a $100,000 purchase deal:

80% First Mortgage (ABC Bank): $80,000 payable at 4% for 30 yrs

15% Second Mortgage (Seller Financed): $15,000 payable at 7% for 5 yrs

Required Cash Down Payment: 5% or $5,000

All-Inclusive Trust Deed (AITD): This is a type of "wraparound mortgage" in which the seller agrees to carry the promissory note and mortgage for the entire balance of the home price, less any down payment. The seller essentially "wraps" the new mortgage instrument around the underlying first mortgage that is still in the seller's name. A **property tax lien** for unpaid property taxes shall take priority over a first, second, or wraparound mortgage lien and be paid off first at any future sale or foreclosure action.

New buyers on wraparound mortgages or conventional purchase transactions may hold title to property as sole and separate, community property, joint tenancy (equal time, title, interest, possession), or in a LLC or corporation. A corporation will likely hold title to a property in severalty (or separate) as if the entity were an individual person. The same ownership rights apply, regardless.

There is a risk that the lender in first position could move forward with its own foreclosure filing notices for the violation of the **alienation clause** (the section of the seller's original promissory note that does not allow the deed to transfer or a change of title to the property without first paying off the loan that is still in the seller's name), ora violation of the **acceleration clause.** If the borrower violates any clauses found in the mortgage note, that could then make the loan "all due and payable" shortly thereafter. However, the odds are quite low that many lenders will actually foreclose as long as they are receiving monthly mortgage payments from any party. But the lender does have the legal right to file foreclosure for an unauthorized or approved deed transfer, so this risk should be formally disclosed to all parties involved in the transaction.

The interest rates charged for seller-financed wraparounds can be much higher than conventional bank loans partly due to increased risk. With a wraparound deal, the seller is receiving interest and principal spreads on both the underlying first mortgage loan at a lower rate and the new equity created in the AITD instrument. Often, there are few alternative investment options available that offer sellers a higher rate of return while the mortgage is secured by a fairly solid asset such as their former primary residence or rental property.

An example of a wraparound mortgage is as follows for a home sales transaction:

Sales Price:	$320,000
Seller's First Mortgage (XYZ Bank):	$240,000
Seller's Interest Rate:	4.25% (30-year fixed)
Seller's First Monthly Payments:	$1,180.66/month

The buyer's new wraparound terms will be as follows in this transaction:

Buyer's Down Payment:	$20,000
Buyer's New Wraparound Mortgage:	$300,000
AITD Wraparound Interest Rate:	7.5%
Wraparound Monthly Payment:	$2,097.64
Total Monthly Net Cash Flow:	$916.98*

* This is the net monthly profit that the seller shall receive each time that the buyer/payor makes his payment. The buyer will be required to pay all necessary expenses associated with the maintenance of homeowner's insurance, property taxes, and housing repairs.

Most mortgage borrowers remain in their loans for somewhere between five and seven years. Even without a balloon payoff amount included in this type of seller-financed loan, many buyers will want to eventually refinance the mortgage debt that is priced 3% to 4.5% higher than the best available mortgage rates these days. If and when the borrower is able to qualify for a conventional bank loan, the seller will receive the principal spread difference between the $300,000 wraparound mortgage and the underlying $240,000 bank loan that is still in the seller's name. If the buyer made payments for 5 years (60 months) prior to refinancing or selling the property, let's review below the potential cash benefits received by the seller over the course of this loan:

Down Payment Received:	$20,000
60 Months of Net Mortgage Profits:	$55,018.80 ($916.98 x 60)
Principal Difference Payoff:	$60,000 ($300,000 - $240,000)
Total Cash Gains for Seller:	$135,018.80

The transaction is usually handled by an escrow, title, or law firm. They will make sure that all of the documents are in place with the correct financial terms while holding the signed grant deed. Sometimes, the grant deed transferring the ownership interest to the new buyer is recorded concurrently with the closing of the AITD transaction. The risk for the seller is that the buyer has yet to pay all of the required installment payment amounts. If the buyer later defaults, the seller will file the three main foreclosure notices or stages (Notice of Default, Notice of Trustee's Sale, Trustee's Sale) in California to legally evict the defaulted buyer from the property.

Sellers and buyers in recorded or unrecorded types of seller-financed transactions should consider appointing a neutral third-party loan collection company to handle the wraparound payment receipt and the payment of the monthly bank mortgage to ensure that all parties are receiving a proper credit and debit each. If the seller collects the AITD payments each month but does not pay the underlying first bank mortgage still in his jor her name, then the bank could file foreclosure, wipe out the existing AITD contract, evict the buyer, and take back the legal and equitable ownership of the property.

Some of these third-party loan collection companies (i.e., an escrow, title, or accounting firm) may charge a small monthly servicing fee to collect and disburse payments to lenders or other designated third parties. These collection firms may automatically send the monthly profits to the seller's bank account each month. They may also send out the appropriate 1099 tax forms for interest income received for the seller and/or 1098 tax forms for potential mortgage-deduction allowances that the buyer may be legally entitled to if their accountant confirms that is the case. It is also wise to have a third party keep accounting records for both parties should any future legal disputes arise over amount of payments actually made.

Land Contract: It is also referred to as a **Contract for Deed**. The "land contract" designation can be a bit confusing because almost any type of real estate can be included in addition to just raw or improved land. A land contract differs from an AITD agreement in that the title to the property does not actually pass over to the buyer at the time of closing.

The buyer holds an "equitable title" interest in the property that is somewhat akin to a temporary shared ownership interest with the seller. The buyer is the contract **payor** while the seller is the **payee** in the transaction. A neutral third party will hold the seller's grant deed up until all required monthly payments and the full payoff amount have been received. At that time, the escrow or title company will record the grant deed that officially transfers all title or ownership interests in the property over to the buyer (**contract payor**).

Which party holds "equitable title" interests in a home under a land contract?

Seller-Financed Property Rule Changes

On July 30, 2008, President George W. Bush signed into law the **Secure and Fair Enforcement for Mortgage Licensing Act (the SAFE Act)**. The SAFE Act requires new licensing, education, and registration of loan originators, especially for owner-occupied residential transactions. On July 21, 2010, as previously discussed in this course, President Barack Obama signed into law the **Dodd-Frank Wall Street Reform and Consumer Protection Act (the Dodd-Frank Act)** which restructured the oversight of financial regulation and provided updated amendments to the Truth-in-Lending Act (TILA).

Both the SAFE Act and the Dodd-Frank Act directly affected conventional and seller financing to varying degrees as it relates to the principals and licensed real estate agents assisting them. While most real estate agents today should be aware of the massive changes made to the mortgage industry since 2008, the seller-financing marketplace has also been affected even though most sellers do not hold active real estate licenses.

It is very important for real estate agents to understand that the Consumer Financial Protection Bureau's **ability-to-repay rule** *also applies to seller-financed deals.* If the seller and his or her listing broker do not work together to thoroughly qualify the buyer as an acceptable credit risk who does have sufficient income and assets to meet the financial demands, the buyer may have the legal right to sue both the seller and listing broker for offering the loan product in the first place even if the buyer defaults on the promissory note and loses the property in foreclosure back to the seller. Yes, even if the buyer defaults and does not meet his or her financial obligations, the buyer still may sue the seller and listing agent for damages due to these new enhanced seller-financing rules that are related to the passage of the SAFE Act and Dodd-Frank.

The licensing of loan originators under California state and federal laws enacted pursuant to the SAFE Act while also meeting certain state and federal guidelines has been a requirement now for several years. HUD had published in previous years the final rules regarding the minimum federal standards that loan originators must meet before engaging in the mortgage origination business.

Unless a real estate broker or salesperson engages in the business of loan originations, they will not have to be licensed as a mortgage loan originator (MLO) with both the state of California and the Nationwide Multistate Licensing System & Registry (NMLS). A "loan originator" is one who takes a loan application from a party and negotiates the terms of the loan in expectation of some type of compensation at the close of the transaction. Remember, some seller-financed transactions will involve the handing over of a completed 1003 loan application, a credit review, and the negotiation of a new financial contract in which the seller must now confirm that the buyer is financially capable of paying during the proposed term of the contract under the ability-to-repay rule. As such, there are now a number of real estate agents engaging in the field of mortgage loan origination without an MLO license in hand. If so, this can be a violation of state and federal laws, and put the agent at risk for future fines by agencies and lawsuits by disgruntled buyers, even if a buyer later defaults on the mortgage payments.

The Department of Housing and Urban Development's (HUD) overall responsibility for the interpretation and enforcement of mortgage-loan origination laws was transferred to the Consumer Financial Protection Bureau (CFPB) on July 21, 2011. These laws that affect mortgage-loan originators exempt or exclude those business professionals who only perform real estate brokerage activities (brokers and salespersons) *unless* they are compensated by a lender, mortgage broker, or other type of loan originator (licensed or unlicensed). Because listing brokers and/or buyer's agents may be compensated by way of a real estate commission from the seller who is also the lender in a seller-financed transactions, a court or governing state or federal agency could rule that the agent was paid by a lender without holding an MLO license.

Title XIV of the Dodd-Frank Act took effect on January 21, 2013. This act states that no creditor is allowed to offer a mortgage loan without making a "reasonable and good faith determination that the customer has the ability to repay the loan." Sellers and agents should consider asking for copies of financial documents, credit reports, and a completed 1003 loan application for any type of seller-financed activity to avoid violating this "ability-to-repay rule." This one rule may be the catalyst or main cause for future potential license restriction issues and/or serious financial losses for real estate agents who do not closely follow these new Title XIV regulations.

An individual, estate, or trust that provides mortgage financing for no more than three (3) properties in any 12-month time period may be exempt from the designation as a mortgage-loan originator if they meet the following rule exclusion guidelines below:

1) The seller did not build the home (i.e., a contractor or developer of one or more properties in a subdivision);

2) The loan is fully amortizing and pays off in full during the life of the loan. (This one clause would have eliminated a high percentage of old seller-financed deals that were structured as amortized over 30 years, but due in one, three, five, or seven years. Most sellers want to be paid off sooner rather than later, which is why so many seller-financed deals had short balloon payoffs.)

3) The seller (and his or her real estate broker) have determined in good faith that the buyer is financially sound enough to repay the loan at some point in the future. The ability-to-repay rule might be more restrictive for individual sellers than for even more-flexible FHA loans, which allow lower FICO credit scores near 580 or 600, gifted down payments, relatively low cash reserves for buyers, and seller credits towards closing costs. There is yet to be a lawsuit won where a disgruntled FHA home loan buyer sued the federal government for approving a loan for property that the buyer later lost in foreclosure. Yet a buyer has the legal right to sue an individual or LLC (limited liability company) seller for offering them a seller-financed deal without sufficiently qualifying the buyer prior to closing the deal.

4) The loan has a fixed rate or is adjustable after 5 or more years. Any adjustable-rate mortgage (ARM) must have "reasonable" annual and lifetime caps.

5) The loan meets other underwriting criteria established by the Federal Reserve Board. Sellers, buyers, and real estate agents should visit the

Fed's various websites to learn about the latest rule changes that could change every so often.

Note that the real estate agents who assist the sellers who provide financing as lenders still might be classified as "unlicensed Mortgage Loan Originators" and subject to fines, license suspensions, or revocations, as well as future lawsuits. As such, licensees should make sure that the buyers can meet the minimal ability-to-repay rule guidelines and thoroughly understand the paperwork that they are signing before the deal closes.

Real estate agents who work on seller-financed deals should strongly encourage their clients to seek out third-party legal and accounting assistance before they allow their clients to sign on the seller-financed contract. Real estate agents may want to get something signed in writing by a buyer's accountant and/or attorney stating that they understand the risks involved with the purchase contract and that these same advisors consider the buyer financially qualified to meet the **ability-to-repay rule**. This way, an unhappy buyer down the road may be less likely to sue the seller and real estate agents involved because even their own financial and legal advisors thought that the buyers were solid, creditworthy buyers.

Buyers who agree to enter into a seller-financed sales contract with some negative credit issues on their credit reports should diligently work to improve their mistakes, errors, or actual past valid delinquency issues. Sometimes, FICO credit scores can jump 50 to 150-plus points in just a few months or less than a year by taking the appropriate steps to clean up the borrower's credit report. Once the credit is near solid A rating, the AITD or land contract payor can later refinance their more expensive mortgage into a much more affordable bank loan at a rate that is two to four percent lower.

Fair Lending and Consumer Protection

The **Equal Credit Opportunity Act (ECOA)** applies to individuals and businesses. This fair lending act was first enacted in 1974. ECOA was implemented in **Regulation B**, and gave the Federal Reserve Board the main responsibility of prescribing and implementing regulation. ECOA prohibits credit discrimination on the basis of race, nation of origin, gender, religion, marital status, age, or because the credit applicant receives some type of public financial assistance such as welfare, food stamps, or social security/disability income.

Mortgage lenders and other types of creditors may ask their borrower applicants for some of the person's racial, gender, and marital status details on the main application for "quality control" or internal office purposes. However, this personal information about the individual and their family members may not be used by the lender or creditor when deciding whether to approve the loan or credit request. The most important factors that creditors must review and analyze include income, expenses, debt-to-income ratios, and credit history.

When a borrower applies for credit, the lender or creditor must follow these basic ECOA standards:

- The lender may not discourage the credit applicant from applying for the loan at the start of the process or reject the application because of the borrower's race, religious beliefs, national origin, gender, or marital status.

- The marital status of a credit applicant should not matter to the lender if the borrower is applying for a separate, unsecured account. However, a lender may have the legal right to ask a loan applicant to confirm whether he or she is single, married, widowed, or divorced if the borrower lives in a **community property** state like California.

- The main questions that a creditor or lender may ask a loan applicant about their spouse if they are currently married include whether or not the spouse will be applying *with* the applicant, if the spouse will be allowed to use the account by way of signing authority or rights, and if the spouse's income, alimony or child support income from a former spouse will be used to help qualify for the new credit or loan.

- Creditors must consider most or all types of consistent and reliable public assistance income the same way as any other type of income such as part or full-time employment income. A lender may not discount the income received by a person due to factors such as gender. For example, a creditor cannot count a man's salary at 100% while discounting a woman's income to 75% because the young married woman is of childbearing age and may possibility quit work in the near future to raise children.

- A lender or creditor may not discount or refuse to consider income from part-time employment, pensions, annuities, social security, welfare, or food stamps. ECOA protects a person from discrimination based on his or her lower-income status or age.

- Lenders or creditors must consider any reliable and consistent alimony, child support, or separate maintenance payments as income. The creditor may ask for proof of this income by reviewing a final divorce decree and/or cancelled checks paid out over the past year.

The additional rights that borrowers have under ECOA when applying for new credit include:

- The option to apply for credit with a cosigner if both parties meet the creditor's underwriting standards;

- The cosigner may be a person other than a spouse;

- The applicant has the right to know within 30 days of filing a complete application why his or her application was accepted or rejected. (Some acceptable reasons for the rejection of a loan or credit application might include that the borrower's income was too low or the applicant hadn't been employed long enough.)

The Dodd-Frank Wall Street Reform and Consumer Protection Act of 2010 transferred the Federal Reserve's primary authority for ECOA over to the Consumer Financial Protection Bureau (CFPB). The Dodd-Frank Act granted new authority to CFPB to supervise the rules established by the Equal Credit Opportunity Act to ensure that individuals and businesses were in full compliance with these equal credit guidelines.

In January 2013, the Consumer Financial Protection Bureau restated the Federal Reserve's original regulations found at 12 CFR Part 1002 (76 Fed. Reg. 79442, December 21, 2011; CFR = Code of Federal

Regulations). The new amended Regulation B rules that were codified in the Dodd-Frank Act require creditors to provide mortgage applicants with free copies of all appraisals and other kinds of written property valuations that were created in connection with all credit applications to be secured by a new proposed first mortgage on a property. This amendment also instructs that all mortgage creditors must notify credit applicants in writing that copies of all appraisals will later be provided to them in the very near term.

Regulation B contains two basic core prohibitions against discriminatory lending practices under 12 CFR 1002.4 and Regulation B which include that:

- A creditor shall not discriminate against a credit applicant due to race, religion, marital status, and other protected classifications regarding any aspect of a credit transaction.

- A creditor may not make any oral or written statement in advertising or elsewhere to current or prospective applicants that would discourage a reasonable person from making or pursuing an application.

Regulation B applies to all persons who, in the ordinary course of business, regularly participate in the credit field and play at least some role in the decision making process. The term "creditor" includes a creditor's assignee (i.e., an investor in the secondary mortgage market) or a transferee (an individual who later purchases the credit or debt). For the purposes related to discrimination or discouragement, 12 CFR 1002.4(a) and (b), the term "creditor" also applies to a person who regularly refers applicants or prospects to creditors such as mortgage lenders.

Some of the most important rules set by **12 CFR Part 1002 (Regulation B)** include the following sections:

§ 1002.4 General rules

A. Discrimination.

B. A creditor shall not discriminate against an applicant on a prohibited basis regarding any aspect of a credit transaction.

B. Discouragement

A creditor shall not make any oral or written statement, in advertising or otherwise, to applicants or prospective applicants that would discourage on a prohibited basis a reasonable person from making or pursuing an application.

C. Written applications

A creditor shall take written applications for the dwelling-related types of credit covered by § 1002.13(a).

D. Form of disclosures

1. GENERAL RULE

A creditor that provides in writing any disclosures or information required by this part must provide the disclosures in a clear and conspicuous manner and, except for the disclosures required by §§ 1002.5 and 1002.13, in a form the applicant may retain.

2. DISCLOSURES IN ELECTRONIC FORM

The disclosures required by this part that are required to be given in writing may be provided to the applicant in electronic form, subject to compliance with the consumer consent and other applicable provisions of the Electronic Signatures in Global and National Commerce Act (E-Sign

Act) (15 U.S.C. 7001 et seq.). Where the disclosures under §§ 1002.5(b)(1), 1002.5(b)(2), 1002.5(d)(1), 1002.5(d)(2), 1002.13, and 1002.14(a)(2) accompany an application accessed by the applicant in electronic form, these disclosures may be provided to the applicant in electronic form on or with the application form, without regard to the consumer consent or other provisions of the E-Sign Act.

E. Foreign-language disclosures

Disclosures may be made in languages other than English, provided they are available in English upon request."

An example of a business professional who would be legally described as a "creditor" might include a real estate broker or salesperson and / or a person holding a mortgage loan originator (MLO) license. Any person who is found to be in violation of these credit discrimination acts can be faced with federal fines, lawsuits, and criminal prosecution. As such, it is critically important for licensed real estate and mortgage professionals to truly understand the basic guidelines for ECOA.

Fair Housing Act

The federal Fair Housing Act was enacted in 1968. One of the main purposes of the act was to protect buyers and tenants of dwelling units from seller or landlord discrimination. The law prohibits and makes it unlawful to refuse to sell, rent to, or negotiate with any person due to the fact that they are part of a protected class of citizens related to race, national origin, gender, disability or handicap status, religion, or familial status (a legal term that describes families with young children).

Under the Fair Housing Act, it is illegal for lenders, real estate agents, and others to do any of the following:

- refuse to provide details about a mortgage loan or credit option;

- deny a loan request based on discriminatory practices; and
- offer different terms or conditions to a borrower due to their protected class status.

Some of the most important text for the Fair Housing Act is listed below:

Fair Housing Act

"Sec. 800.[42 U.S.C. 3601 note] Short Title

This title may be cited as the "Fair Housing Act".

Sec. 801.[42 U.S.C. 3601] Declaration of Policy

It is the policy of the United States to provide, within constitutional limitations, for fair housing throughout the United States.

Sec. 802.[42 U.S.C. 3602] Definitions

As used in this subchapter--

> *(b) "Dwelling" means any building, structure, or portion thereof which is occupied as, or designed or intended for occupancy as, a residence by one or more families, and any vacant land which is offered for sale or lease for the construction or location thereon of any such building, structure, or portion thereof.*

> *(c) "Family" includes a single individual.*

> *(d) "Person" includes one or more individuals, corporations, partnerships, associations, labor organizations, legal representatives, mutual companies, joint-stock companies, trusts,*

unincorporated organizations, trustees, trustees in cases under title 11 [of the United States Code], receivers, and fiduciaries.

(e) "To rent" includes to lease, to sublease, to let and otherwise to grant for a consideration the right to occupy premises not owned by the occupant.

(f) "Discriminatory housing practice" means an act that is unlawful under section 804, 805, 806, or 818 of this title.

(g) "State" means any of the several States, the District of Columbia, the Commonwealth of Puerto Rico, or any of the territories and possessions of the United States.

(h) "Handicap" means, with respect to a person--

(i) "Aggrieved person" includes any person who--

(j) "Complainant" means the person (including the Secretary) who files a complaint under section 810.

(k) "Familial status" means one or more individuals (who have not attained the age of 18 years) being domiciled with--

The protections afforded against discrimination on the basis of familial status shall apply to any person who is pregnant or is in the process of securing legal custody of any individual who has not attained the age of 18 years.

(l) "Conciliation" means the attempted resolution of issues raised by a complaint, or by the investigation of such complaint, through informal

negotiations involving the aggrieved person, the respondent, and the Secretary.

(m) "Conciliation agreement" means a written agreement setting forth the resolution of the issues in conciliation.

(n) "Respondent" means--

(o) "Prevailing party" has the same meaning as such term has in section 722 of the Revised Statutes of the United States(42 U.S.C. 1988).

(2) a record of having such an impairment, or

(3) being regarded as having such an impairment, but such term does not include current, illegal use of or addiction to a controlled substance (as defined in section 102 of the Controlled Substances Act (21 U.S.C. 802)).

(2) believes that such person will be injured by a discriminatory housing practice that is about to occur.

(2) the designee of such parent or other person having such custody, with the written permission of such parent or other person."

The illegal act of **redlining** is also prohibited under the Fair Housing Act. Redlining occurs when a lender refuses to make a loan in a certain neighborhood due to racial or ethnic mix concerns. Examples may include when a bank refuses to offer purchase or refinance loans in an older downtown neighborhood that is comprised primarily of people of color or other protected-class members. Lenders might state that they are concerned about the future neighborhood values falling, so they will avoid funding loans in that specific region. Whether true or not at the time, the lender's concerns may become self-fulfilling prophecies in that values may actually fall due to such limited access for mortgage loans in the area.

Community Reinvestment Act (CRA)

The Community Reinvestment Act (CRA) is law enacted in 1977 with the intent to encourage depository institutions to help meet the credit needs of surrounding communities that were mainly located in low and moderate-income neighborhoods. This act was designed partly to offset redlining actions taken by lenders to avoid certain ethnically mixed neighborhoods. The Community Reinvestment Act requires federal regulators to review the records of each bank or savings bank to determine if it is lending in as many different types of neighborhoods as possible. This records assessment will then be used to further evaluate the applications for any future bank merger, branch openings, or new state or federal charter requests. Banks that were considered to be engaging in discriminatory lending practices would not likely be approved by federal or state regulators for future expansion plans .

Home Mortgage Disclosure Act

The Home Mortgage Disclosure Act (HMDA) became law in 1975. It created a new way for the federal government to monitor whether or not lenders were fulfilling their obligations by offering equal credit access to all members of their local community. HMDA applies to commercial banks, community banks, credit unions, thrifts or savings banks, and to independent mortgage companies. Lenders must submit annual reports to to the federal government outlining what types of residential loans they made over the past year, including purchase loans, home-improvement loans, and refinancing transactions.

The HDMA requires that each of these financial institutions maintain a detailed report in their office that must also be sent to federal agencies, and be publicly disclosed and easily accessible by consumers who are interested in seeing the results. This information must specifically include the details about the customer's race, gender, and family background if the customer has willingly agreed to include that information on their 1003 loan application. The Dodd-Frank Act transferred the HDMA rulemaking authority from the Federal Reserve Board to the Consumer Financial Protection Bureau on July 21, 2011.

Predatory Lending

State and federal banking regulators are keeping a close eye on financial institutions and mortgage brokers who knowingly take advantage of their borrowers by offering them high-cost loans with outrageously high rates and fees. Since the near financial implosion back in the fall of 2008, **negative amortization** loans (where the original loan balance can increase in size as the customer defers unpaid interest) were outlawed. Most types of short-term **balloon loans** (loans with one, two, or three-year due dates) have been made illegal in recent years as well. Additionally, many conforming residential loans for owner-occupants have their total fee and closing costs capped at combined levels as low as 3% as seen with certain **Qualified Mortgage** loans.

Lenders and real estate agents must work together to ensure that a client is truly qualified for a conventional, government-backed, private, or seller-financed loan. Both lenders and agents should think about the potential negative consequences associated with not properly following the **ability-to-repay** rule for consumers. If that $500,000 purchase loan might make the buyer's agent $15,000 in commission (3% rate) after the agent engaged in **predatory steering** (guiding a client to a more expensive property or loan so that the agent can earn higher fees), then the same agent may later end up being sued by both the borrower and federal agencies with a team of attorneys and regulators behind them.

The access to finance is usually the most important factor involved in the vast majority of real estate transactions. There may literally be tens or hundreds of different loan products available for a real estate agent's client. To make sure that the client is treated fairly and that no state or federal laws are being violated, real estate and mortgage agents should stay on top of the latest financial rule changes so that they are not jeopardizing their clients or their own personal real estate licenses.

Chapter Twelve Summary

- **Capital gains** can be payable over several years instead of one lump sum by using some kind of installment sale. These installment sale options can include new first or second mortgages, land contracts, and AITD (all-inclusive trust deed) transactions.

- A **1031-tax deferred exchange** can defer an investor's capital gains after the sale of one or more non-owner occupied properties if the same investors rolls the gains into one or more new properties within six (6) months of the original closing date. The property or properties must be identified within 45 days.

- A mortgage or deed of trust that is handed by the buyer to the seller instead of to a third-party financial institution is often called a **purchase money loan**. This occurs in various types of seller-financed deals.

- **All-Inclusive Trust Deed (AITD):** A "wraparound mortgage" in which the seller agrees to carry the promissory note and mortgage for the entire balance of the home price, less any down payment. The seller "wraps" the mortgage instrument around the underlying first mortgage that is still in the seller's name. The grant deed may or may not be transferred in the owner's name at the time of closing or later at the end of the installment sales contract.

- An unrecorded **land contract** can differ from an AITD in that the grant deed is not signed over to the buyer until after the seller's loans are all paid off.

- **The Dodd-Frank Wall Street Reform and Consumer Protection Act (the Dodd-Frank Act)** changed the rules for conventional, government, and seller-financed mortgage deals. All lenders and their affiliate real estate agents must keep a close eye on the **ability-to-repay rule** before closing a seller-financed transaction. Otherwise, the borrower may have the legal right to later sue the seller and the agents involved for offering him or her the loan in the first place.

- The amended **Regulation B** rules that were included within the Dodd-Frank Act made it a requirement that creditors provide mortgage applicants with free copies of all appraisals and other kinds of written property valuations.

- The **Fair Housing Act** was signed into law in 1968. The purpose of this law was to protect buyers and tenants of dwelling units from seller or landlord discrimination.

- **Redlining**, an illegal action under the Fair Housing Act, happens when a lender refuses to make a loan in a certain neighborhood due to racial discrimination.

- The **Home Mortgage Disclosure Act (HMDA)** was signed into law in 1975. It requires lenders to keep track of the type of loans they offer to their borrowers of various backgrounds, race, gender, and national origin. Each lender must provide annual statements to government agencies as well as make these details easy to find for consumers.

Chapter Twelve Quiz

1. Which tax is usually paid on the sale of a property where the owner takes all of the profits in the year of sale?
    A. Capital gains
    B. Installment gains
    C. 1031 deferral taxes
    D. Short-term taxes

2. A seller financed deal in which the mortgage or deed of trust is handed by the buyer to the seller instead of to a third-party financial institution is called a ____.
    A. 1031 exchange
    B. Purchase money loan
    C. Barter exchange
    D. Seller rollover

3. A second mortgage is also called a ____.
    A. Seller carryback
    B. Junior lien
    C. Primary loan
    D. Both A and B

4. Which type of sales transaction is the least likely to have the grant deed recorded from the seller to buyer on the original closing date?
    A. Purchase money loan
    B. Land contract
    C. AITD
    D. Conventional sale

5. Which party holds "equitable title" interests in a home under a land contract?

  A. Buyer
  B. Seller
  C. Trustee
  D. Payee

6. What lending guideline of the Consumer Financial Protection Bureau, that is related to sufficiency of the borrower's income to pay back the debt must a conventional bank lender follow before approving a loan?

  A. TRID
  B. Ability-to-repay rule
  C. Funding Verification Rule
  D. RESPA

7. Which group had the most power to enforce the Equal Credit Opportunity Act (ECOA) and Regulation B when it took effect in 1974?

  A. SEC
  B. HUD
  C. Federal Reserve
  D. FDIC

8. After the Dodd-Frank Act was passed in 2010, the primary authority for the Equal Credit Opportunity Act transferred to which group?

  A. HUD
  B. Federal Housing Finance Agency
  C. Consumer Financial Protection Bureau
  D. FDIC

9. Which act was passed in 1968 to protect buyers and tenants of dwelling units from seller or landlord discrimination?

  A. Equal Credit Opportunity Act
  B. Fair Lending Act
  C. Fair Housing Act
  D. Housing Assistance Act

10. What is the illegal act that occurs when a lender refuses to make a loan in a certain neighborhood due to racial or ethnic mix concerns?
    A. Steering
    B. Redlining
    C. Profiling
    D. Diversion

11. A mortgage loan with a relatively short term that includes a final payoff amount that is much larger than the other monthly loan amounts is called a ____.
    A. Fully amortized loan
    B. Partially amortized loan
    C. Interest-only loan
    D. Balloon loan

12. Which federal law requires that each financial institution maintains a detailed report in its own office that must also be sent to federal agencies and publicly disclosed?
    A. Home Mortgage Disclosure Act
    B. Fair Housing Act
    C. Fair Lending Act
    D. Equal Lending Act

Answer Key:

1. A	6. B	11. D
2. B	7. C	12. A
3. D	8. C	
4. B	9. C	
5. A	10. B	

Glossary

Acceleration clause: Provision in a real estate financing instrument allowing the lender to declare the full debt due immediately if the borrower breaches any of the provisions of the loan agreement. Also referred to as a call provision.

Accession: The process of manufactured or natural improvement or addition to property.

Accrued depreciation The difference in cost between the replacement value of a new building and its current appraised value. Depreciation which accumulates over time.

Acquisition cost: Amount of money required to acquire title to a property; it includes the purchase price as well as the closing costs, legal fees, escrow, service charges, title insurance, recording fees, and other such expenses.

Actual age: Number of years since a building was completed; also called *historical* or *chronological* age.

Ad valorem: Latin phrase meaning "according to value," referring to taxes assessed on the value of property.

ADA: Americans with Disabilities Act.

Adjacent: Next to, nearby, bordering, or neighboring (not necessarily in real contact).

Adjustable-rate mortgage (ARM): Loan in which the interest rate increases or decreases periodically to reflect changes in the cost of money.

Adjusted cost basis: A property's income tax cost basis, plus additional costs such as improvements and subtractions, such as depreciation in value.

Adjusted gross income Gross income with federal and state income taxes and Social Security subtracted.

Adjustment period: Time period between when the interest rate or monthly payment for an adjustable-rate mortgage is changed.

Administrative agency: Government agency administering a complicated area of law and policy, implementing and enforcing detailed regulations that have the force of law. For example, the Department of Real Estate is the administrative agency charged with regulating the real estate business.

Advances: Funds provided by the beneficiary to pay taxes to safeguard the lender's interest according to the trust deed.

Affirm: (a) To confirm or approve. (b) To make a sincere declaration that is not under oath.

After-acquired title: If a title is acquired by a grantor only after a conveyance to a grantee, the deed to the grantee becomes effective at the time the grantor actually receives title.

Agreement: Contract between two or more persons to do or not do a certain thing, for consideration.

Air rights: The right to unobstructed use and possession of the air space over a parcel of land. This right may be transferred separately from the land.

Alienation: The transfer of ownership or an interest in property from one person to another, in any way.

Alienation, Involuntary: Transfer of an interest in property against the will of the owner, or without any action by the owner (ensuing through operation of law, natural processes, or adverse possession).

Alienation, Voluntary: When an interest in property is voluntarily transferred by the owner to someone else (generally by deed or will).

Alienation clause: A security instrument provision giving the lender the right to declare the full loan balance due immediately if the borrower sells or transfers the security property; also termed as due-on-sale clause.

All-inclusive deed of trust: *See*: Wrap-around Loan.

Amenities: The features of a property that adds to the pleasure and/or convenience of owning it, such as a swimming pool, a beautiful view, a gym, etc.

Americans with Disabilities Act: Federal law mandating that public facilities must be accessible to disabled people.

Amortization, Negative: The adding of interest-not-paid to the principal balance of a loan.

Amortize: To pay off a debt gradually, with installments that include both principal and interest.

Annual percentage rate (APR): All the charges paid by the borrower for the loan (including interest, origination fee, discount points, and mortgage insurance costs), expressed as an annual percentage of the amount borrowed.

Annuity: Sum of money received in a series of payments at regular intervals (usually annually).

Anti-deficiency rules: Laws prohibiting a secured lender from suing the borrower for a deficiency judgment in certain circumstances.

Apportionment: A division of property or liability into proportionate parts (may not be equal parts).

Appraisal: An estimate of the value of a piece of property as of a specific date.

Appraiser: Person who evaluates the value of the property, especially a trained and experienced person who has expertise in this field.

Appraiser, Fee: A self-employed appraiser who is hired to appraise real estate for a fee, as opposed to an appraiser who works for a lender, a government agency, or some other entity as a salaried employee.

Appreciation: An increase in value; the opposite of depreciation.

Appropriation: Keeping property or reducing it to a personal possession, excluding others from it.

Appurtenances: Rights that go along with ownership of a particular piece of property, such as air rights or mineral rights. These are generally transferred with the property, but in some cases they may be sold separately.

Appurtenances, Intangible: Rights concerning ownership of a piece of property that does not comprise physical objects or substances. An access easement is a good example of this.

APR: Annual Percentage Rate.

Area: (a) Locale or region. (b) The size of a surface, normally in square units of measure, as in square feet or square miles.

Arranger of credit: A real estate licensee or attorney who arranges a transaction where credit is extended by a seller of residential property.

Artificial person: A legal unit, such as a corporation, treated as an individual having legal rights and responsibilities by the law; as distinguished from a normal being, a human. An artificial person is also called a legal person.

Assessment: Property valuation for taxation purposes.

Assessor: Officer responsible for determining the value of the property for taxation.

Asset: A thing of value owned by a person.

Assets, Capital: Assets that a tax payer holds, other than (a) property held for sale to customers, and (b) depreciable property or real property used in the taxpayer's trade or business. Real property is a capital asset if it is used for personal use or for profit.

Assets, Liquid: Any assets or cash that can be turned into cash (liquidated), such as stock in a company.

Assign: Transfer of rights (particularly contract rights) or interests to another.

Assignee: One to whom rights or interests are assigned.

Assignment: (a) Transferring contract rights from one person to another. (b) In case of a lease, the transfer of the entire leasehold estate by the original tenant to another.

Assignment of contract and deed: The instrument through which a new vendor is substituted for the original vendor in a land contract.

Assignor: Someone who assigns his rights or interest to another.

Assumption: Action by a buyer to take on personal liability for paying off the seller's existing mortgage or deed of trust.

Assumption fee: A fee paid to the lender, generally by the buyer, when a mortgage or deed of trust is assumed.

Attachment: Court-ordered seizure of property belonging to a defendant in a lawsuit, so it will be available to satisfy a judgment if the plaintiff wins. An attachment creates a lien in case it is real property.

Auditing: Verifying and examining records, particularly the financial accounts of a business or other organization.

Back-end ratio: The borrower's mortgage payments added to any other regular monthly financial obligations, divided by total gross income

Bad debt/Vacancy factor: A percentage deducted from a property's potential gross income to find the effective gross income, estimating the income that will probably be lost due to vacancies and non-payment of rents by the tenants.

Balance, Principle of: An appraisal principle which holds that the maximum value of real estate is achieved when the agents in production (labor, capital, land, and coordination) are in proper balance.

Balloon payment: A payment on a loan (usually the final payment) that is substantially larger than the regular installment payments.

Bankruptcy: (a) A condition resulting when the liabilities of an individual, corporation, or firm exceeds assets. (b) A court declaration that an individual, corporation, or firm is insolvent, resulting in the assets and debts being administered under bankruptcy laws.

Base line: Main east-west line in the government survey system from which township lines are established. Each principal meridian has one base line associated with it.

Basis: Figure used in calculating the gain on the sale of real estate for federal income tax purposes; also called the cost basis.

Basis, Adjusted: The initial basis of the owner in the property, plus capital expenditures for improvements and minus any allowable depreciation deductions.

Basis, Initial: The amount of the owner's original investment in the property: the cost of acquiring the property including closing costs and other expenses along with the purchase price.

Bearer: A person in possession of a negotiable instrument.

Benchmark: A surveyor's mark at a known point of elevation on a stationery object, used as a reference point in calculating other elevations in a surveyed area, most often a metal disk set into cement or rock.

Beneficiary: (a) One for whom a trust is created and on whose behalf the trustee administers the trust. (b) The lender in a deed of trust transaction. c) Someone who is entitled to receive real or personal property under a will (a legatee or devisee).

Beneficiary's Statement: Document in which a lender confirms the status of a loan (the interest rate, principal balance, etc.) and describes any claims that could affect an interested party.

Bill of sale: A document used to transfer title to personal property from a seller to a buyer.

Blanket mortgage: Mortgage that includes more than one property parcel as security.

Block: A group of lots surrounded by streets or unimproved land in a subdivision.

Bond: (a) A written obligation, normally interest bearing, to pay a certain sum at a specified time. (b) Money put up as a surety, protecting against failure to perform, negligent performance, or fraud.

Bonus: An additional payment, over and above the due payment.

Broker, Associate: Someone who is qualified as a broker and is affiliated with another broker.

Bundle of rights: The rights inherent in ownership of property, including the right to use, lease, enjoy, encumber, will, sell, or do nothing with the property.

Buy down: Discount points paid to a lender to reduce (buy down) the interest rates charged to a borrower, especially when a seller pays discount

California Fair Housing Law: Law that guarantees equal treatment for everyone in all business establishments, often referred to as the Rumford Act.

CalVet loans: State-sponsored residential finance program utilized to provide cheap home and farm loans to veterans,

Call: A specification that describes a segment of the boundary in a metes and bounds description; for example, "south 20° west 100 feet" is a call.

Cap: A limit on how much a lender may raise an Adjustable Rate

Mortgage interest rate or monthly payment per year, or over the life of the loan.

Capital: Money or other forms of wealth available for use in producing more money.

Capital assets: Assets held by a taxpayer other than property held for sale to customers in the normal course of the taxpayer's business. It also comprises depreciable property or real property used in the taxpayer's trade or business. Therefore, real property is a capital asset if owned for personal use or for profit.

Capital expenditures: Money spent on improvements and alterations that add to the value of the property and/or prolong its life.

Capital gain: Profit achieved from the sale of a capital asset. It is a long-term capital gain, if the asset was held for more than one year and it is a short-term capital gain, if the asset was held for one year or less.

Capital improvement: Any improvement so designed that it becomes a permanent part of the real property or that will have the effect of prolonging the property's life significantly.

Capitalization: A method of appraising real property by converting the anticipated net income from the property into the present value; also called the income approach to value.

Capitalization rate: A percentage used in capitalization (Net Income = Capitalization Rate x Value). It is the rate believed to represent the proper relationship between the value of the property and the income it produces; the rate that would be a reasonable return on an investment of the type in question; or the yield necessary to attract investment of capital in property like the subject property. It is also called the cap rate.

Capital loss: A loss that is a result of a sale of a capital asset. It may either be long-term (held for more than one year) or short-term (held for one year or less).

CAR: California Association of Realtors®.

Carry-back loan: *See*: Purchase money mortgage.

Cash flow: The residual income after deducting all operating expenses and debt service from the gross income.

CC&Rs: A declaration of covenants, conditions, and restrictions that is generally recorded by a developer to place restrictions on all lots within a new subdivision.

Certificate of discharge: Document given by the mortgagor to the mortgagee when the mortgage debt has been paid in full, acknowledging that the debt has been paid and the mortgage is no longer a lien against the property; also called a satisfaction of mortgage or mortgage release.

Certificate of eligibility: Document issued by the Department of Veterans Affairs regarding the veteran's eligibility for a VA-guaranteed loan.

Certificate of reasonable value (CRV): Based on an appraiser's estimate of the value of a property, it is mandatory for a VA-guaranteed home loan to be authorized; the amount of the loan cannot be more than the CRV.

Certificate of sale: Document given to the purchaser at a mortgage foreclosure sale, unlike a deed which is replaced with a sheriff's deed only after the redemption period expires.

Chain of title: Record of encumbrances and conveyances pertaining to a property.

Chattel: An article of personal property.

Chattel mortgage: Using personal property as security for a debt.

Chattel real: Personal property closely associated with real property. A lease is a good example.

Client: Someone who employs a broker, lawyer, appraiser, or any other professional. A real estate broker may have a client who is either is a seller, buyer, landlord, or tenant.

Closing: The last stage of a real estate transaction when the seller receives the purchase money and the buyer receives the deed with the title transferred to him. It may also be called a settlement.

Closing costs: Expenses incurred while transferring real estate in addition to the purchase price.

Closing date: Date on which all the terms of a purchase agreement have to be met, or else the contract is terminated.

Closing statement: Accounting of funds from a real estate purchase, furnished to both seller and buyer.

Cloud on title: A claim, encumbrance, or apparent defect that makes the title to a property unmarketable.

Collateral: Anything of value used as security for a debt or obligation.

Collusion: Agreement between two or more persons to defraud another.

Color of title: Appears to be of good title, but in fact, is not.

Commercial bank: Type of financial institution that has traditionally emphasized commercial lending (loans to businesses), and also makes residential mortgage loans.

Commercial property: Property that is zoned and used for business purposes, such as restaurants, or office buildings. Set apart from residential, industrial, and agricultural property.

Commission: (a) Compensation received by a broker for services provided in connection with a real estate transaction (normally a percentage of the sales price). (b) Group of people gathered for a purpose or a function (generally a governmental body, as in a planning commission).

Commitment: A lender's promise to make a loan in real estate finance; loan may be firm or conditional. (A conditional loan is based on fulfillment of certain conditions, such as a satisfactory credit report on the borrower.)

Co-mortgagor: Family member (generally) who accepts responsibilities for the repayment of a mortgage loan, along with the primary borrower, to help the borrower qualify for the loan.

Comparable: In appraisal, a property that is similar to the subject property and which has been sold recently. The sales prices of comparables provide data for estimating the value of the subject property using the sales comparison approach.

Comparative market analysis: Estimate of property value for appraisals based on indicators from the sale of comparable properties.

Condition: (a) A provision in a contract that makes the parties' rights and obligations depend on the occurrence (or nonoccurrence) of a particular event; also called a contingency clause. (b) A provision in a deed that makes title-conveying subject to compliance with a particular restriction.

Condominium: A subdivision that provides an exclusive ownership (fee) interest in the airspace of a particular portion of real property, and an interest in common in a section of that property.

Confirmation of sale: Court approval of a sale of property by an executor, administrator, or guardian.

Conforming loan: Home mortgage loan in which the borrower and real estate conform to Fannie Mae and Freddie Mac guidelines, with a lower interest rate than a non-conforming loan.

Conformity, principle of: This principle holds that property values are boosted when buildings are similar in design, construction, and age.

Consideration: Something of value provided to induce entering into a contract—money, personal services, love. Without consideration, a contract is not legally binding.

Construction lien: *See*: Mechanic's lien.

Consumer Price Index: An index that tracks changes in the cost of goods and services for a typical consumer.

Contiguous: Adjacent, abutting, or in close proximity.

Contingency clause: *See*: Condition.

Contract: A written or oral agreement to do or not do specified things, in return for consideration.

Contract, Land: A contract for the sale of real property in which the buyer (the vendee) pays in installments. The buyer obtains possession of the property immediately while the seller (the vendor) retains legal title until the full price of the property has been paid. It is also called the conditional sales contract, installment sales contract, real estate contract, or contract for deed.

Contract of adhesion: A one-sided contract that is unfair to one of the parties.

Contract of deed: *See*: Contract, Land.

Contractual capacity: The legal capacity to enter into a binding contract. A mentally competent person who has attained the age of majority is a person with contractual capacity.

Contribution, Principle of: An appraisal principle which holds that the value of real property is at its best when the improvements produce the highest return proportionate with their cost—the investment.

Conventional loan: A mortgage loan not guaranteed by a governmental agency, such as the Veterans Administration.

Conversion: (a) Misappropriating property or funds belonging to another (for example, converting trust funds to one's own use). (b) The process where an apartment complex is changed to a condominium or cooperative.

Conveyance: Transfer of title of real property from one person to another through a written document (usually a deed).

Cooperating agent: A member of a multiple listing service who finds a buyer for property listed for sale by another broker.

Cooperative: Building owned by a corporation, in which the residents are the shareholders. Each shareholder receives a proprietary lease for an individual unit along with the right to use the common areas.

Cooperative sale: A transaction in which the listing agent and the selling agent work together but for different brokers.

Corporation: Legal entity that acts via its board of directors and officers, usually without liability on the part of the person or persons owning it.

Correction lines: Guide meridians running every 24 miles east and west of a meridian, and standard parallels running every 24 miles north and south of a base line, used to correct inaccuracies in the rectangular survey system of land description caused by the earth's curvature.

Cost approach to value: One of the three key methods of appraisal. An estimate of the subject property's value is determined by estimating the cost of replacing the improvements, and deducting the estimated accrued depreciation from it while adding the estimated market value of the land.

Cost basis: *See*: Basis.

Cost recovery deductions: *See*: Depreciation.

Covenant: An agreement or a promise to perform or not perform certain acts (generally imposed by deeds). *See*: CC&Rs.

Credit arranger: A mediator between prospective borrowers and lenders negotiating loans, such as a mortgage broker.

Credit bidding: When the lender obtains a property by bidding the amount the borrower owes in a foreclosure sale.

Credit history: Credit accounts which demonstrate a loan applicant's past record of meeting financial obligations.

Credit report: Credit history of loan applicants compiled by companies in the credit reporting industry; used to determine creditworthiness.

Credit scoring: Evaluation method for assessing the creditworthiness of loan applicants.

Credit union: Financial institution that may serve only members of a certain group (as in a labor union or a professional association) and has traditionally emphasized consumer loans.

Damages: (a) Losses suffered by a person due to a breach of contract or a tort. (b) An amount of money the defendant is ordered to pay to the claimant in a lawsuit.

Debit: A charge or debt owed to another.

Debtor: Someone who owes money to another.

Debt service: The amount of funds required over a period of time to cover the repayment of interest and principal on a debt.

Debt-service ratio: A measure for debt service showing the proportion of gross income a debtor is currently using for housing payments

Declaration of Abandonment: An owner-recorded document that voluntarily releases a property from homestead protection.

Declaration of Homestead: A recorded document that creates homestead protection for a property that would otherwise not receive it.

Deduction: Amount on which income tax is not required to be paid.

Deed: Correctly executed and delivered written instrument that conveys title to real property (from the grantor to the grantee).

Deed, Gift: Deed in which there is no support of valuable consideration; most frequently listing "love and affection" as the consideration.

Deed, Grant: The most commonly used type of deed in California, it uses "grant" in its words of conveyance and holds certain implied warranties that the property is not encumbered and has not been deeded to someone else.

Deed, Quitclaim: Deed conveying any interest in the property that a grantor may have at the time of executing the deed, without warranties.

Deed, Tax: A deed that a buyer of a property obtains at a tax foreclosure sale.

Deed, Trustee's: A deed that a buyer of a property receives at a trustee's sale.

Deed in lieu of foreclosure: A deed given to the lender by the borrower (who has defaulted) to avoid foreclosure proceedings by the lender.

Deed of reconveyance: Once the debt has been repaid, the security property is released from the lien that is created by a deed of trust. The instrument used is called the deed of reconveyance.

Deed of trust: To secure the repayment of a debt, an instrument is used that creates a voluntary lien on real property. This lien includes a power of sale clause that allows non-judicial foreclosure. The parties to this deed are the grantor (borrower), the beneficiary (lender), and the trustee (neutral third party).

Deed restrictions: Provisions in a deed that set restrictions on the use of property. It may either be covenants or conditions.

Default: When one of the parties to a contract fails to fulfill one or more of the obligations or duties as enforced by the contract.

Deferred maintenance: Curable depreciations that ensue due to maintenance or repairs that were postponed and thus caused physical deterioration.

Deficiency judgment: Determination by the court that the borrower owes more money when the security for a loan does not completely satisfy a debt default.

Delinquency: Failing to make timely mortgage payments.

Delivery: When a deed is legally transferred from the grantor to the grantee, thus transferring title.

Demand: One of the four elements of value (other three being scarcity, utility, and transferability). It is a desire to own along with the ability to afford.

Demise: (a) Conveying an interest in real property via the terms of a lease. (b) Transferring an estate or interest in property to someone for a long time period, for life, or at will.

Department of Housing and Urban Development (HUD): Federal agency responsible for public housing programs, FHA-insured home mortgage loans, and enforcing the Federal Fair Housing Act. The FHA and Ginnie Mae both are part of HUD.

Depreciable property: Related to the federal income tax codes, it is property that qualifies for depreciation deductions because it might wear out and may have to be replaced.

Depreciation: (a) A loss in value as a result of physical deterioration, functional obsolescence, or external obsolescence. (b) Allocating the cost of an asset over a period of time for the purpose of income tax deductions.

Developer: Someone who subdivides land or improves land to obtain a beneficial use.

Development loans: Loans which finance the purchasing of real property and the accompanying buildings.

Disbursements: Money spent or paid out, usually on a construction schedule.

Disclaimer: Denying legal responsibility.

Discount points: Percentage of the principal amount of a loan that is collected by the lender or withheld from the loan amount when the loan is originated. This is done to increase the lender's revenue on the loan.

Discount rate: Interest rate charged when a member bank borrows money from the Federal Reserve Bank.

Discrimination: Unequal treatment given to people on the basis of their race, religion, sex, national origin, age, or some other attribute; prohibited by state and federal law.

Disintegration: Period of decline in a property's life cycle, when the property's current economic usefulness is ending and constant maintenance becomes inevitable.

Disintermediation: The rapid outflow of money from banks into financial institutions perceived to provide a higher rate of return.

Down payment: Portion of the purchase price of a property that is paid in cash by the buyer, generally the difference between the purchase price and the financed amount.

Due-on-sale clause: A provision in a trust deed allowing the lender to call the entire loan balance due if the borrower transfers title. *See*: Acceleration clause.

Dwelling: A place of living, a house or a home.

Earnest money: Deposit made by a real estate buyer demonstrating her good faith.

Easement: Right given to another person or entity to trespass upon property that is not owned by that person or entity.

Easement, Access: An easement that allows the holder of the easement to reach (and leave) his property (which is the dominant tenement) by passing through the servient tenement; also called an easement for ingress and egress.

Easement, Appurtenant: An appurtenant easement is a right to use an adjoining property. The one benefitting from the easement is the dominant tenement.

Easement by express grant: Easement that is voluntarily created in a deed, will, or other written instrument.

Easement by express reservation: When an easement is created in a deed by which the property is divided by the landowner, the servient tenement is transferred while the dominant tenement is retained.

Easement by implication: Easement that is created by law so as to provide access to a landlocked parcel of land.

Easement by necessity: Such an easement is most commonly implied in favor of grantees that do not have any access to their land except over the land owned by the grantor.

Easement in gross: Easement benefitting a person rather than a piece of land. There is a dominant tenant, without a dominant tenement.

Economic life: Time period when an improved property yields a return on investment apart from the rent due to the land itself; also called the useful life.

Economic obsolescence: Loss of value due to factors stemming from beyond the property.

Effective age: Age of a structure as its condition indicates and the remainder of its usefulness (as opposed to its actual age). Effective age of a building may be increased if maintained well.

Ejectment: Legal action through which possession of real property is recovered from someone who has illegally taken possession of it; also called an eviction.

Emblements, Doctrine of: Law allowing an agricultural tenant to enter the land for harvesting crops even after the lease period ends.

Eminent domain: Right of the government to take title to real property for public use by condemnation. The property owner receives just compensation for property.

Encroachment: Unlawful intrusion onto neighborhood property, often due to a mistake regarding boundary location.

Encumber: Placing a lien or encumbrance against the title to a property.

Encumbrance: Non-possessory interest in real property, such as a mortgage (loan), a lien (voluntary or involuntary), an easement, or a restrictive covenant that limits the title.

Entitlement: In terms of a VA loan, it is the amount of the borrower's guaranty.

EPA: Environmental Protection Agency.

Equal Credit Opportunity Act: Federal law prohibiting lenders from discriminating against loan applicants on the basis of race, color, religion, national origin, sex, marital status, or age, or because the applicant's income is generated from public assistance.

Equitable remedy: Judgment granted by a civil lawsuit to a complainant that is not an award of money/damages which could be an injunction, rescission, or a specific performance.

Equitable right of redemption: Real estate owner's right to take back property after default but before foreclosure, by paying all debt, costs, and interest.

Equity: Difference between the current market value of the property and the liens against the property.

Escalation clause: Provision in a lease agreement that allows an increase in payments on the basis of an increase in an index, such as the consumer price index.

Escheat: Reverting of a property to the state in case there are no capable heirs found.

Escrow: Agreement that a neutral third party will hold something of value (money or a deed) until the provisions of a transaction or a contract may be carried out.

Escrow agent: Neutral third party entrusted by a seller and purchaser to hold a something of value pending the fulfillment of conditions needed to close a transaction.

Escrow instructions: Directions that a party to a transaction gives to an escrow agent specifying the terms under which the escrow is to be conducted.

Estate: Interest held by the property owners, it may be a freehold or a leasehold property.

Estate at sufferance: Unlawful occupation of a property by a tenant after their lease has terminated.

Estate at will: Occupancy of real estate by a tenant for an indefinite period, which either party can terminated at will

Estate for years: Interest in real property that permits possession for a certain, established time.

Estate of inheritance: Estate that may be passed on to the heirs of the holder, as in a fee simple.

Estoppel letter: Document used in mortgage negotiations to establish facts and financial obligations.

Expenses, Fixed: Recurring property expenses such as real estate taxes or hazard insurance.

Expenses, Maintenance: Cost of cleaning, supplies, utilities, tenant services, and other administrative costs for properties that produce income.

Fair Credit Reporting Act: Consumer protection law regulating the disclosure of consumer credit reports.

Fair Employment and Housing Act: Civil rights law in California prohibiting all housing discrimination on the basis of race, color, religion, sex, marital status, national origin, sexual orientation, familial status, source of income, or disability; also called the Rumford Act.

Fair Housing Act: Also called Title VIII of the Civil Rights Act of 1968; federal law that makes discrimination illegal on the basis of race, color, religion, sex, marital status, national origin, sexual orientation, familial status, source of income, or disability for the purpose of sale or rental of residential property (or just land that may be used for constructing a residential building).

Fair market value: The price that a buyer and seller, willing but not compelled to sell or buy, would pay.

Federal Deposit Insurance Corporation (FDIC): Federal agency that insures accounts in savings and loans and commercial banks, bolstering confidence in the banking system.

Federal Home Loan Bank System (FHLB): Twelve regional wholesale banks that loan funds to FHLB members to bolster local community lenders.

Federal Home Loan Mortgage Corporation (FHLMC; Freddie Mac): Federally sponsored agency that buys mortgages on the secondary market, then bundles and sells them to investors.

Federal Housing Administration (FHA): Federal agency that insures lenders for the repayment of real estate loans.

Federal National Mortgage Association (FNMA; Fannie Mae): Federally sponsored agency that buys and sells residential mortgages, thereby enhancing liquidity in the mortgage market.

Federal Reserve (the Fed): Government body that regulates commercial banks and implements monetary policy in order to stabilize the national economy.

Federal Reserve System: Twelve Federal Reserve Banks, which make loans to member banks.

Federal Trade Commission (FTC): Federal agency with the responsibility for investigating and terminating unfair and misleading business practices; in charge of enforcing the Truth in Lending Act.

Fee: *See*: Fee simple.

Fee simple: Recognized as the highest form of estate ownership in real estate. Duration of this ownership is unlimited and can be conveyed in a will to the owner's heirs.

Fee simple absolute: A form of freehold ownership, not subject to termination.

Fee simple defeasible: A form of fee simple estate subject to termination in case of a condition not being fulfilled or if there is an occurrence of a specified event; also called a qualified fee.

Fee simple subject to a condition subsequent: Form of estate ownership that can only be terminated by legal action in case a condition is not fulfilled; also called a conditional fee.

FICO score: The credit scoring system used by most mortgage lenders to evaluate the credit worthiness of applicants for mortgage loans.

Finance charge: A fee charged for the use of credit; charges that are paid separately from the loan proceeds

Financial Institutions Reform, Recovery, and Enforcement Act (FIRREA) of 1989: Federal law that refurbished the regulatory system for savings institutions

Financial statement: Summation of facts that show the financial condition of an individual (or business), including a detailed list of assets and liabilities.

Finder's fee: A referral fee paid to someone who directs a buyer or a seller to a real estate agent.

First lien position: Mortgage or a deed of trust that has a higher lien priority than any other mortgage or deed of trust against the property.

Fiscal year: Twelve-month period that is used as a business year for accounting, tax, and other financial activities, in contrast to a calendar year.

Fixed disbursement plan: Financing arrangement in a construction project where loan proceeds are to be disbursed in a series of preset installments at different phases of the construction.

Fixture: Personal property that is permanently attached to land or improvements so that it becomes a part of the real property.

Forbearance: A temporary delay in foreclosure actions granted by a lender or creditor that postpones monthly payments

Foreclosure: Sale of real property by mortgagee, trustee, or other lien-holder when a borrower defaults.

Foreclosure, Judicial: (a) Sale of property as ordered by the court. (b) Lawsuit that is filed by a mortgagee or deed of trust beneficiary to foreclose on the security property of a defaulting borrower.

Foreclosure, Non-judicial: Trustee's foreclosure under the power-of-sale clause in a deed of trust.

Forfeiture: Failure to perform a duty or condition leading to a loss of rights or something else of value.

Freehold: Estate in land where ownership is for an indefinite length of time, such as a fee simple or a life estate.

Front money: Money needed to initiate a project, including expenses such as attorney's fee, loan charges, feasibility studies, and a down payment.

Functional obsolescence: Loss of value from causes within the property, excluding any due to physical deterioration.

Garnishment: Legal procedure through which a creditor acquires access to the funds or personal property of a debtor previously under the control of a third party.

General plan: Long-term, comprehensive plan for development of a community implemented through zoning and other laws; also called a comprehensive plan or master plan.

Gift funds: Money given by a relative (or a third party) of a buyer who himself does not have enough cash to close a transaction.

Good faith deposit: Deposit provided by a prospective buyer to the seller as evidence of his good intention of closing the transaction; also called an earnest money deposit.

Goodwill: Intangible asset of a business it acquires from having a good reputation with the public. Goodwill is generally as indication of future business.

Government National Mortgage Association (GNMA) (Ginnie Mae): One of the three main secondary market agencies, this federal agency is part of the Department of Housing and Urban Development.

Government-sponsored enterprise: GSEs are private corporations chartered and managed by the federal government. Secondary market agencies Fannie Mae and Freddie Mac are the most important GSEs in the real estate industry.

Government Survey System: System of grids made up of range and township lines dividing the land into townships, which are further subdivided into sections. Identification of a particular property is done through its location within a particular section, township, and range; called the Rectangular Survey System.

Grant: To transfer or convey an interest in real property through a written instrument.

Grantee: Person receiving a grant of real property.

Granting clause: Words in a deed that points out the grantor's granting clause.

Grantor: Person conveying an interest in real property.

Gross income multiplier: Figure multiplied by the gross income of a rental property to calculate an estimate of the property's value; also called the gross rent multiplier.

Gross income multiplier method: Way of appraising residential property according to its rental value; also called gross rent multiplier method.

Guardian: Person appointed by a court to manage the affairs of a minor or an incompetent person.

Guide meridians: Lines running north-south (parallel to the principal meridian) at 24-mile intervals in the Government Survey System.

Habitability, Implied warranty of: Warranty implied by law in every residential lease that states that the property is fit for habitation.

Hard money loan: Usually made by a private lender with a high rate of interest, the loan is backed by the value of the property, not the borrower's creditworthiness.

Highest and best use: Legal and physically possible use of a property that, at the time it is appraised, is most likely to generate the greatest return over a particular time period.

Holder in due course: One who has taken a note, check, or similar asset prior to it being overdue—in good faith and for value—and with no knowledge that it had previously been dishonored.

Holdover tenant: Tenant who keeps possession of leased property after the lease term has expired.

Home equity line of credit (HELOC): Credit account secured by equity in the borrower's home, enabling him to borrow up to a specified credit limit.

Home equity loan: Loan secured by a second mortgage on a principal residence, usually used for a non-housing purpose.

Homeowners association: Non-profit organization comprising homeowners from a particular subdivision, responsible for enforcing CC&Rs and managing other community affairs.

Homestead: Dwelling occupied by the owner along with any appurtenant outbuildings and land.

Homestead Law: State law providing limited protection to homestead properties against judgment creditor's claims.

HUD: *See* Department of Housing and Urban Development.

Hypothecation: Using real property as collateral for a debt without having to give up possession of it.

Impounds: Borrower's funds collected and kept in a reserve account by the lender.

Improvements: Additions to land property that are manmade.

Imputed knowledge: Legal doctrine stating that a principal is considered to have notice of information that the agent has, even if the agent never told the principal.

Income, Disposable: Income that remains after the payment of taxes.

Income, Effective gross: Measure of a rental property's capacity to generate income calculated by subtracting a bad debt/vacancy factor from the economic, rent-potential gross income.

Income, Gross: Total income of a property before making any deductions such as bad debts, vacancies, operating expenses, etc.

Income, Net: Income that is capitalized to estimate the value of a property. It is calculated by subtracting the operating expenses (i.e., fixed expenses, maintenance expenses, and reserves for replacement) of the property from the effective gross income.

Income, Potential gross: Economic rent of the property, the income the property would earn if it were available for lease in the current market.

Income approach to value: One of the three main methods of appraisal in which an estimate of the property value is based on the net income it produces; also called the capitalization method or the investor's method of appraisal.

Income property: Property which generates rent or other income for the owner, referred to as property held for the production of income in the income tax code.

Income ratio: Criteria used for qualifying a buyer for a loan, to find if his income is sufficient. The buyer's debt and proposed housing expenses should not be over a specified percentage of his income.

Increment: An increase in value, the opposite of which is decrement.

Independent contractor: Contractor who is self-employed and whose method of work is not controlled by another.

Index: Changes in the cost of money indicated in a published statistical report, which can be used to make adjustments in such areas as wages, rental figures, and loan interest rates.

Inflation: Decrease in money's purchasing power, measured by the Consumer Price Index; real estate is considered a hedge against inflation because it generally holds its value.

Installments: Portion of a debt paid in successive period, usually to reduce a mortgage.

Installment sales contract: Real estate purchase structured to be paid in installments with title retained by seller until all payments are made; also called contract of sale and land contract.

Institutional lender: A commercial bank, savings bank, thrift or insurance company that makes real estate loans

Instrument: Written document formulated to set the rights and liabilities of the parties; examples are a will, lease, or promissory note.

Interest: Money charged by bank or other lending institution for the use of money. Also, a partial degree of ownership.

Interest rate: Percentage of an amount of money that is the cost of using it, usually expressed as a monthly or yearly percentage.

Interim loan: A short-term loan made generally to finance construction.

Investment property: Property acquired for its capacity to produce income or anticipated resale value, such as office buildings or undeveloped land.

Involuntary lien: Lien applied against a property without the owner's agreement, such as unpaid taxes.

Joint tenancy: Ownership of a property interest by two or more parties, each of whom has an undivided interest with the right of survivorship (sharing equally with the surviving tenants in the interest of a deceased joint tenant).

Joint venture: Agreement to invest in a single property or business by two or more parties.

Judgment: A court ruling directing that one party is indebted to another one and setting the amount of indebtedness.

Judgment creditor: Party who has received a judgment from the court for money owed to her.

Judgment debtor: Party whom a judgment has been directed against for money owed.

Judgment lien: Claim upon the property of a debtor as the result of a judgment, enabling the judgment creditor to have the property sold for payment to satisfy the judgment.

Junior mortgage: Mortgagee whose claims on a property will be addressed only after previous mortgages have been settled.

Land: Earth's surface area that is solid, and not composed of water.

Land contract: Installment agreement for the purchase of real estate in which the buyer may use and occupy the land, without the passage of deed or title until all or a portion of the selling price is conveyed.

Landlord: Person, the lessor, who rents property to another person, the lessee.

Landmark: A stationary object that serves a boundary or reference point for a land parcel.

Late charge: Amount assessed by a lender against a borrower who misses making an installment payment when due.

Lease: Contract agreement in which an owner of real property, in exchange for the consideration of rent, passes the rights of possession to the property to another party for a specified time period.

Leasehold estate: Tenant's ownership interest in the property that is leased to her.

Leasehold improvements: Fixtures attached to real estate that are installed by the tenant and which can be moved by him after the lease's expiration, if their removal does not damage the property.

Legal description: Legally proper identification of realty by one of three agreed-upon methods: the government rectangular survey, metes and bounds, lot and block number.

Lessee: Person to whom property is rented under a lease; a tenant.

Lessor: Person who rents property to another person; a landlord.

Leverage: Using borrowed funds to raise purchasing power and enhance profitability of an investment.

License: Having the right granted by the state of California to work as a real estate broker or salesperson.

Licensee: Person who hold a real estate license, which conveys the privilege to accept compensation for helping with a real estate transaction.

Lien: Encumbrance against property rendering it security for the payment of a debt, mortgage, or other money judgment.

Life estate: Freehold land interest that terminates upon the death of the owner or other designated person.

Life tenant: Individual who is permitted to possess property for her lifetime or during the lifetime of another specified person.

Liquidated damages: Amount designated in a contract that one party will owe the other party in case of a breach of contract.

***Lis pendens*:** Recorded notice that the rights to the possession of real property is the subject of litigation, thus impacting disposition of its title.

Listing: Employment contract in writing between an agent and principal, authorizing the agent to conduct services for the principal regarding the principal's property. Also, a record of the property for sale by the broker authorized by the owner to sell it.

Loan origination, Retail: Loan processing done wholly by local banks and small-scale lenders.

Loan origination, Wholesale: Loans originated by mortgage brokers and mortgage correspondents who subsequently sell the loans to large, "wholesale" lending institutions

Loan origination fee: The cost a lender charges for originating a loan, usually in the form of "points"

Loan package: Documents considered by the lender comprising important information regarding the loan, such as property description, the agreed-upon purchase price, and sale terms.

Loan-to-value ratio (LTV): Ratio calculated by dividing the mortgage principal by the property value.

Lock-in: Agreement to maintain a certain rate or price for a specified time period.

Lot and block number: Method of land description that relies on the placement of recorded plats.

MAI: Professional membership in the Appraisal Institute.

Margin: Figure added to an index in order to adjust an interest rate on an adjustable-rate mortgage.

Marginal property: Realty that generates barely enough income to cover the cost of using it

Marketable title: Title that a court will assess as being free enough from defect so it will enforce its acceptance by buyer.

Market data approach: One of the three methods of appraisal, it compares recently sold properties to the property being appraised. *See*: Sales comparison approach.

Market price: Actual price paid for a property in a transaction.

Market value: Highest price a willing buyer will pay for a property and the lowest a willing seller will accept, assuming no undue, outside pressures.

Mechanic's lien: Lien created by law against real property as security for payment for the labor and materials used for the improvement of a property.

Meridian: North-south line used in government rectangular survey.

Metes and bounds: Land description method that relies on land boundary lines, utilizing those lines with their terminal points and angles.

Mineral rights: Authorization to amass income from the sale of gas, oil, and other resources underground.

Monument: Fixed object and point specified by surveyors to establish land locations, such as boulders or unusual trees.

Mortgage: Written instrument that establishes a lien on real estate as security for payment of a designated debt.

Mortgage banker: Person who originates, finances, sells, closes, and services mortgage loans, which are generally insured or guaranteed by a private mortgage insurer or government agency.

Mortgage broker: Places loans with investors for a fee, but does not service them.

Mortgage commitment: Agreement between a borrower and a lender to set up a loan at a later date, dependent on the conditions specified in the agreement.

Mortgage loan disclosure statement: Statement on a form approved by the Real Estate Commissioner that discloses to a potential borrower the terms and conditions of a mortgage loan; required by law to be proffered by mortgage brokers before the borrower is bound by the loan terms.

Mortgage-backed securities: Investment instrument based on a pooling of mortgages.

Mortgagee: Someone who receives a mortgage from a mortgagor to secure a loan or performance of a duty; also called a lender or creditor.

Mortgagor: Person who provides a mortgage on property to a mortgagee to secure a loan or the mortgagee's performance of a duty.

Multiple listing: Arrangement between real estate brokers to co-operate by providing information to each other regarding listings and to split commissions between the listing and selling brokers.

Negative amortization: Increase in a loan's outstanding balance due to periodic debt service payments not covering the total amount of interest attached to the loan.

Negative cash flow: A situation where the income generated by a property is less than the outflow of cash necessary to sustain it.

Negotiable instrument: A written unconditional promise or order to pay a certain amount of money at a defined time or on demand.

Net income: Actual earnings remaining after deducting all expenses from gross income.

Net operating income: The income from realty or a business after deducting operating expenses but before deducting tax payments on interest and principal payments.

Non-conforming loan: Mortgage loan that does not meet the criteria for being funded by Fannie Mae or Freddie Mac.

Non-institutional lenders: Other sources of real estate loans besides banks, thrifts, and insurance companies—such as mortgage bankers, mortgage brokers, pension funds, and private individuals.

Note: Written instrument acknowledging a debt and promise to pay.

Notice, Actual: Implied or express factual knowledge.

Notice, Constructive: Fact which should have been discovered due to one's actual notice and/or inquiries that a reasonably prudent person would be expected to make.

Notice, Legal: Notice required by law to be given.

Notice to quit: Notice provided to a tenant to vacate property.

Obsolescence: Decline in value to a reduction in desirability and usefulness of a structure because its design and construction become obsolete or decline due to a structure becoming outmoded; not in keeping with current needs.

Offer to purchase: Proposal to a property owner by a potential purchaser to acquire the property under previously stated terms.

Open-end loan: Type of loan under which an additional amount of money may be loaned to a borrower under the same trust deed.

Open-end mortgage: Mortgage including a clause under which the mortgagor may obtain additional funds from the mortgagee after some loan payments have been made.

Open listing: Listing provided to a number of brokers without a duty to compensate any besides the particular broker who first secures a buyer ready, willing, and able to accept the listing's terms or obtains the seller's acceptance of a different offer.

Open mortgage: Mortgage that has matured or whose payments are late, so that it is open to being foreclosed upon.

Operating expenses: Funds used to maintain property, such as insurance and repairs, but excluding depreciation or finance costs.

Option: Right without the obligation, to lease or purchase a property upon specified terms during a specified period.

Optionee: One who receives or acquires an option.

Optionor: One who gives or sells an option.

Oral contract: An agreement not in writing, usually unenforceable.

Overall capitalization rate: Rate calculated by dividing net operating income by the property's purchase cost.

Package loan: Mortgage created in which the principal loan amount is raised to include improvements and movable items, such as appliances, along with real estate.

Partially amortized note: A periodic payments schedule on the principal amount is set, so that the interest accruing during the loan term and other surplus unpaid principal is to be paid at the end of the term.

Pass-through securities: Securities originated by the VA and FHA to support the secondary mortgage market; guaranteed by Ginnie Mae.

Percentage lease: Property lease with the rental amount based on a percentage of sales made on the premises, with a set minimum amount; usually used by retailers.

Periodic estate: Lease based on a specified calendar amount of days, like month to month or year to year; also known as a periodic tenancy.

Personal property: All property that is not realty; also known as personalty.

Physical depreciation: Decline in value stemming from age, wear and tear, and the elements.

Planned Unit Development (PUD): Zoning or land-use plan for large tracts that includes intensive development of common and private areas, designed as one integrated unit.

Plottage: Increasing the value of a plot of land that has been assembled from smaller plots under a single ownership.

Points: Fees provided to lenders to attract a mortgage loan. One point equals one percent of the principal loan amount, which lowers the funding amount advanced by the lender, effectively raising the interest rate.

Positive cash flow: The situation where the income generated by a property is greater than the outflow of cash necessary to sustain it.

Premises: Land and buildings; an estate.

Prepayment clause: Mortgage clause conveying the privilege to a borrower to pay her entire debt prior to its maturity.

Prepayment penalty: Charges levied against a borrower for paying her entire debt prior to its maturity, if there is no prepayment clause.

Primary mortgage market: The market for consumers to directly obtain a mortgage loan.

Prime rate: Short-term interest rate that a bank charges its most creditworthy business customers.

Principal: (a) Employer of a broker or agent. (b) Amount of money from the mortgage or other loan, apart from the interest due on it. (c) One of the main parties in a real estate deal.

Private lender: One who invests his own money into real estate loans, directly or via brokers.

Private mortgage insurance (PMI): Mortgage guarantee insurance that protects conventional lenders in case of default, with premiums paid by the borrower.

Probate: To prove the validity of a will of a deceased person.

Processing: The compilation of loan application documents for the consideration of a lender.

Procuring cause: Legal term for the cause resulting in the objective of a real estate broker or agent procuring a ready, willing, and able realty purchaser; used to determine who is entitled to a commission.

Promissory note: Borrower's signed promise to repay the loan to a specific person under specific terms.

Property: Rights that a party has to use and possess land or chattel to the exclusion of anyone else.

Proprietorship: Business ownership, including the management of real estate, by a person, as opposed to a corporation or partnership.

Proration: Allocation between seller and purchaser of proportional shares of a debt that has been paid, or due to be paid, regarding a realty sale, such as property taxes and insurance.

Purchase capital: Funds used to purchase realty, from whatever source.

Purchase money mortgage: Mortgage provided by a buyer (grantee) to a seller (grantor) in partial payment of a real estate purchase price.

Quiet enjoyment: Right of an owner or tenant to the use of a property without any interference to their possession.

Quiet title: Court action to remove a defect or cloud on an owner's legal right to a piece of realty.

Quitclaim deed: Conveyance establishing only the grantor's interest in real estate, with no ownership warranties.

Range lines: Used in the government rectangular survey method of land description as lines parallel to the principal meridian, demarcating the land into six-mile strips called ranges.

Real estate: Land and all permanent attachments to it.

Real Estate Advisory Commission: Ten-member board that makes recommendations to the Real Estate Commissioner on pertinent issues.

Real estate investment trust (REIT): Mutual fund authorized by law to be immune from corporate taxes if most of its profits are distributed to individual investors who are taxed.

Real property: All the rights inherent in ownership to use real estate.

Real Estate Settlement Procedures Act (RESPA): Federal law requiring lenders to offer information to borrowers on settlement costs.

Realtor: Real estate professional who follows the code of ethics pursuant to their membership in the National Association of Realtors.

Recapture clause: Contract clause allowing party granting an interest or right in real estate to re-take it under specific conditions.

Recording: Act of entering documents regarding title to real estate in the public record.

Recourse: Authority of a lender to assert a claim to funds from a borrower in default, besides the property pledged as collateral.

Redlining: Unlawful policy of a lender denying to make loans in certain areas with high minority populations, due to perceived lending risks, without considering the creditworthiness of each applicant.

Refinance: The replacement or renewal of a current loan with new financing.

Regulation Z: *See*: Truth-in-Lending Law.

Reinstatement: The curing of a default on a loan secured by a trust deed.

Release clause: A provision of a blanket loan, allowing the release of a particular land parcel on repayment of a specified part of the loan.

Rent: Compensation paid for the use of realty.

Replacement cost: In appraisals, the cost of construction to replace or serve the same function as a similar, previous building.

Reproduction cost: In appraisals, the cost of construction of a replica of a property as of a certain date.

Reserve requirement: Controlled by the Fed, the amount of reserve funds that banks and thrifts must have on hand to safeguard depositors.

Reversion: Lessor's right to take possession of leased property upon the end of a lease.

Right of survivorship: Right of a surviving joint tenant to take the interest of a deceased joint owner.

Right of way: Easement right-to-use of specific path for access or passage, as well as the subdivision areas allocated to government use for streets and other types of public access.

Riparian rights: Rights regarding water use on, under, or adjacent to a person's land, providing reasonable use of such water.

Rollover mortgage: Loan in which the interest rate and the monthly payment are renegotiated, generally every five years.

Rumford Act: *See*: Fair Housing Law.

Sale-and-leaseback: Seller retains occupancy of land by leasing it back simultaneously with its sale, generally for a long-term lease.

Sales comparison approach: In appraisals, estimating value through analysis of comparable properties' recent sale prices.

Salesperson: One licensed to perform any act authorized by the state's Real Estate Law, if employed by a broker also licensed.

Satisfaction piece: Written instrument recording and acknowledging a mortgage loan's last payment.

Secondary trust deed: Loan is secured by a trust deed favoring the seller, and recorded subsequent to the first trust deed.

Secondary mortgage market: The buying and selling of pools of mortgages by lending institutions, which generates funding for primary lenders to provide new loans to consumers.

Section of land: Square mile in the government rectangular survey description of land.

Security instrument: Realty interest permitting a property to be sold if the obligation for which the security interest was created is defaulted upon.

Separate property: As distinguished from community property, property owned by a spouse prior to marriage; acquired by gift or bequest; or, by proceeds from other separate property.

Servicing: The administration of an existing loan.

Straight-line depreciation: Method of depreciation which uses equal yearly reductions to estimate a property's book value.

Subdivision: Land tract divided into plots appropriate for the construction of homes, as per the state's Subdivided Lands Law.

"Subject to" mortgage: Method to take title to mortgaged realty without being personally liable for payment of amount due on the promissory note. If the new buyer fails to make payments going forward, the most he will lose is his equity in the property.

Subordination clause: Instrument allowing a mortgage recorded at a subsequent date to take precedence over an earlier mortgage.

Surety: One who guarantees another's performance; a guarantor.

Survey: Procedure under which a parcel of land is measured and its area calculated.

Swing loan: A temporary, short term loan, made on a borrower's equity in his present home.

Tax: Charge assessed against individuals, corporations, and organizations to fund government.

Tax-free exchange: Trade of one property for another that is excluded from tax liability on any profit when the trade occurs.

Tax sale: Property being sold after a period of unpaid taxes.

Tenancy at sufferance: Tenancy created when a lawful tenant retains possession of a property after the lease terminates.

Tenancy at will: License to possess realty and tenements for an indefinite period, at the owner's will.

Tenancy by the entireties: Estate that exists just between spouses, with each having equal right of possession and with right of survivorship.

Tenancy in common: Ownership of real property by two or more persons, with each having an undivided interest but without the right of survivorship.

Tenant: Person given possession of real property belonging to someone else for a fixed term or at will.

Thrifts: Savings banks, savings and loans and other institutions which specialize in investments in real estate deeds of trust.

Tight money market: When the demand for money is greater than the supply, interest rates rise and standards that borrowers need to meet become tougher.

Time of the essence: A contract condition requiring that all references to specified dates regarding performance be followed exactly.

Title: Establishes that a land owner has lawful possession of a property, having all the elements of ownership.

Title insurance: Insurance policy providing protection from losses caused by possible defects in the title.

Title search: Public records inquiry to ascertain any issues of ownership and encumbrance regarding realty.

Topography: Surface of the land; may be hilly, flat, rocky.

Township: Six-mile, square tract located between two range lines and two township lines established by government rectangular survey.

Trade fixtures: Articles annexed to rental structures by a commercial tenant in the course of operating their business, removable by the tenant.

Trust deed: Conveyance of realty to a neutral third party (trustee) which that person holds for another party's benefit.

Trustee's sale: A non-judicial foreclosure sale done by the trustee; it takes place only when a trust deed includes a power of sale clause.

Trustor: Party who gives property to a trustee to be held on a beneficiary's behalf, so that the trustor becomes the owner of real estate and the lender is the beneficiary.

Truth-in-Lending Law (Regulation Z): Federal law enacted to inform borrowers regarding the complete cost of a loan.

Underwriting: Process of evaluating an applicant's capability to meet the obligations of a real estate loan.

Unit in place method: Projecting the cost of building a structure based on estimating the price of its individual components, such as the foundation, floors, walls, and cost of labor.

Unity: Four unities are needed to establish a joint tenancy: interest, possession, time, and title. Thus, joint tenants are required to have equal interests created by a conveyance, the identical undivided possession, and the same use during the same time.

Unruh Act: State law requiring real estate borrowers be provided with explicit notices of default on a mortgage to safeguard homeowners from losing their residences due to default on retail installment purchases.

Unsecured loan: In an unsecured loan, the lender receives a promissory note from the borrower but without a security (such as a trust deed or mortgage) for payment of the debt.

Urban property: City; closely-settled realty.

Usury: Interest rate impermissibly set higher than allowed by law.

Utility: One of the elements of value, the capability to provide gratification, inciting the wish to possess a property.

Valid: Having legally sufficient force; enforceable by a court.

Value: What something is worth to a particular party.

Variable expenses: Operating costs for a property that rise upon occupancy.

Vendee: Buyer; a purchaser.

Vendee's lien: Lien applied to property according to a contract of sale, to secure buyer's deposit.

Vendor: Seller.

Verification of Deposit (VOD): Form used by loan applicant's bank to establish the existence and history of funds that can be used for the loan's down payment and other charges.

Verification of Employment (VOE): Confirming the loan applicant's employment information by obtaining current data from the employer, such as pay stubs and tax forms.

Warranty: Promise or guaranty included in a contract.

Warranty deed: Instrument that includes a covenant declaring the grantor will protect the grantee from claims on title.

Without recourse: Phrase employed in endorsement of a note or bill indicating that the holder cannot expect payment from the debtor personally if non-payment occurs.

Wrap-around loan: *See:* All-inclusive deed of trust. Wraps an existing loan with a new one, with the borrower making one payment for both loans.

Yield: Interest rate earned by a lender on the loan amount.

Zoning: Governmental authority designating an area for a particular use.

INDEX